S. T. GILL, Artist, &c., late Draftsman and Water Color Painter to the Hubard Profile Gallery of London, begs to announce to his friends and the public generally of Adelaide and its vicinity that he has opened rooms in Gawler-place, where for the present he solicits the attendance of such individuals as are desirous of obtaining correct likenesses of themselves, families, or friends. Parties preferring attendance at their residences may be accommodated without additional charge. Correct resemblances of horses, dogs, &c., with local scenery, &c. executed to order. Residences sketched and transferred to paper suited for home conveyance. Orders executed in rotation.

Open daily from eleven till dusk.

S.T. GILL

THE SOUTH AUSTRALIAN YEARS
1839-1852

Ron Appleyard · Barbara Fargher · Ron Radford

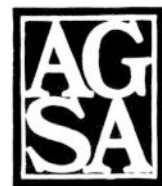

ART GALLERY OF SOUTH AUSTRALIA

ADELAIDE 1986

S.T. Gill, The South Australian Years 1839–1852

Published on the occasion of an exhibition at the Art Gallery of South Australia, shown from 16 July as a contribution to South Australia's Jubilee 150 year.

Cataloguing-in-publication data
National Library of Australia

Appleyard, Ron, 1920–
    S.T. Gill : The South Australian years 1839–1852.

    ISBN 0 7308 0790 8
    ISBN 0 7308 0794 0   (pbk)

    1. Gill, S.T. (Samuel Thomas), 1818–1880 — Exhibitions. 2. Painting, Australian — South Australia — Exhibitions. 3. Painting, Modern — 19th century — South Australia — Exhibitions. I. Gill, S.T. (Samuel Thomas), 1818–1880. II. Fargher, Barbara, 1932–   . III. Radford, Ron, 1949– IV. Art Gallery Board of South Australia. V. Title.

759.994'074'0994231

Designed by Michael Deves
Typeset by Adelaide Phototype Bureau
Printed by Colour Printing House, Adelaide.

Art Gallery of South Australia, North Terrace, Adelaide, South Australia 5000, Australia. Telephone (08) 223 7200.

Cover illustration:
Invalid's tent, salt lake 75 miles north-west of Mount Arden, watercolour on paper 21.4 x 34.2 cm, Art Gallery of South Australia.

The Art Gallery of South Australia acknowledges the sponsorship of Colliers International Property Consultants and the assistance of the South Australia Jubilee 150 Board.

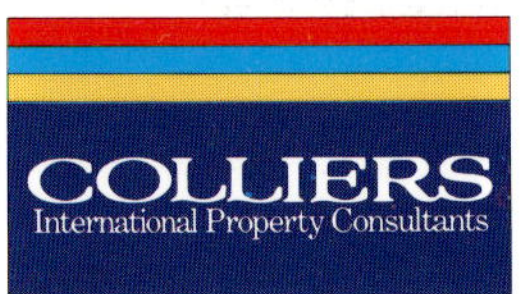
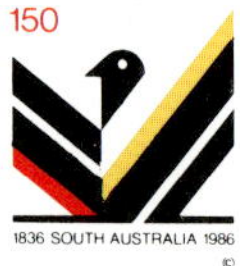

Contents

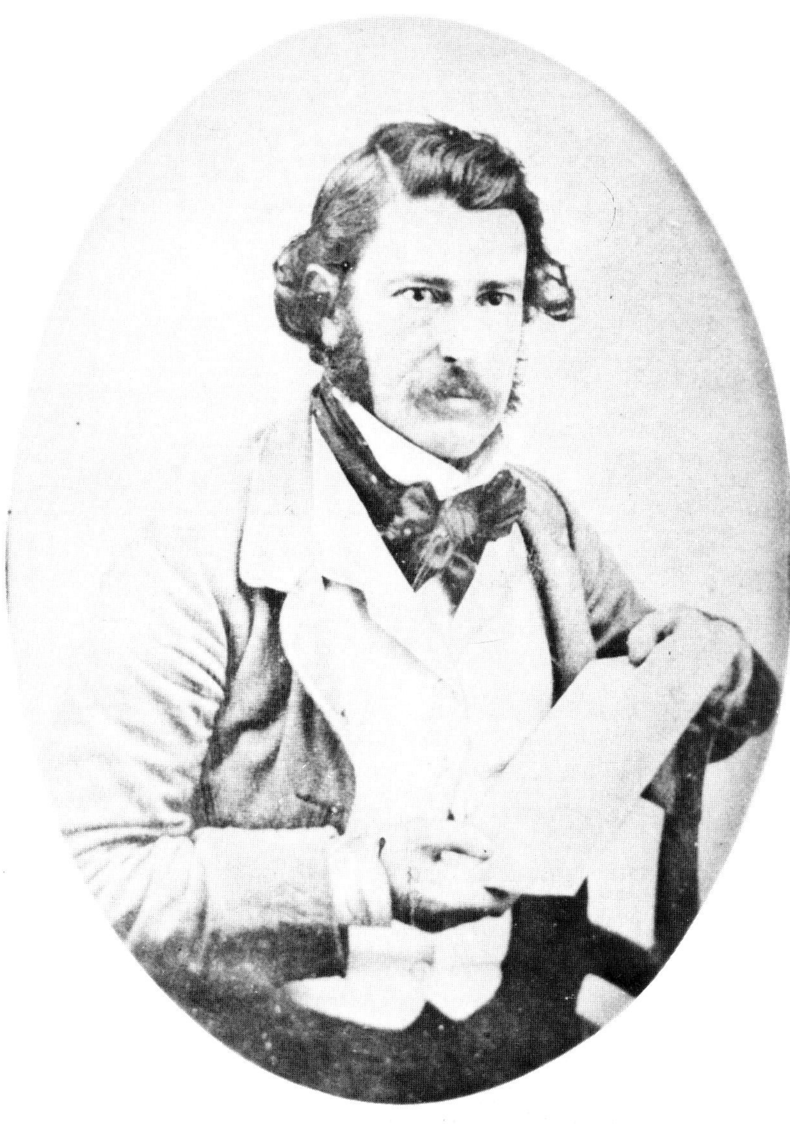

Early photograph of S.T. Gill.
Private collection, Adelaide

Acknowledgements

Many people and institutions have readily given of their knowledge and assisted with research in the preparation of this book. In particular, Dr John Tregenza, Historian, History Trust of South Australia, who besides his personal assistance on many points, made available the South Australian Historical Pictures Index; Mr C.M. Thompson, a great-nephew of S.T. Gill, who made available various family papers; Mr K.T. Borrow who provided important material from his extensive research notes; Mr Ralph Grandison and his wife Sue who have expended considerable time and energy locating Gill's painting sites in the Flinders Range and have given freely of that knowledge; Barbara Perry, Pictorial Librarian, National Library of Australia, Margaret Calder and Elizabeth Imasher, Mitchell Library, Sydney; Christine Downer and Wendy Prior, La Trobe Library, Melbourne, and John Love, Brian Baldwin and other staff members of the South Australian Archives (now Public Record Office and Mortlock Library), have all made available pictures and documents, and have patiently answered many enquiries; Necia Gilbert spent many hours searching newspapers; Mary Horrocks assisted with family papers; Ian Auhl, R.J. Noye, Carl Collison, Graeme Pretty, Peter Morgan, Brian Samuels and Len Marquis all contributed information resulting from their own researches in particular fields. In Britain the Hon. Jane Roberts, Royal Library, Windsor Castle, the staff of the Plymouth Central Library and the Devon Record Office also the Reverend G.W. Rusling of the Baptist Union, London, and other officers of that Church were all exceedingly helpful.

Black and white photography of works held in South Australia was by Clayton McWhinney and colour photography by Richard Humphrys. Many works were restored in time for the exhibition by Kerry McInnes and Heather Mansell.

At the Art Gallery of South Australia, the authors wish to thank the following: David Thomas, former Director of the Gallery, Jane Hylton who helped with the publication management, James Schoff who helped with gaining sponsorship, Ellaine Rankine and Sandy Fawcett who typed most of the text, and the Director, Daniel Thomas, for the editorial style and his constant encouragement.

The two standard references often consulted were K.M. Bowden, *Samuel Thomas Gill, Artist*, Melbourne, privately published, 1971, and Geoffrey Dutton, *S.T. Gill's Australia*, Melbourne, Macmillan, 1981. Both authors readily answered questions and provided information relating to the original sources they had consulted.

Ron Appleyard
Barbara Fargher
Ron Radford

Foreword

S.T. Gill, whose Australian career began in South Australia, and another watercolour painter, Conrad Martens, who worked in New South Wales, are the only Australian colonial artists whose work always remained part of the nation's cultural consciousness. Perhaps watercolour seemed, to post-Centennial Australians, a more appropriate medium for migrants and pioneers than oil painting. Perhaps their lighter style was less alien than Eugene von Guérard's intense romanticism to the popular taste for impressionism which dominated from the 1880s for nearly a century. Perhaps the topographical intentions in some of their work made it accessible to later generations as history rather than as art.

The artistic excellence of Gill's best work has been insufficiently appreciated. Since the best work was produced during his years in South Australia, the celebrations in 1986 of the Sesquicentenary of the colony/state founded at Adelaide in 1836 are a happy occasion for reassessment of Gill's art.

The South Australia Jubilee 150 Board provided a substantial grant for conservation of many watercolours, hitherto in unfit condition for display or reproduction, and another to assist the book. Colliers International Property Consultants, Adelaide, also provided substantial assistance to the production cost of this exhibition book. Without the support of those two sponsors the exhibition could not have taken place nor the book been published.

The Art Gallery Board eagerly maintains a policy of presenting and publishing South Australian art and is delighted to add this to its previous monographs on Horace Trenerry, Hans Heysen, Dorrit Black, Margaret Preston, George French Angas, James Cant and Eugene von Guérard. The Art Gallery Board especially thanks the many owners who have contributed loans of Gill's work to this exhibition and allowed their works to be reproduced here.

The large holdings of Gill's paintings in the Art Gallery of South Australia, received by gift as well as purchase, are the result of continuing local affection for his work over more than a century and are the prime cause of the project. The immediate cause, however, is the presence of the three curator-authors who prepared the exhibition and wrote its book.

Ron Radford, since 1980 the Gallery's Curator of Paintings and Sculptures, conceived, co-ordinated and selected the exhibition and contributed the Appreciation which reassesses Gill's art. Barbara Fargher, a founder in 1972 of the volunteer Gallery Guides and now a part-time and occasional Assistant Curator very much at home with the Gallery's collections, re-catalogued the holdings of Gill's work and also contributed special insights from her own experience as a watercolour painter.

Most important is Ron Appleyard's contribution. First employed at the Art Gallery in 1937, retired from its Deputy Directorship in 1982, a lifetime of familiarity with Gill's work has been crowned by intensive recent research. Gill's biography is now immensely improved. The paintings have been sometimes re-titled; dating is far more accurate. Gill's confusing repetitions and variants are for the first time clearly identified. Mr Appleyard's research is at the heart of this exhibition and its book.

I thank all who have contributed to *S.T. Gill: The South Australian Years 1839–1852*. But the warmest thanks are due to Ron Appleyard, the Art Gallery's guiding spirit for many years past and for as long into the future as he tolerates our demands. We dedicate the exhibition and the book to Ron Appleyard.

Daniel Thomas
Director, Art Gallery of South Australia

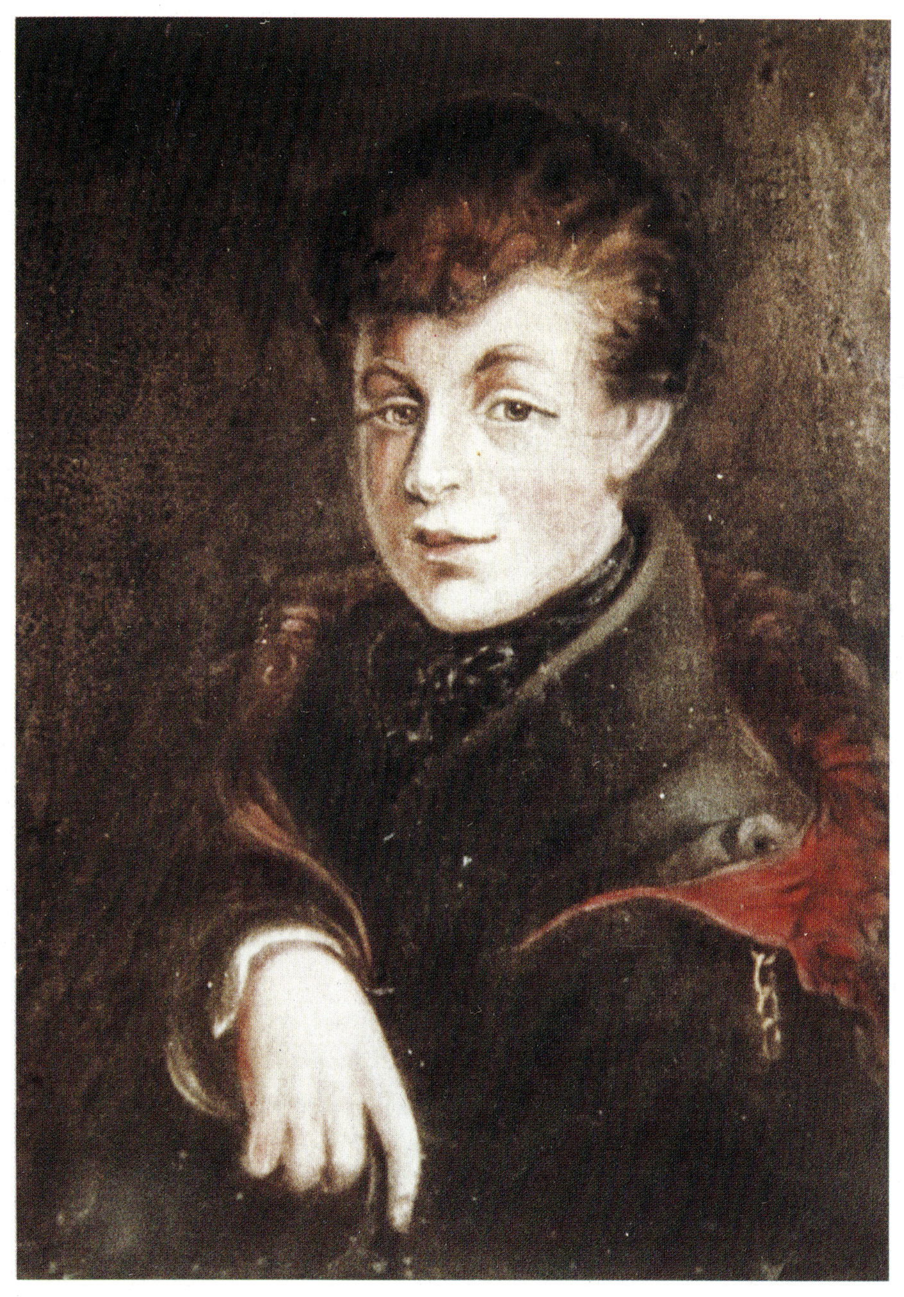

Self portrait, oil, size unknown, painted
21 February 1835. Destroyed by fire 1948.

S.T. Gill
An Appreciation

In the Melbourne General Cemetery, Carlton, there stands a grand and impressively constructed memorial which marks the grave of the now much-loved Australian colonial artist S.T. Gill. Buried in October 1880 in a common grave with the bodies of three other paupers, his remains were later traced, transferred and elaborately commemorated in October 1913. The inscription on the gravestone reads: 'Samuel Thomas Gill/ The Artist of the Gold-fields/ . . .'

S.T. Gill is still best known for his animated illustrations of the goldfields of Victoria, yet during his long Australian career of forty years — longer than any other nineteenth-century Australian professional artist with the exception of Conrad Martens — he spent a total of little more than two years on the goldfields at Ballarat, Bendigo and Mount Alexander. Furthermore, most of the Victorian goldfield subjects were repetitions, executed sometimes more than twenty years after his visit to those areas in the early 1850s. The largest group of these works, including some of his most famous, was commissioned by the Public Library of Victoria, Melbourne, in 1869. Well into the 1870s he repeated this goldfield series and individual works from it. In fact, Gill spent by far the longest part of his career in the boom city of Melbourne. It is not well known that he also lived for eight years from 1856 to 1864 in Sydney.

However, S.T. Gill spent his first twelve years in Australia, from the end of 1839 to the beginning of 1852, in the colony of South Australia, where he has been known principally as an artist who in the 1840s, painted the now historic early views of Adelaide and Port Adelaide. These lively city scenes have been shown regularly since the 1890s at the Art Gallery of South Australia and have been reproduced more often than any other colonial South Australian subjects by Gill, or by any of his fellow artists. But just as it is inaccurate to regard S.T. Gill only as an artist of the goldfields, so also is it very limiting to regard Gill's South Australian work as confined to scenes of Adelaide. Most of his city views were, after all, the result of a single commission in 1845 from James Allen (see Appendix A). Indeed they are a relatively small part of his South Australian oeuvre. He painted and made lithographs of a vast range of subjects including copper mining, houses, portraits, inland exploration, natives, sporting and other special events and numerous and extraordinarily beautiful South Australian landscapes. It was only after Gill left the colony that his figures became larger and assumed a greater importance than their landscape surroundings and it is no great exaggeration to see him in South Australia principally as a landscape painter.

It is clear that when the confident twenty-one-year-old artist first advertised his abilities in *The South Australian Register* in March 1840, he was willing to tackle any subject on commission. His advertisement reads:

S.T. Gill, Artist, &c., late Draftsman and Water Colour Painter to the Hubard Profile Gallery, London, begs to announce to his friends and the public generally of Adelaide and its vicinity, that he has opened rooms in Gawler Place where for the present he solicits the attendance of such individuals as are desirous of obtaining correct likenesses of themselves, families or friends. Parties preferring attendance at their residences may be accommodated without additional charge. Correct resemblances of horses, dogs, etc., with local scenery etc., executed to order. Residences sketched and transferred to paper suited for home conveyance. Orders executed in rotation. Open daily from eleven to dusk.

In his twelve years in South Australia, Gill successfully undertook all the subjects advertised and more. S.T. Gill was a pioneer of many subjects later tackled on a very grand scale by other artists during the growth of Australian nationalism at the end of the nineteenth century.

S.T. Gill helped form the beginnings of the bush mythology as represented in Australian art. His watercolour paintings of stockmen, explorers, bush-rangers, prospectors and other pioneers are forerunners of many illustrations and, more importantly, they establish themes which Tom Roberts, Frederick McCubbin and John Longstaff made artistically monumental in large-scale oil painting, as did Henry Lawson and Banjo Paterson in literature.

Before 1842, Gill became the first artist to paint the Australian subject of sheep-shearing[1], a theme which many others, including Tom Roberts, later were to interpret as heroic for the Australian experience.

Gill was also the first Australian artist to use mining as a subject when, in the mid 1840s, he depicted the excavation of South Australian copper. The subject of mining (particularly of gold) remained significant in Australian art and illustration until the end of the nineteenth century.

Although there are a very few isolated horse portraits and scenes of coursing and other sporting events by other artists before the 1840s, Gill was the first in Australia regularly to depict such scenes, still a great source of admiration and pride in the self-perceived sporting nation of Australia.

S.T. Gill was not only a forerunner. His work often exerted a direct influence inasmuch as his lithographs and watercolours were widely circulated and easily accessible, and not only those seen at the Public Library in Melbourne. Gill's work was readily seen and admired whereas that of John Glover, George French Angas and Alexander Schramm was unknown to the outdoor painters of the 1880s and 1890s and the romantic landscape paintings of Eugene von Guérard, Nicholas Chevalier and Conrad Martens were quickly forgotten by them. It is true that Gill's reworkings of his earlier themes in the late 1860s and 1870s differ from his eye-witness accounts of the 1840s and 1850s, but they are a kind of history painting rather than illustration. As the figures in his later work loom larger and the landscape backgrounds diminish, so does the nationalistic sentiment grow.

In spite of the myth of the bush and the outback, Australians have always been city dwellers and recordings of Australian towns were a feature of Australian art from the very earliest days of settlement. S.T. Gill continues this tradition but he was the first artist to imbue the cities and towns of Adelaide, Melbourne, Ballarat, Mount Alexander, Bendigo, Geelong, Sydney and others with a robust activity which brings them bustling to life. We are indebted to Gill not only for our knowledge of what the buildings and streets looked like, but also what the people from all walks of life and all ages wore, what they carried, what dogs and horses they owned, how they stood and how they moved. Gill left us an invaluable record of life in Australia in the mid nineteenth century.

S.T. Gill's South Australian subjects are discussed in more detail here under eleven headings: S.T. Gill's Sketchbook, The Seasons and The Months, Landscapes and Rural Scenes, The Natives, Adelaide and Port Adelaide, Sturt's Expedition, Mining, Sport and Recreation, the Horrocks Expedition, Houses, Portraits of the Colonists.

Gill was twenty-one when he arrived in the three-year-old British colony of South Australia with his parents at the end of 1839. Early signs of an artistic talent had been encouraged by his father, the Reverend Samuel Gill, who was an amateur artist. S.T. Gill had finished his education at a boarding school in Plymouth, a town conscious of its artistic heritage and which had produced such notable artists as Joshua Reynolds, Samuel Prout and Charles Eastlake. Regular exhibitions were held in Plymouth and there were good art schools. Gill had received training from competent art teachers of landscape and portrait painting at the school which he left aged about sixteen. He then worked with a carver and gilder in Plymouth where he could observe fine paintings as they came in to be framed. Bent on an artistic career, he went to London to take further lessons and found work at the successful Hubard Profile Gallery which specialised in the cut-paper landscapes and silhouette portraits characteristic of the time. As well as working on profiles Gill also filled in backgrounds to portraits and other designs. By the time he arrived in South Australia he had gained sound experience as an artist and illustrator within the English watercolour tradition. Gill would have seen numerous exhibitions in London including those at the Royal Academy and paintings by the old masters at the National Gallery; there he surely would have admired also the boisterous work of William Hogarth. Even before his stay in London he would have come across and admired the satirical prints of Thomas Rowlandson, James Gillray, Isaac and George Cruikshank and other English humorous illustrators with whom he has been compared.

S.T. Gill's English sketchbook, now in the collection of the Art Gallery of South Australia, was begun when he was seventeen and concludes when he was nearly twenty; it demonstrates his development under his father's encouragement and contains some of his father's well-intended poems which S.T. Gill illustrated. The sketchbook reveals Gill's interest in contemporary illustration and is full of human interest and wit. And it includes compositions which appear later in his South Australian works.

What appear to be the earliest known Australian works by S.T. Gill, probably executed well within his first two years in South Australia, are his four paintings of each of the seasons and his twelve works (one is lost) based on each of the months. The four seasons are a frequently occurring subject in European art from classical times to the nineteenth century and the regular labours of the months have been depicted since the early Christian era. Pieter Brueghel's *Months* are best known to us today and S.T. Gill could have come across Brueghel's work in London in the form of engraved prints which have always been widely circulated.

Gill's robust colonists toiling with the new land are reminiscent of Brueghel's lively, hefty peasants in the fields and are equally entertaining. Gill's works show the same earthly cycles appropriate to the months of the year, reversed for the southern hemisphere, but there is no mistaking that these are an Australian equivalent of an oft-interpreted European theme. Gill has observed in accurate detail the characteristic Australian vegetation, the bright light, the golden pastures of the summer months and the distinctive colonial architecture and dress. In each of the four seasons, the energetic and progressive colonists are quietly observed from afar by Aborigines. This hints at Gill's awareness that the land so eagerly worked by the colonists has been thoughtlessly appropriated from a less aggressive people.

Summer (cat. 14) is one of the most endearing of the seasonal group and, like many of Gill's works, is packed with activity. The labourers are energetically scything the golden wheat of a good harvest and abundance is further emphasized by distant vineyards and foreground ripe melons. This is the colonists' promised land of plenty but there is a threat on the horizon. Smoke from a bush or grass fire can be seen in the distance.[2]

These vignettes of the seasons and months show Gill responding to every aspect of his new environment. Gill, the boy-illustrator from London's Hubard Gallery, is becoming a mature colonial artist, full of new things to express about his adopted country.

The history of colonial art in Australia is often the history of conventional, competent European artists whose art has been transformed by the fresh stimulus of an unfamiliar and sometimes dramatic Australian landscape and by the optimism of a new life in what for Europeans was a virgin continent. Professionally trained artists like John Glover, Eugene von Guérard, Louis Buvelot, who arrived in their maturity, created their best work in Australia; the stimulus was especially important for younger and more impressionable artists like William Westall, Augustus Earle, Conrad Martens, John Skinner Prout, George French Angas, William Strutt and S.T. Gill.

Gill was soon painting with relish almost every aspect of colonial life. His best works were his rural landscapes, his exploration landscapes of the ill-fated Horrocks expedition and his well known scenes of Adelaide and its new port.

One of his most intriguing landscapes is *A Native*

Corroboree at night (cat. 37). In this painting Gill has reversed the role of the Aborigines as observers of the busy settlers depicted in *The Seasons* and here the settlers observe the ancient rites of the indigenous race. At the foot of the majestic mountain illuminated in the mysterious light of the full moon and a fire, the Australian Aborigines perform their dance. Giant gums and native vegetation surround and guard this eerie scene. Scenes of dusky Aborigines in the evening are the subject of other colonial artists' work, the masterpieces of which are John Glover's *A corrobery of Natives in Mills Plains* (c.1832) and Eugene von Guérard's *Stony Rises, Corangamite* (1857), both in the Art Gallery of South Australia. In what is possibly the first South Australian oil painting, the amateur artist John Michael Skipper (who usually worked in watercolour) recorded at the beginning of the 1840s an Aborigines' corroboree being watched by settlers in his *Corroboree, South Australia*.[3] Gill was well aware of Skipper's paintings and of the work of E.C. Frome, both of whom were active at the time of Gill's arrival.

Gill painted numerous other South Australian landscapes like *Approach to Mount Crawford* (cat. 20), *Rhodes's Cattle Station on the Gawler* (cat. 23) and *Mounted Police chasing Bushrangers* (cat. 18). These paintings show acute understanding of the unique qualities of the Australian landscape. Before Gill, only Glover in Tasmania had consistently rendered the true colouring and structure peculiar to Australian vegetation, the gnarled old gums, the spindly casuarinas, the distinctive grass-trees, banksias and other flora. Gill's landscapes go beyond mere topographical recordings and capture the very silence of the bush.

Gill's most remarkable and dramatic landscapes, however, are his paintings from the Horrocks Expedition beyond the Flinders Ranges. E.C. Frome, the Surveyor General, was the first to paint the Flinders Ranges in the early 1840s. Gill would have known Frome's watercolours, which were the first glimpse in art of Australia's vast interior desert. These works could have inspired Gill to seek similar subjects and he eagerly volunteered to join the Horrocks Expedition. In so doing he was fulfilling standard procedure for naval and inland expeditions, which usually included an artist-recorder.

S.T. Gill's least typical and least known landscapes, part of his Horrocks Expedition series, are his rocky mountainous views of the Flinders Ranges. *Stony Creek, Mount Remarkable Survey, from above the fall* (cat. 89) is one of the most haunting of these landscapes and hints at the influence of Frome's treatment of similar subjects. It is an evocative work. The starkly angular, rocky outcrops, like ancient ruins, form a romantic, dark ravine inhabited by Aborigines, seen here in the foreground. The arid and worn mountains seen in the distance and the one flying cockatoo in the ravine emphasize the sense of brooding isolation.

Perhaps the most arresting of Gill's expedition works is *Invalid's tent, salt lake* (cat. 98). One is immediately struck by the desolation of the scene. The small tent is the only protrusion in a vast, flat wilderness. Gill has painted himself reclining outside the tent; his wounded, dying leader Horrocks is inside. At the time this subject was first conceived, Gill was not sure that they would be rescued and he has captured the sense of melancholoy which goes beyond the simple, accurate description of the distant salt lake and the grey scrub on the red earth. The grazing camel, the first ever used on an Australian expedition (and, in fact, the unwitting cause of Horrocks's accident) is oblivious to the tragic atmosphere.

Contrasting with his lonely desert images are the populated city views for which Gill is popularly known. Like a producer of an operetta or a director on a film set, he skilfully manipulates his large cast of extras against the well lit backdrop of the city of Adelaide. So convincing are these compositions that we forget that they are not a suspended moment in time, like a cinematic still, but are the result of carefully arranged figures and domestic animals. In *North Terrace, Adelaide, looking south-east from Government House Guardhouse* (cat. 43), for example, we are drawn into the painting as if entering King William Street from North Terrace on horseback. We are following the soldier on his horse and the tramp dragging his stick. Across our path a boy is running with scampering dogs, about to upset a stationary man intently reading his newspaper; the man's vertical presence stops our eyes moving off the picture plane to the right. From the middle distance we are approached by a successful young man and his lady in a horse and gig. Individuals and groups are appropriately and casually scattered along the street. The whole composition is carefully orchestrated, not only by the arrangement of the figures but also by the choice of the colour of their costumes. With the reds of the soldiers' coats and the tramp, the blues of the trousers of the running boy and the coat of the reading man, Gill successfully distributes colour accents through the foreground. Touches of ochre-coloured walls and orange brick buildings add to the satisfying colour arrangement of the whole composition.

These light-filled city views of Adelaide and the views of the harbour of Port Adelaide were the result of a commission by James Allen to help promote South Australia abroad, yet there is no hint of the topographical drudgery in merely fulfilling the patron's wishes. We feel that Gill has revelled in the lively action of a city he clearly loves.

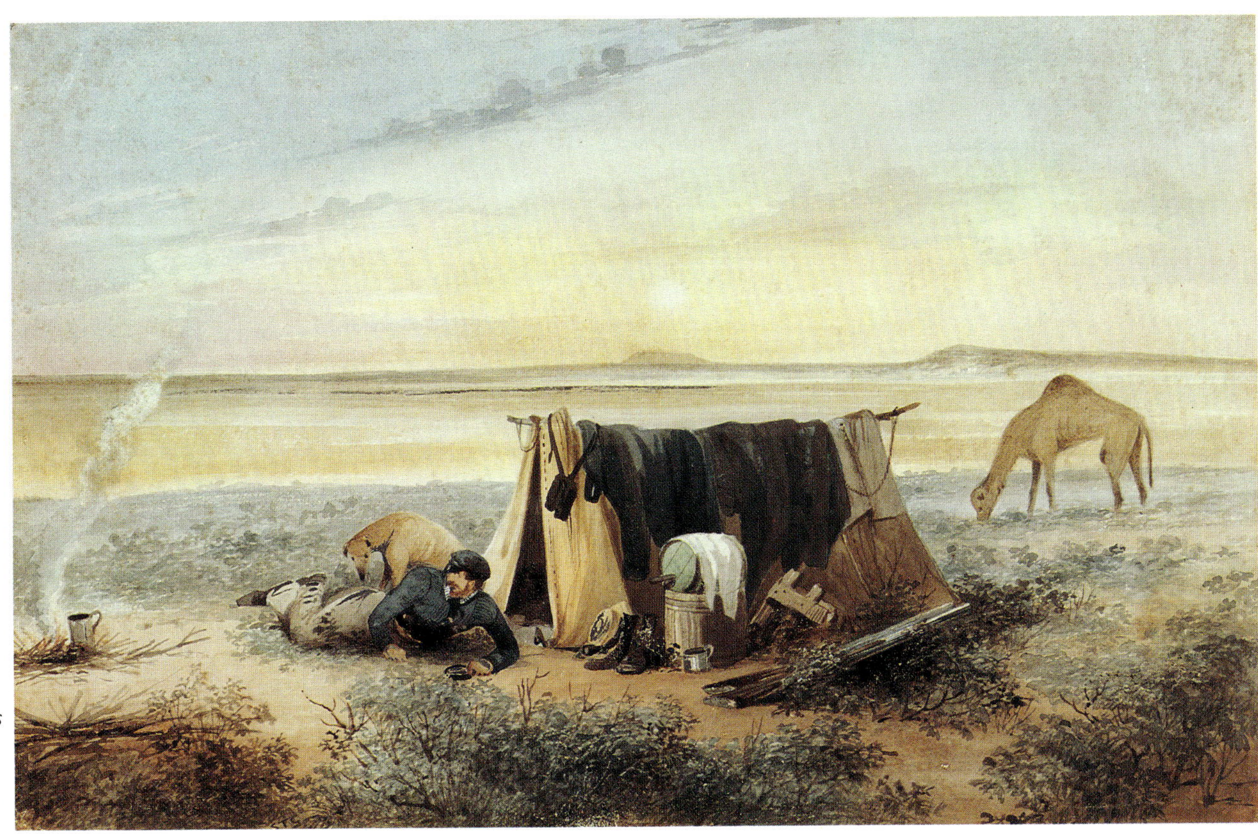

98 *Invalid's tent, salt lake 75 miles north-west of Mount Arden,* watercolour on paper 21.4 x 34.2 cm, Art Gallery of South Australia.

S.T. Gill's familiar subjects, especially these cityscapes, are not only much loved by the public for nostalgic reasons but have also been of particular use to social historians. However, the historical significance of Gill's work has often overshadowed and distorted its aesthetic importance. He is now the best known Australian colonial artist but the great affection that his works evoke today has little to do with their quality or merit as works of art. In his standard work *Australian Painting 1788-1960* (first published 1962) Bernard Smith writes of Gill and his art as forming

. . .a most valuable commentary upon life of the times, a commentary which is expressed with much gusto and great humour. Gill is the first artist whose work expresses a distinctly Australian attitude to life; the sardonic humour, the nonchalance of the irreverent attitude to all forms of authority, so frequently remarked upon by the students of Australian behaviour, are all present in his work.

Nevertheless, 'a most valuable commentary upon life of the times', does not necessarily make a fine work of art. Robert Hughes, in his *The Art of Australia*, 1966, refers to Gill as '. . . The most robust and "Australian" of all Colonial artists' and speaks of 'his proletariat humour' and his 'eye of a journalist'. In *Outlines of Australian Art: The Joseph Brown collection*, 1973, Daniel Thomas also speaks of Gill as 'a democratic pictorial journalist who might have taken up photography at a later age'. (S.T. Gill was in fact the first to briefly experiment with photography in South Australia in the early 1840s). Thomas goes on to say that 'Nobody in Australian art has captured the cheerful animation of the city crowds, of mining or outback workers so well'.

Alan McCulloch in *Artists of the Goldfields*, 1976, states 'What Mark Twain was to the American short story, S.T. Gill was to Australian drawing and painting'.

The South Australian author Geoffrey Dutton, in his *S.T. Gill's Australia*, 1981, reminds us of Gill's gentle character in spite of a popular belief of him as a fairly 'rough customer'. Dutton states 'He had a shy detachment. . . He was the quiet man in the corner sketching, not the bully-boy at the bar'. It is only Dutton who attempts to place him as an aesthetically important artist. 'Even now', writes Dutton, 'Gill is underrated as an artist'. Dutton offers a number of reasons for this, among them being that Gill painted smaller watercolours rather than grander oils and that satirical artists are frequently not taken very seriously by art historians. Dutton suggests that Gill's drunken life-style has detracted from his reputation as an artist and that he is judged by his best known works, which are sometimes unfortunately also his most inferior. Dutton's claims are partly true, but the quality of Gill's work varied enormously and he produced a great number of potboilers , that is, works made for quick sale. He was an extremely prolific artist and is believed to have produced at least 1,500 works, making his oeuvre one of the largest of any Australian artist.

One must be prepared to compare the quality of Gill's best work with that of his contemporaries. Art historians have tended to avoid doing this mainly because S.T. Gill's interesting subjects and character studies can be seen as an individual and separate category of illustrative art. But Gill's aesthetically important landscapes bear comparison with those of his contemporaries working in South Australia, with those of John Glover and John Skinner Prout working in Tasmania, Conrad Martens in New South Wales and, later in Victoria, the works of William Strutt, Eugene von Guérard, Nicholas Chevalier, Thomas Clark and Louis Buvelot.

During S.T. Gill's forty-year career from 1840 to 1880, the landscape paintings of two Australian artists tower above the rest in concept and quality. They are the works of John Glover in the 1830s and von Guérard from the 1850s to the 1870s. John Glover learned from the works of the great seventeenth-century masters of European landscape. This knowledge, coupled with a renewed vision inspired by the totally unfamiliar landscape of his newly adopted country, produced Australia's first great landscape paintings in the first half of the 1830s. Von Guérard also learned much from the tradition of European landscape and was trained in the German romantic manner. He created a vision of the sublime landscape in Australia and was the nineteenth-century artist who most often gave the landscape symbolic significance. He was Australia's greatest nineteenth-century artist. Beside the work of these giants S.T. Gill's intimate watercolour landscapes of the 1840s pale.[4] It is more realistic, however, to compare his work with that of his other contemporaries and it then stands favourably.

Conrad Martens was S.T. Gill's exact contemporary in Sydney and was the only artist in the nineteenth century to have a longer Australian career than Gill. Martens arrived four years before Gill and died two years before him. In fact when Gill was in Sydney between 1856 and 1864, he was Martens's greatest rival. Gill attempted some of the sweeping panoramic views of Sydney harbour which Martens had mastered, but Gill's approach was too prosaic. The overall atmospheric effect and general space and structure of the land in Martens's work makes Gill's look too preoccupied with topographic accuracy. On the other hand, Martens's work, in his efforts to depict the romantic and panoramic vision of Sydney Harbour, often became artificial and mannered while Gill's focus was often directed towards the more intimate aspects of nature, rather akin to the commonplace subjects chosen by Buvelot some years later in Melbourne. Gill's most successful Sydney works were his street scenes and his house portraits and only in these genres could Martens not equal him.

Martens's strongest artistic rival prior to Gill's arrival in Sydney had been the watercolourist John Skinner Prout, who came to Sydney early in 1840, only weeks after Gill had arrived in Adelaide. Prout's more modern, lively style, with its assertive, broken brushwork seemed to unnerve Martens. But Prout early in 1844 moved to Hobart where his influence encouraged a school of landscape painting in watercolour before his return to Britain in 1848. Prout, like Gill, had a greater interest than Martens (who used the figure as mere staffage) in incorporating characters as part of his landscapes and cityscapes, but Prout's best works are of fern glades and intimate sketches of the native bushland. Prout's work was more painterly and his compositions often more enclosed than Gill's open, illustrative compositions generally painted with smoother washes. In his attempts to capture the flickering light and moods of nature, Prout, with his deft brushwork, sacrifices stable composition. Unlike Gill's more careful arrangements, much of Prout's Australian work rarely rises above the quick, but delightfully fresh, sketch. When Prout enlarges his works, often years after the initial sketch, they are frequently comparatively lifeless and structurally weak.

S.T. Gill's most immediate artistic competitor in South Australia was George French Angas, the son of the wealthy chairman of the South Australian Company, George Fife Angas. George French Angas arrived in South Australia in 1844[5] and made inland trips in that and the following year, recording images of the Aborigines and their customs, the landscape and the fauna, which he exhibited in the colony's first one-man show in June 1845. Angas's landscapes and Aboriginal subjects are more objective and descriptive than S.T. Gill's work, his intention being to have them made into attractive hand-coloured lithographs. They were to impart information about the new colony and its progress. But his landscapes are not only topographical. He did structure his work, yet compared with Gill's compositions, Angas's lack vitality. Gill was skilled in bringing a simple landscape to life with human interest. His work is rarely boring. Even in Angas's dramatic views of the Coorong or the craters of Mount Gambier, where he attempts to elevate the scenes to the romantically poetic, they never quite achieve the drama present in Martens's best harbour views. Instead they fall between the topographical and the picturesque and are rarely saved, as are Gill's works, by points of anecdotal interest.

By the mid 1840s there were, apart from Angas, other artists (most of them amateurs) working in South Australia, namely John Michael Skipper, E.C. Frome, W.A. Cawthorne, George Hamilton, F.R. Nixon, Martha Berkeley and E.A. Opie. By the time of the goldrush to

Victoria, Adelaide, with a population of only just over 10,000 people, had gained further artists. These professional artists included J.A. Gilfillan, Alexander Schramm, James Shaw, Richard Read (Junior), Samuel Calvert and John Crossland. With the copper boom and the recovery of rural industry, for a few years from the late 1840s to about 1852, Adelaide was briefly the centre of Australian art. Artists were attracted to the young, civilised community from other colonies as well as from overseas. Unfortunately, there were far too many artists for the small population to support and as a consequence Gill failed to gain enough commissions; in September 1851 he had to face the debtors' court and was declared insolvent. With the discovery of gold in the eastern colonies, thousands of South Australians, including Gill and other artists, rushed to the goldfields.

Within a few months of his arrival in Victoria, Gill was to take the opportunity of publishing a small book of lithographs of the goldfields. This was the commencement of the series of goldfield works for which he has become so popular today. Most artists went to the goldfields in search of gold but, when this proved fruitless, returned to producing art. Victoria, like South Australia previously, now had too many artists and Melbourne in particular had numerous landscape painters, all of whom produced more saleable work than Gill. Gill could not compete with von Guérard's sublime views, Thomas Clark's sophisticated Gainsborough-like landscapes or Nicholas Chevalier's large, popular illustrations in oil. Gill was a better landscape painter and composer of figure subjects than Chevalier but, by the second half of the 1850s and through the 1860s, wealthy Melbourne citizens and prosperous pastoralists wanted large and impressive decorations for their new homes, not small watercolours. In Melbourne J.A. Gilfillan produced some large city views in oil similar to those he had done in Adelaide but Gill did not receive many commissions of this kind.

William Strutt, Australia's most professionally trained figure and animal painter of the nineteenth century, was established in Melbourne before the goldrushes and must have been a great rival. It was difficult enough even for Strutt, who had connections, to secure enough commissions by which to live. This created tough competition for Gill who worked in the same genre. Gill had an instinct for crowds and movement but Strutt had been academically trained in Paris as a history painter and skilfully composed many watercolours as well as some figure subjects in oils. None of these have Gill's vivacity or atmosphere, but the draughtsmanship is better and they have more convincing form.

It is understandable why Gill, with his ability to record the spontaneous and his acute understanding of human nature, was the perfect artist for the rough and tumble of the goldfields. Undoubtedly he is the best of the scores of artists who recorded mining activities but by the second half of the 1850s, when alluvial mining was declining, he had saturated his own market with his watercolours and lithographs. It is probably for this reason, as well as the stiff competition in Melbourne, that he moved to Sydney in 1856. When he returned to Melbourne eight years later, he began repeating his earlier goldmining themes and bush subjects and continued to do so into the 1870s. As mentioned, these late works on earlier themes virtually became history paintings.

In his last years in Melbourne Gill also painted large watercolour landscapes of South Australia. They were based on sketches from the 1840s and his very good visual memory. It is interesting to note that although the small community of the colony of South Australia was well-endowed with landscape painters for its first fifteen years (Colonel Light, Adelaide's founder, was also the colony's first landscape painter), there was no major resident landscape painter from the 1850s to the end of the century. Instead, in Adelaide there were numerous figure and portrait painters like John Crossland, Alexander Schramm, Charles Hill, John Irvine, Andrew MacCormac, John Upton and Louis Tannert. This was unusual for· an Australian colony for, as is well known, in the second half of the nineteenth century, Australia's strong landscape tradition was well established. It was not until the beginning of the twentieth century that the landscape tradition in South Australia was revived, principally by Hans Heysen. S.T. Gill therefore, while working in Melbourne during the 1860s and 1870s, sent many landscapes to South Australia as did the Melbourne painter and photographer H.J. Johnstone who worked up oil landscapes from photographs. Von Guérard produced South Australian landscape paintings and lithographs based on his earlier 1855 and 1857 drawings. Thomas Clark also produced oil paintings of South Australian landscapes from his own drawings. Gill's late South Australian landscape subjects, like nearly all his late works, are competent but dull compared with his lively earlier work. There is a coarseness about them which is absent from his smaller refined works of the 1840s.

Gill was usually unsuccessful when working on a larger scale. Unlike Alexander Schramm, William Strutt, Eugene von Guérard or Louis Buvelot, his training and inclination were never towards large-scale compositions. Furthermore, as has been mentioned, his strength lay in the spontaneity of his drawings and watercolours done on the spot or while his inspiration was still fresh. One can sense Gill's delight in the placement of figures, dogs, horses and the peculiar native vegetation depicted in these early works. In a darker Melbourne city studio far away in time and place from the South Australian landscapes of his youth, he became the producer of scores of large pastiches of South Australian and other landscapes, goldmining and bush subjects. It is sad that it is these last works by which he has been best known. They say a lot about the character of Australia and Australians of the time and are authentic social commentaries, but they are artistically disappointing.

It has not been emphasized forcefully that S.T. Gill's South Australian paintings of the 1840s are by far the best works of his long Australian career. He is clearly the best of all the South Australian artists of the 1830s and 1840s. But his South Australian works are not well known, mainly because there are fewer of them and they rarely appear on the market. There is also the fact that South Australian nineteenth-century art is generally less known than that of the equivalent period in the eastern colonies. Many of Gill's 1840s works are held in the pictorial collections of libraries, namely the Mitchell Library, Sydney, and the National Library of Australia, Canberra, and are therefore somewhat overlooked as artistic achievements. The largest number of his South Australian works are in the Art Gallery of South Australia and many are in poor condition, partly because their over-exposure in less conservation-conscious days has resulted in fading.

The imperfect preservation of many of these works has not helped Gill's reputation. Fortunately, over twenty-five of the best works in the Gallery's collection have been restored to something like their former freshness in time for the sesquicentenary of South Australia.

This book and the large exhibition which is the occasion of its publication will place S.T. Gill's oeuvre more accurately in context. It is hoped that Gill's work will now be seen not only as an invaluable record of the nation's history but also, and more importantly, as a unique and fine contribution to the tradition of the art of painting in Australia.

S. T. GILL, Artist, &c., late Draftsman and Water Color Painter to the Hubard Profile Gallery of London, begs to announce to his friends and the public generally of Adelaide and its vicinity that he has opened rooms in Gawler-place, where for the present he solicits the attendance of such individuals as are desirous of obtaining correct likenesses of themselves, families, or friends. Parties preferring attendance at their residences may be accommodated without additional charge. Correct resemblances of horses, dogs. &c., with local scenery, &c executed to order. Residences sketched and transferred to paper suited for. home conveyance. Orders executed in rotation.
Open daily from eleven till dusk.

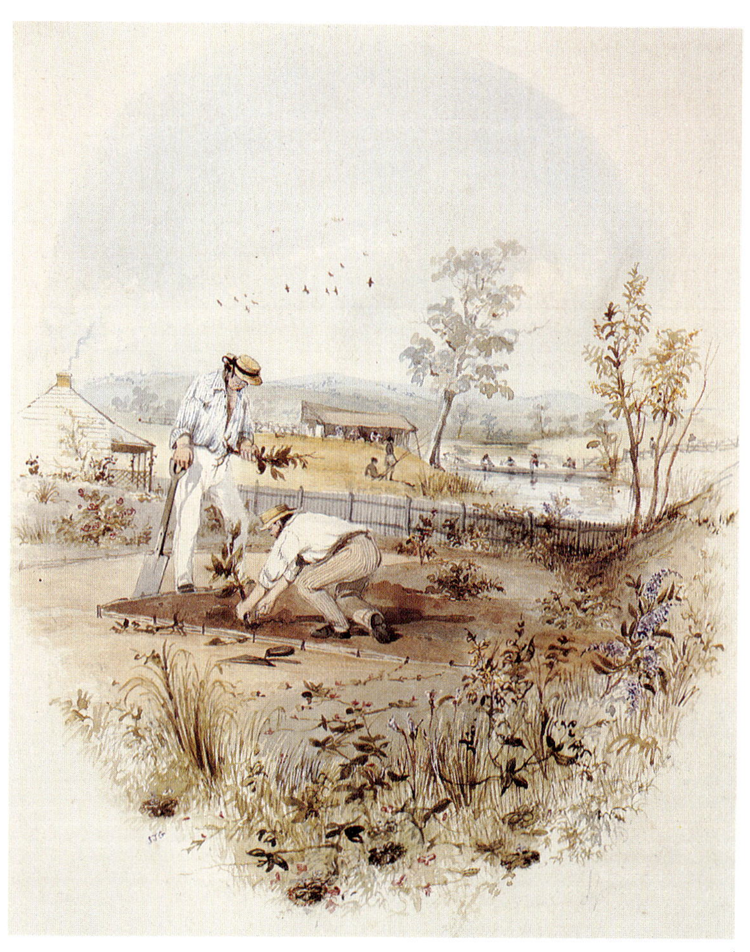

13 *Spring*, watercolour on paper, 29.3 x 21.8 cm, National Library of Australia.

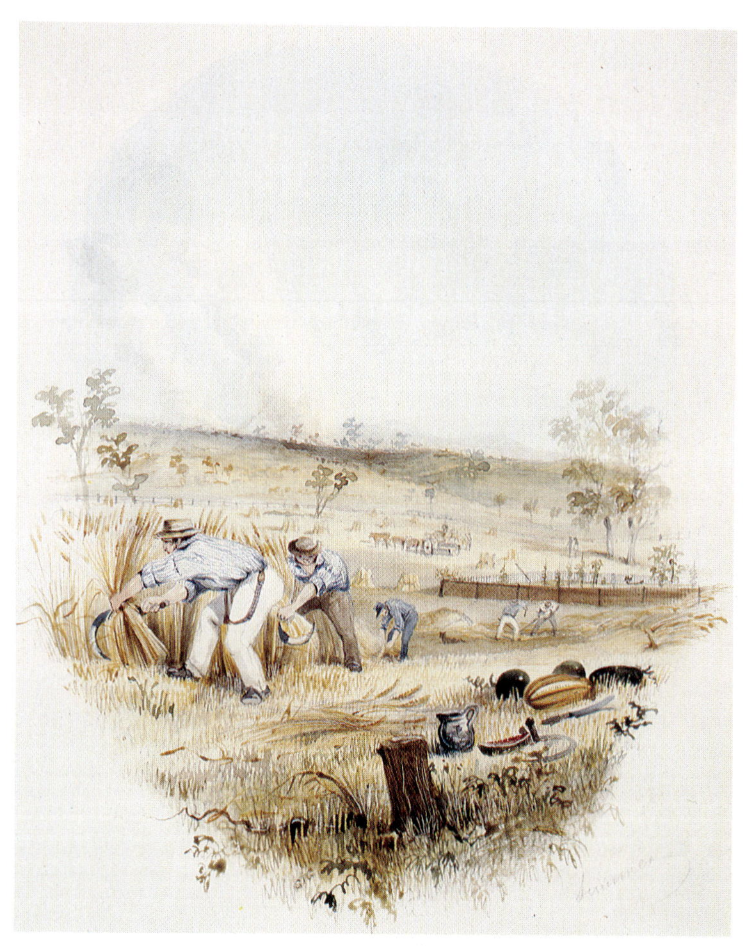

14 *Summer*, watercolour on paper, 29.3 x 21.8 cm, National Library of Australia.

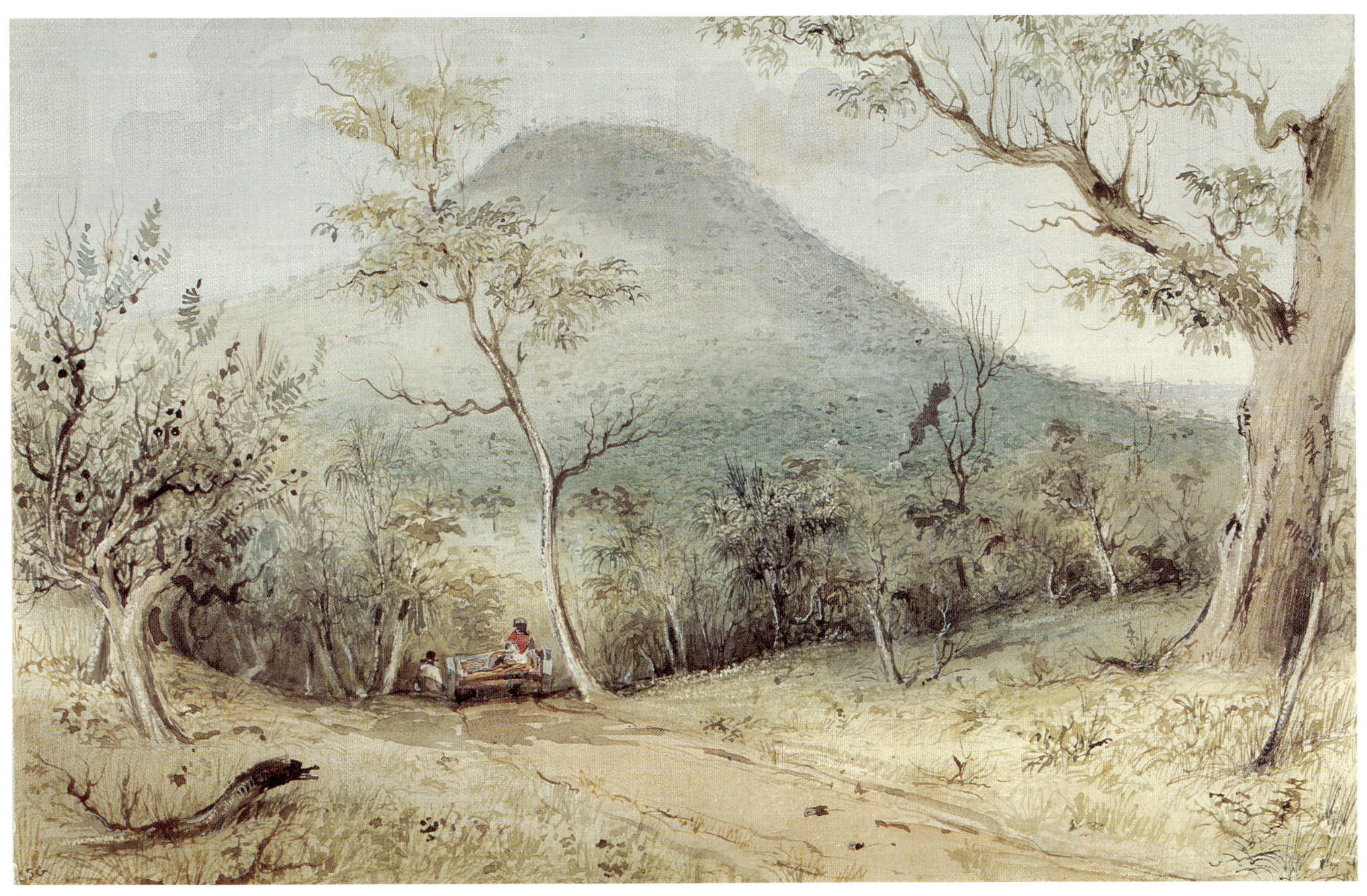

20 *Approach to Mount Crawford*, watercolour on paper, 20.1 x 31.4 cm, Art Gallery of South Australia.

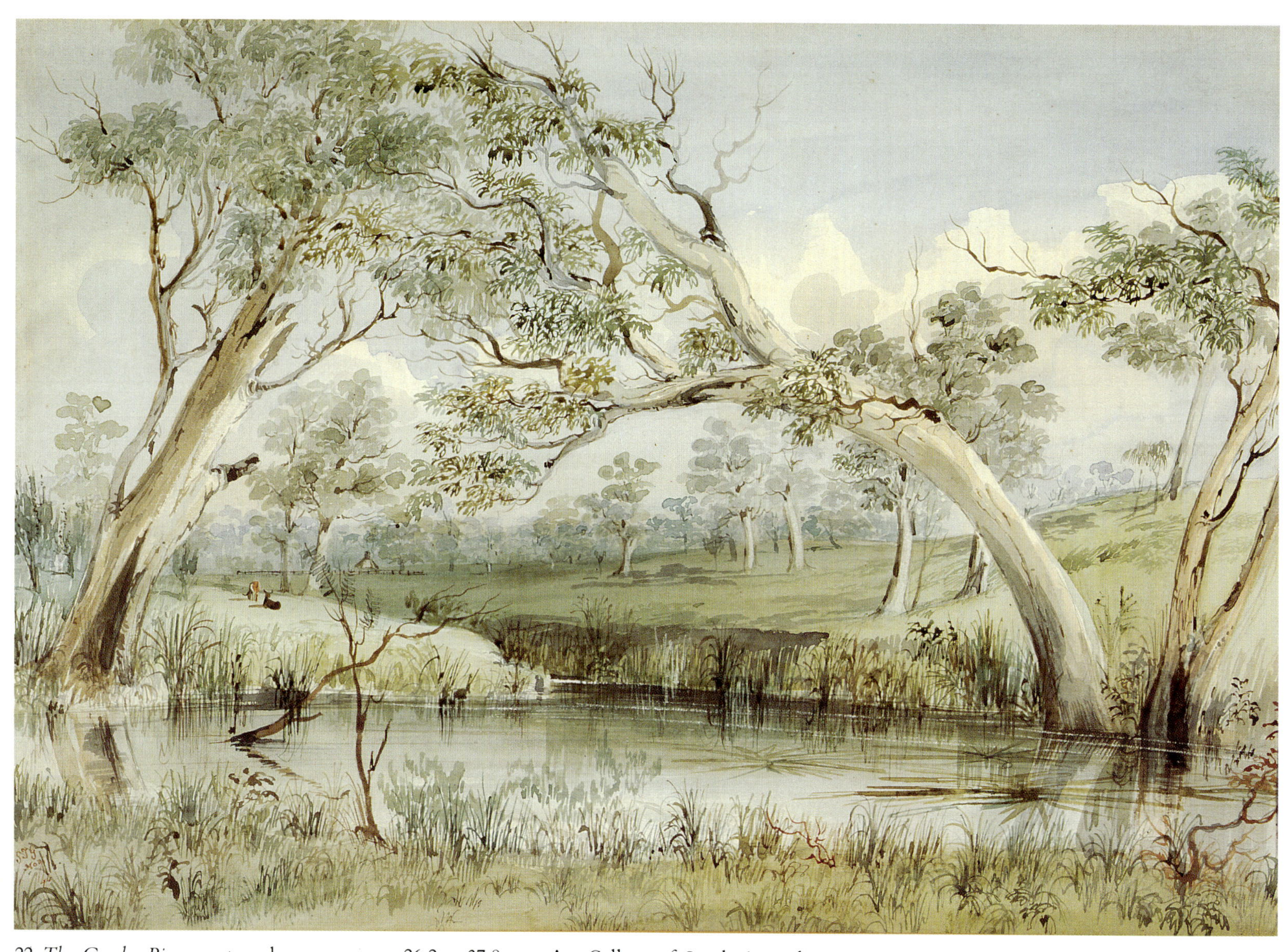

22 *The Gawler River*, watercolour on paper, 26.2 x 37.8 cm, Art Gallery of South Australia.

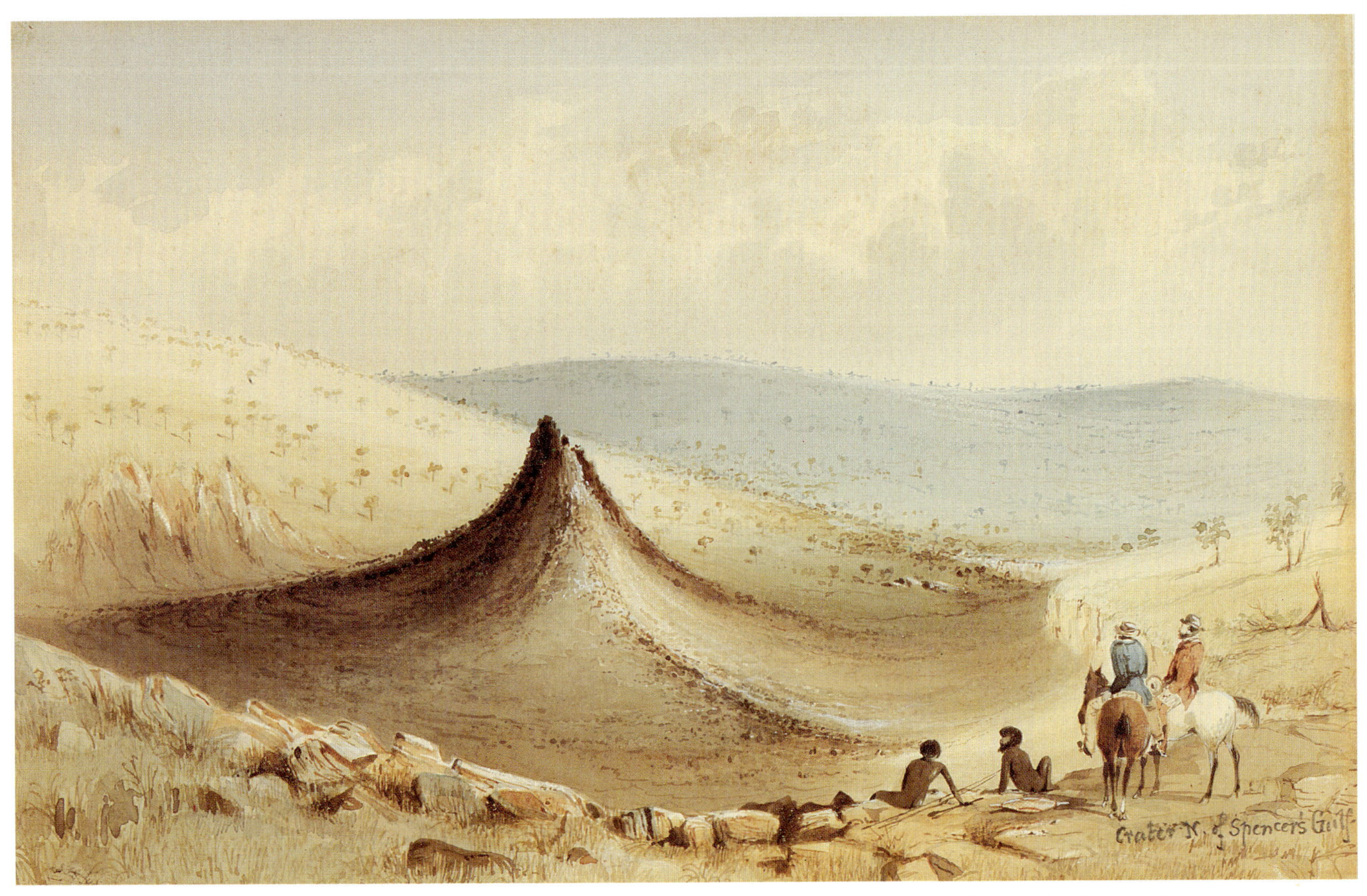

27 *Extinct Crater, North of Spencer Gulf, South Australia*, watercolour on paper, 17.8 x 28.5 cm, Art Gallery of South Australia.

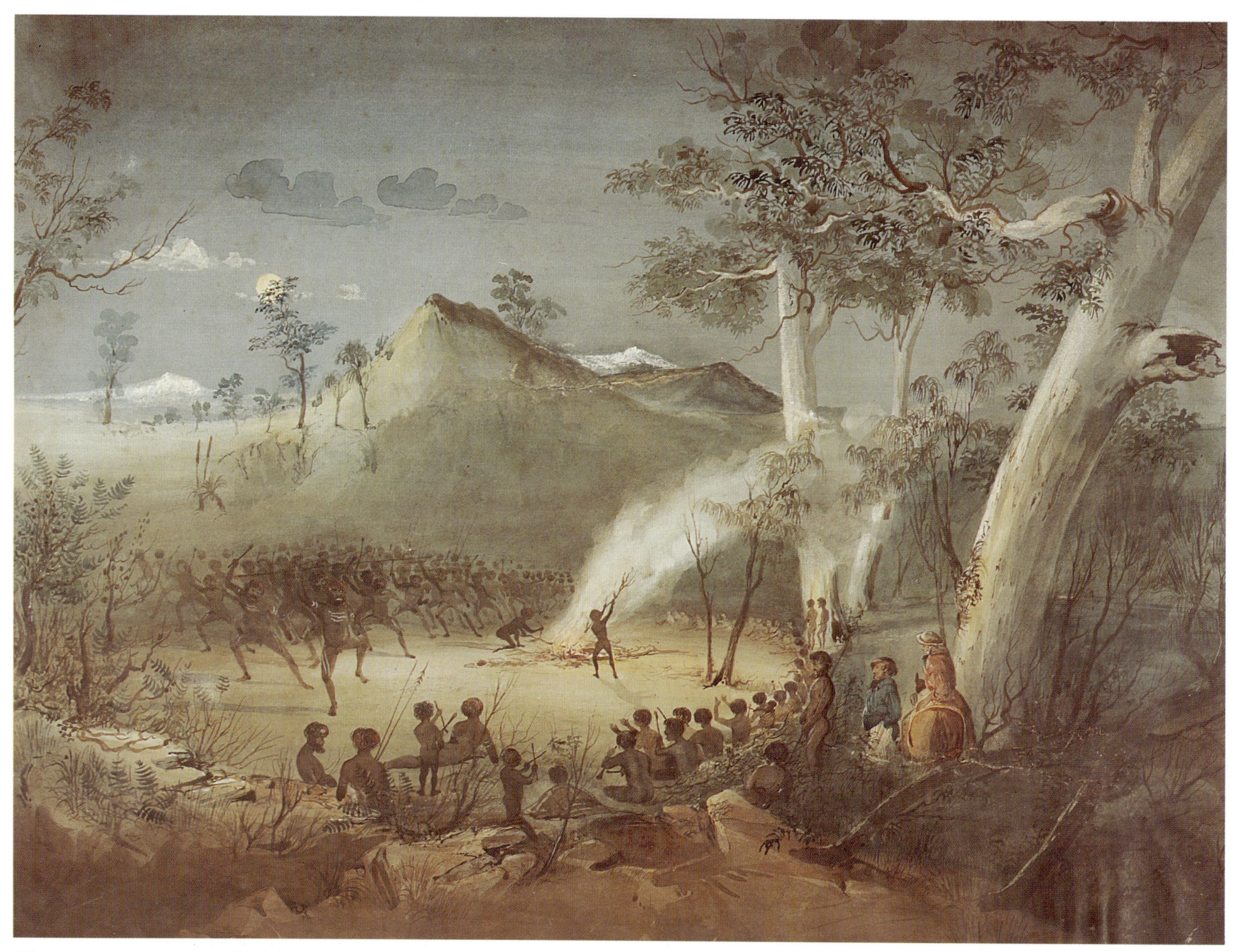

37 *A native corroboree at night*, watercolour on paper, 42.7 x 63.5 cm, National Library of Australia.

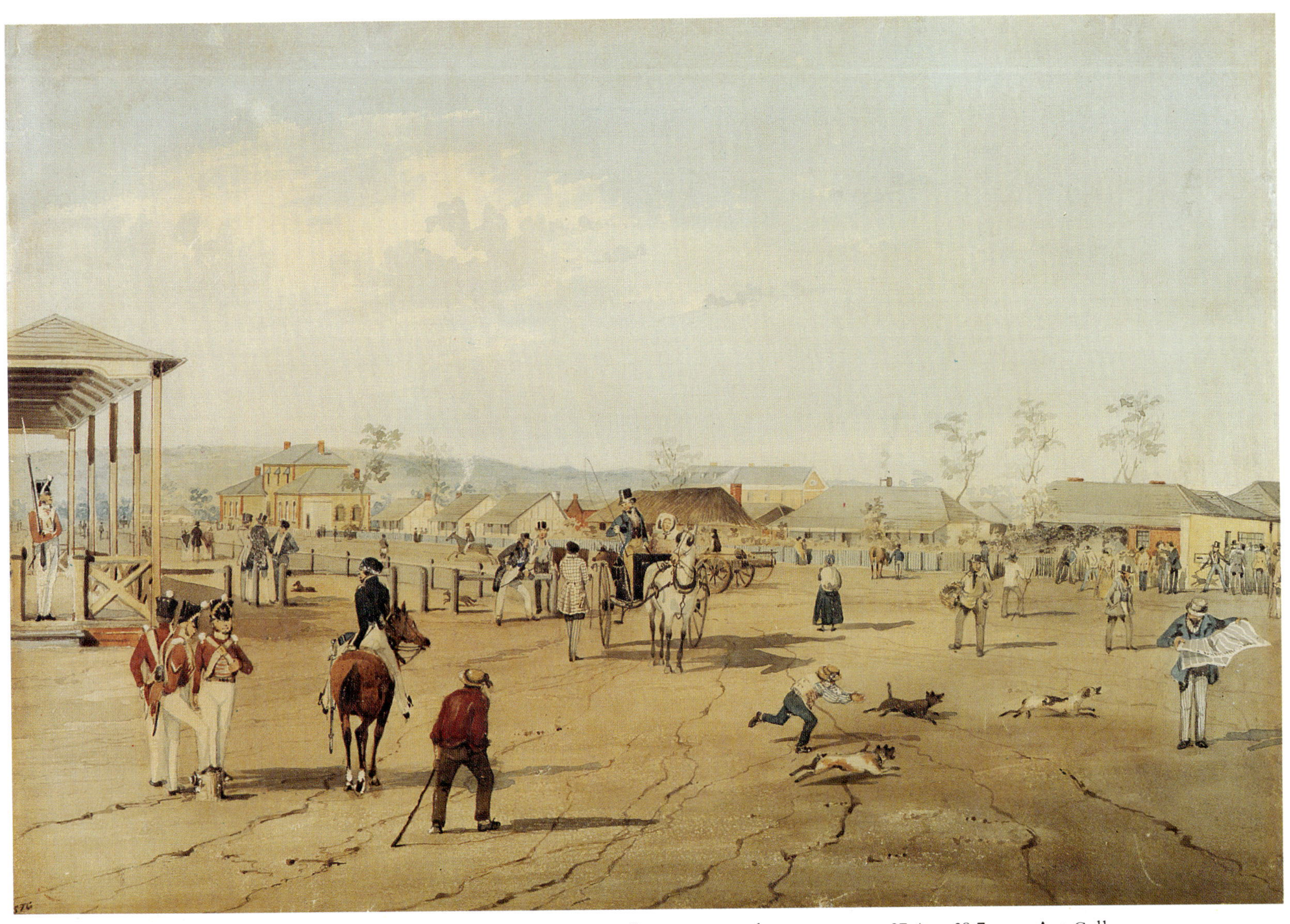

43 *North Terrace, Adelaide, looking south-east from Government House Guardhouse*, watercolour on paper, 27.4 x 39.7 cm, Art Gallery of South Australia.

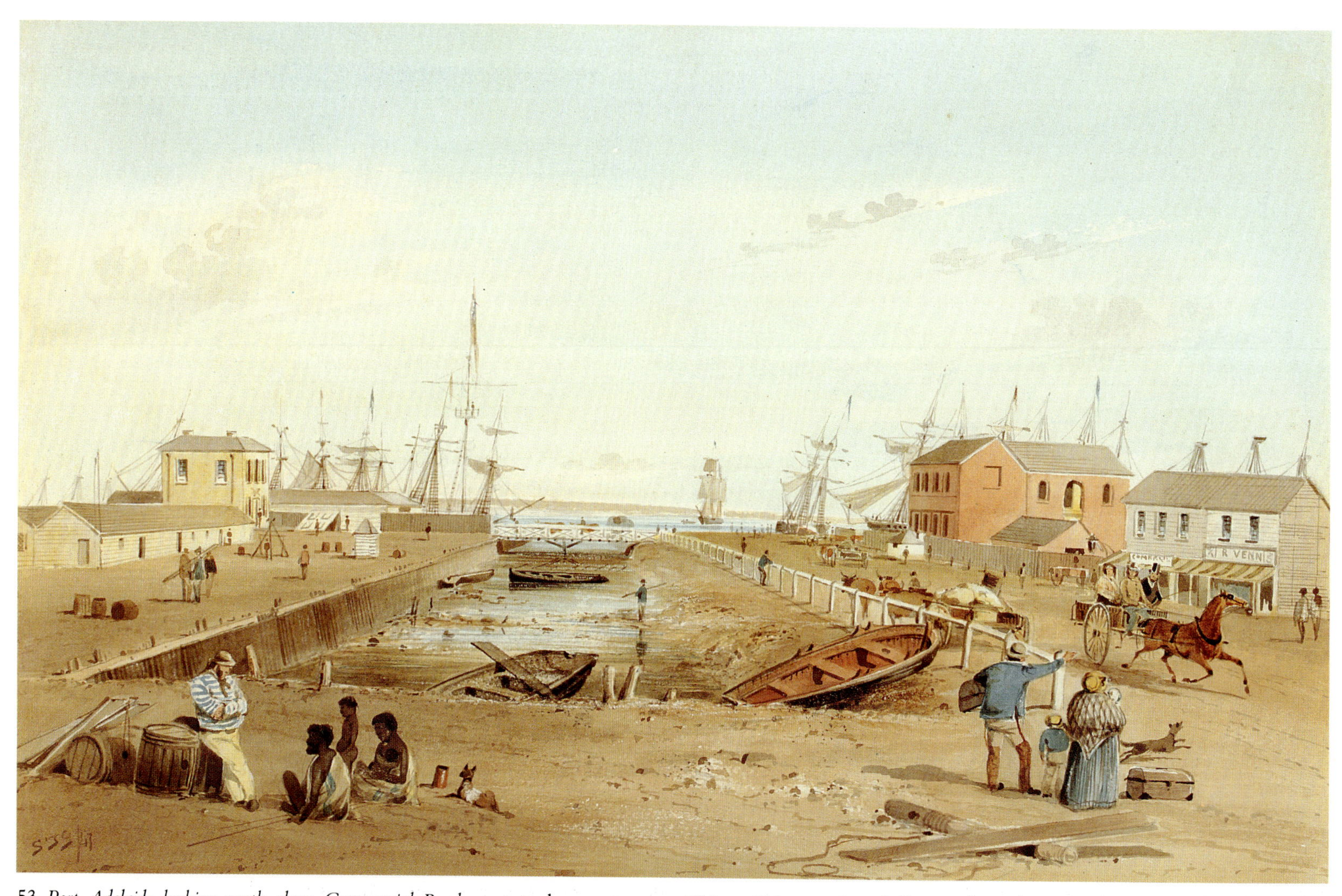

53 *Port Adelaide looking north along Commercial Road*, watercolour on paper, 20.3 x 32.0 cm, Art Gallery of South Australia.

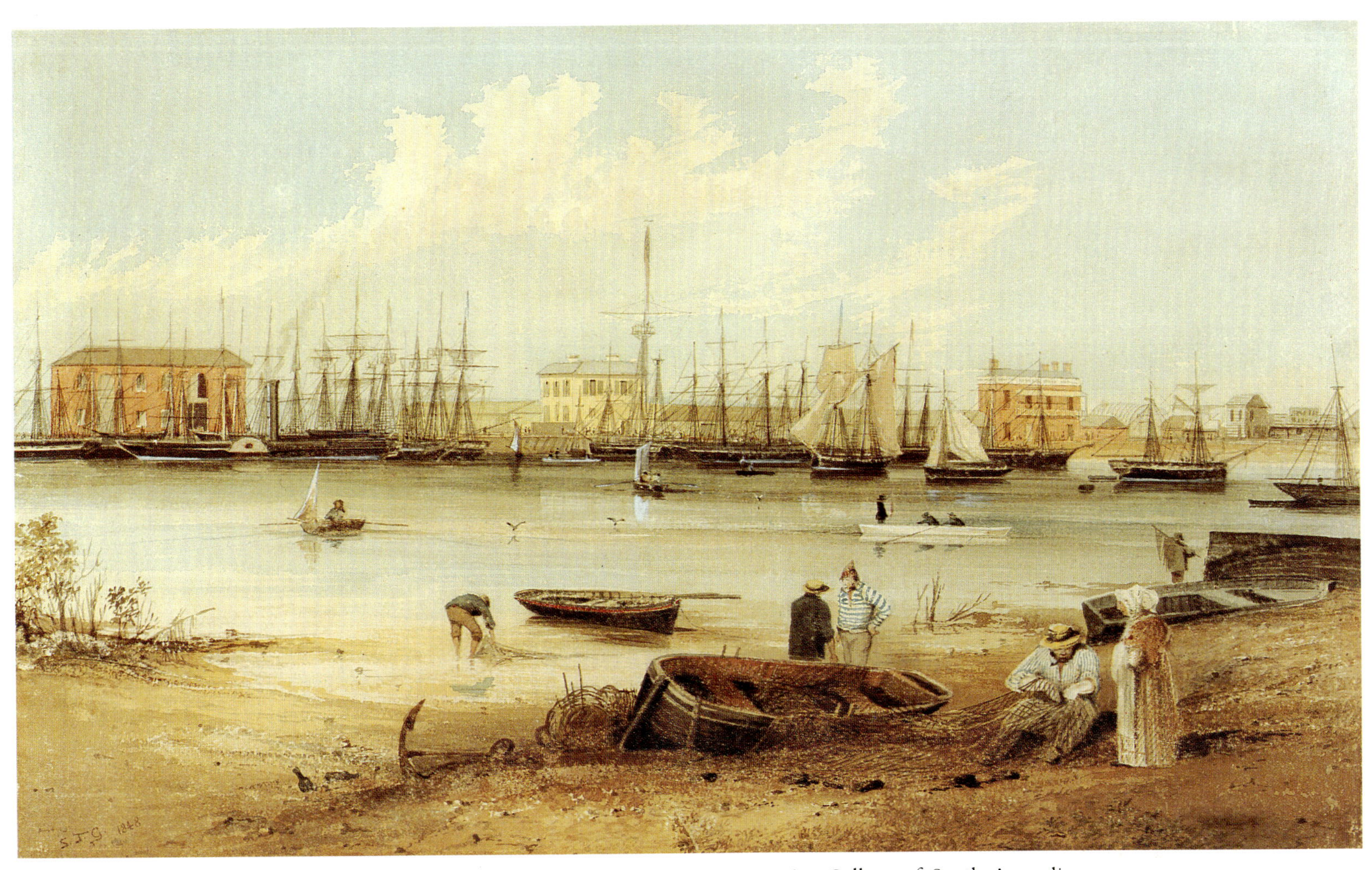

55 *Port Adelaide looking across Gawler Reach*, watercolour on paper, 28.2 x 46.1 cm, Art Gallery of South Australia.

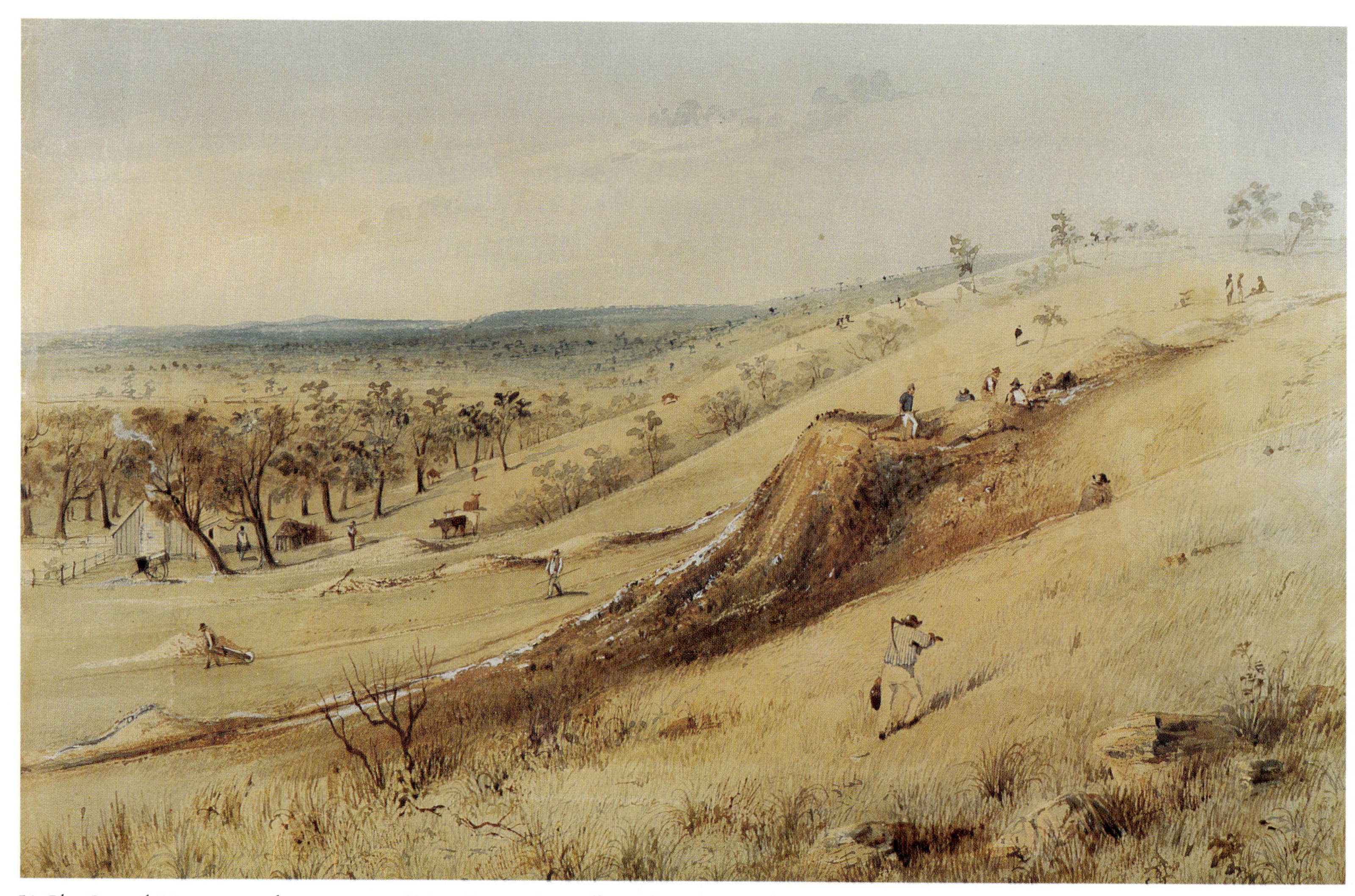

56 *Glen Osmond Mine*, watercolour on paper, 27.3 x 39.7cm, Art Gallery of South Australia.

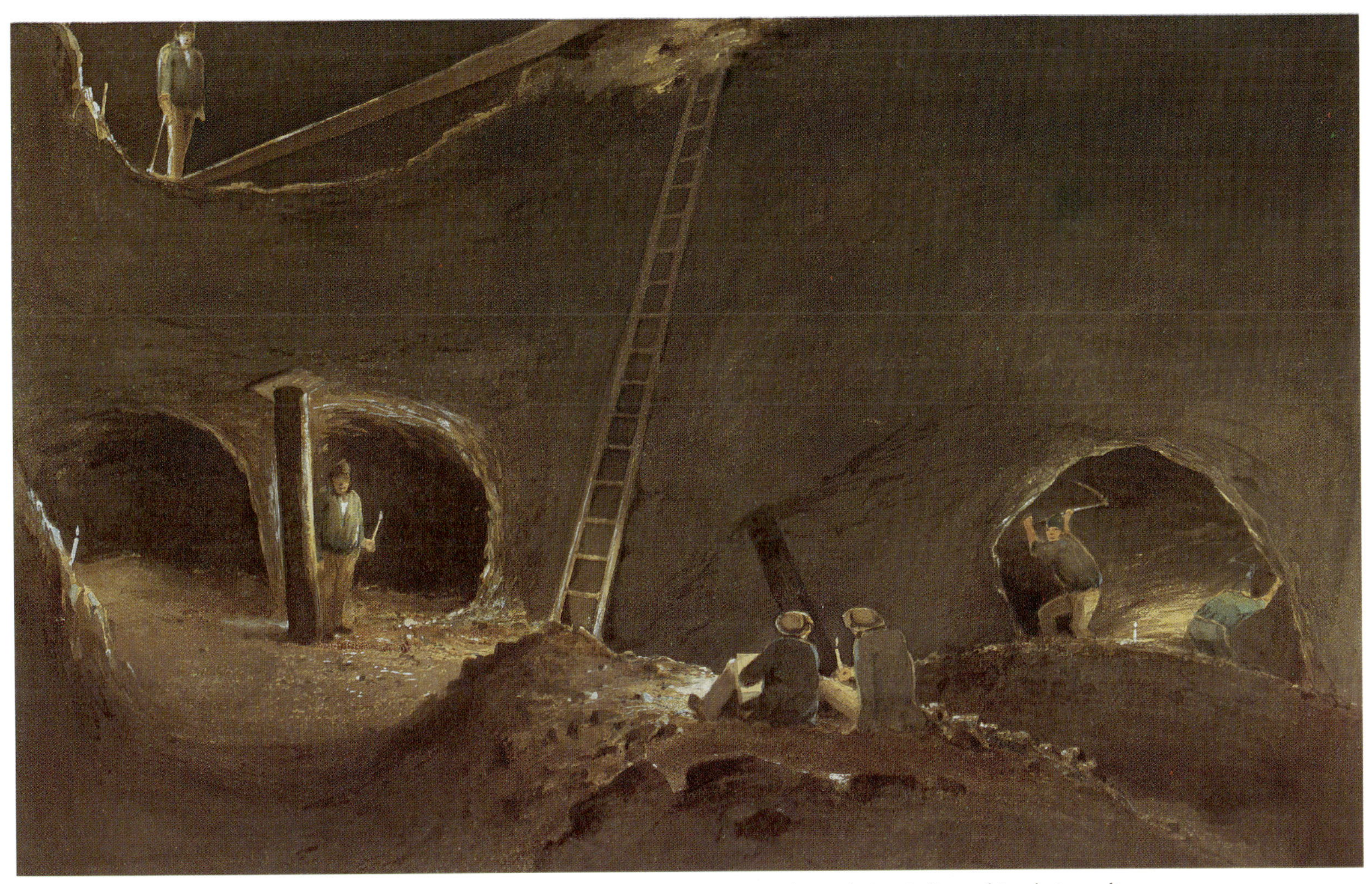

63 *Neales's Stopes, Burra Burra Mine, April 12th 1847*, watercolour on paper, 19.5 x 31.3 cm (image), Art Gallery of South Australia.

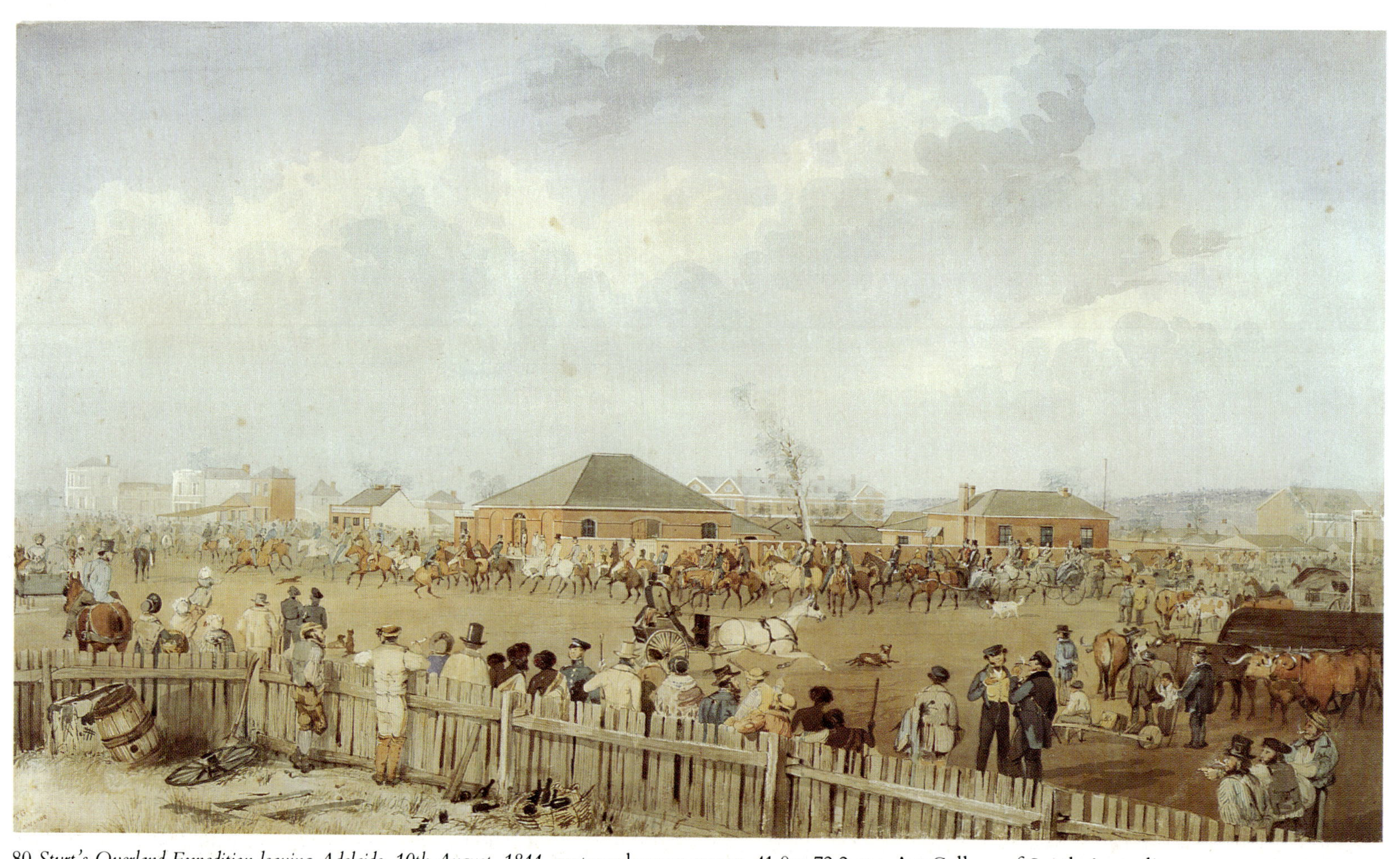

80 *Sturt's Overland Expedition leaving Adelaide, 10th August, 1844*, watercolour on paper, 41.0 x 72.2 cm, Art Gallery of South Australia.

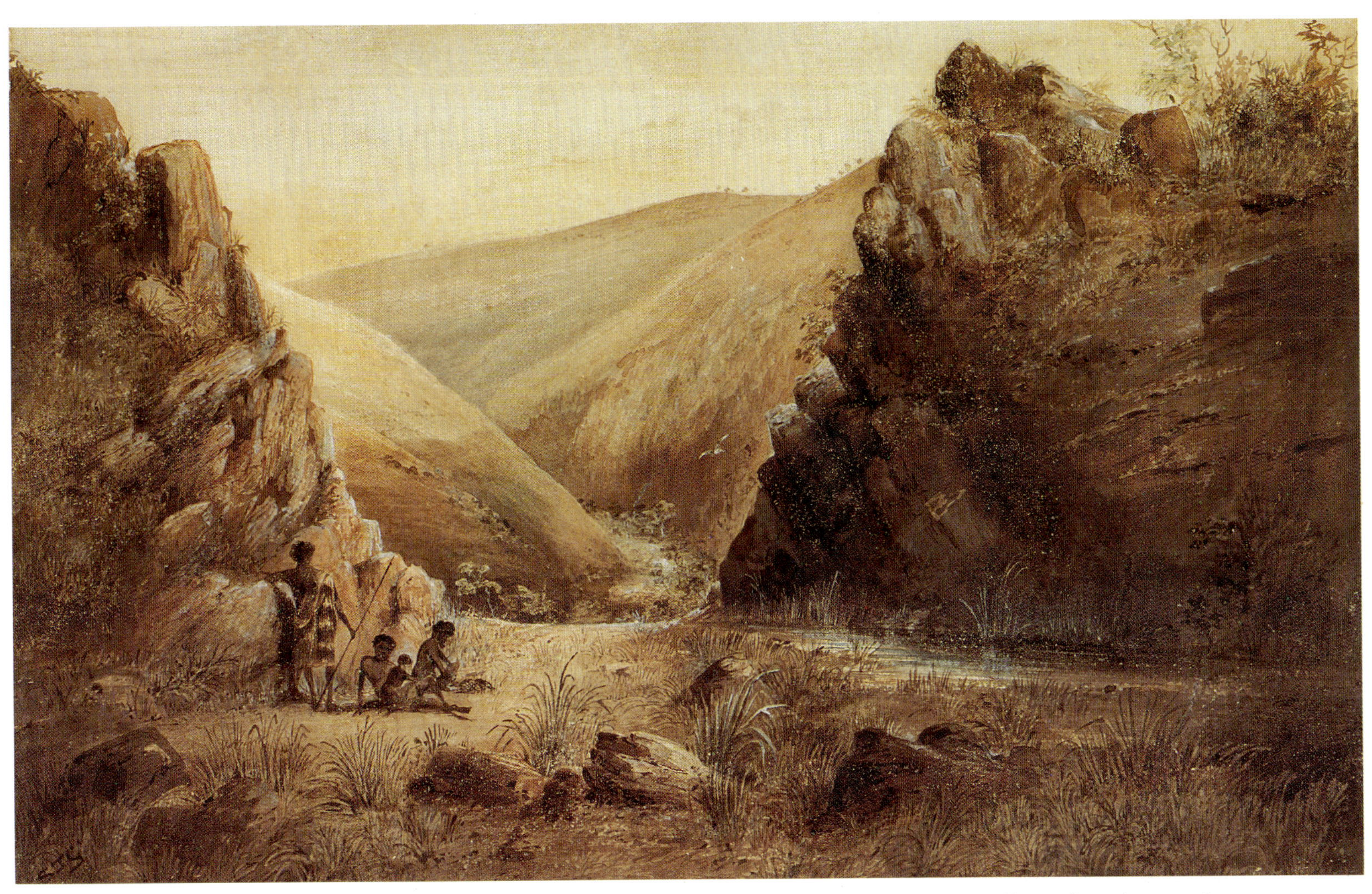

89 *Stony Creek, Mount Remarkable Survey, from above the fall,* watercolour on paper, 26.3 x 39.2 cm, Art Gallery of South Australia.

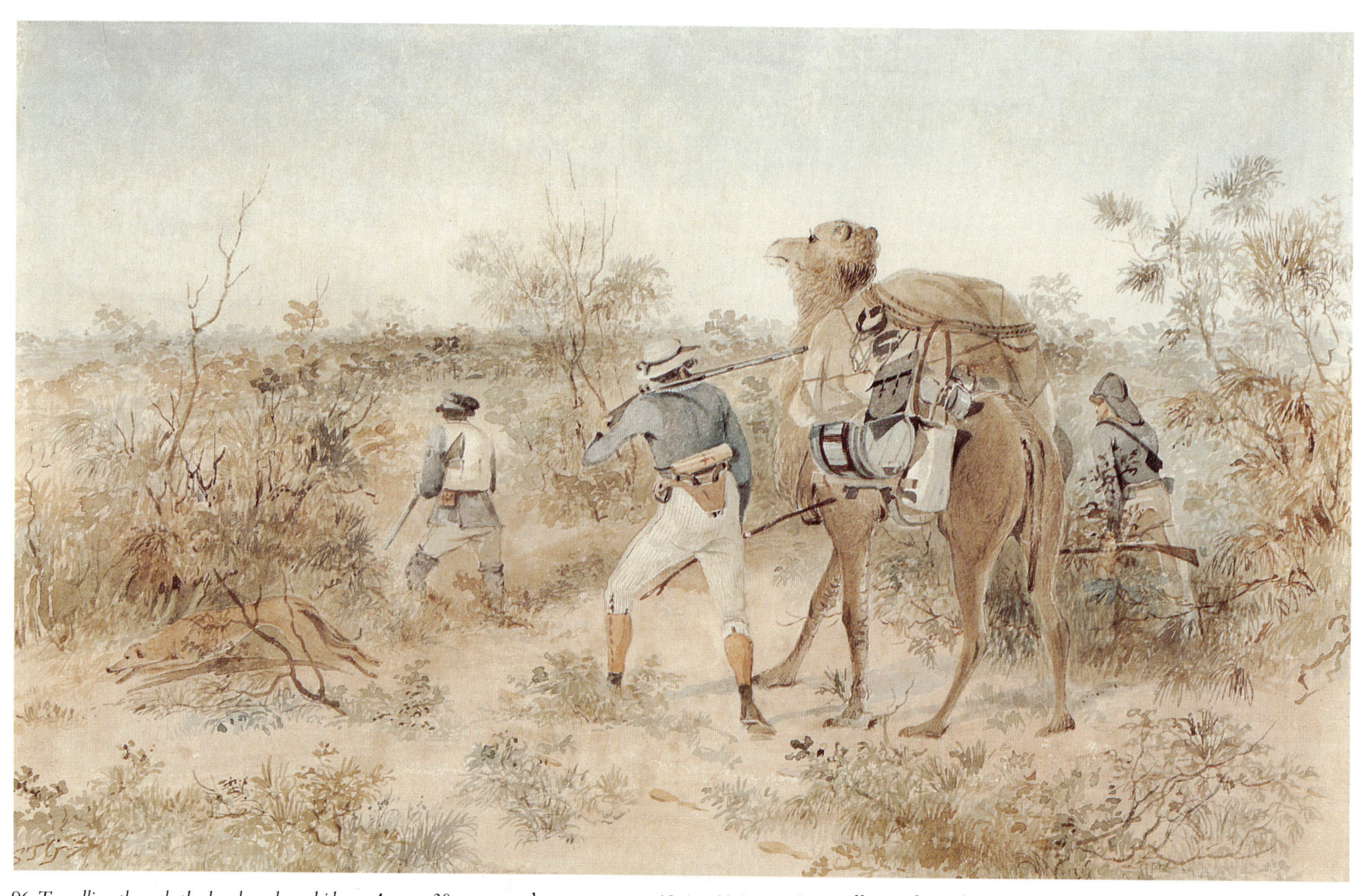

96 *Travelling through the brush and sandridges, August 30*, watercolour on paper, 18.6 x 30.3 cm, Art Gallery of South Australia.

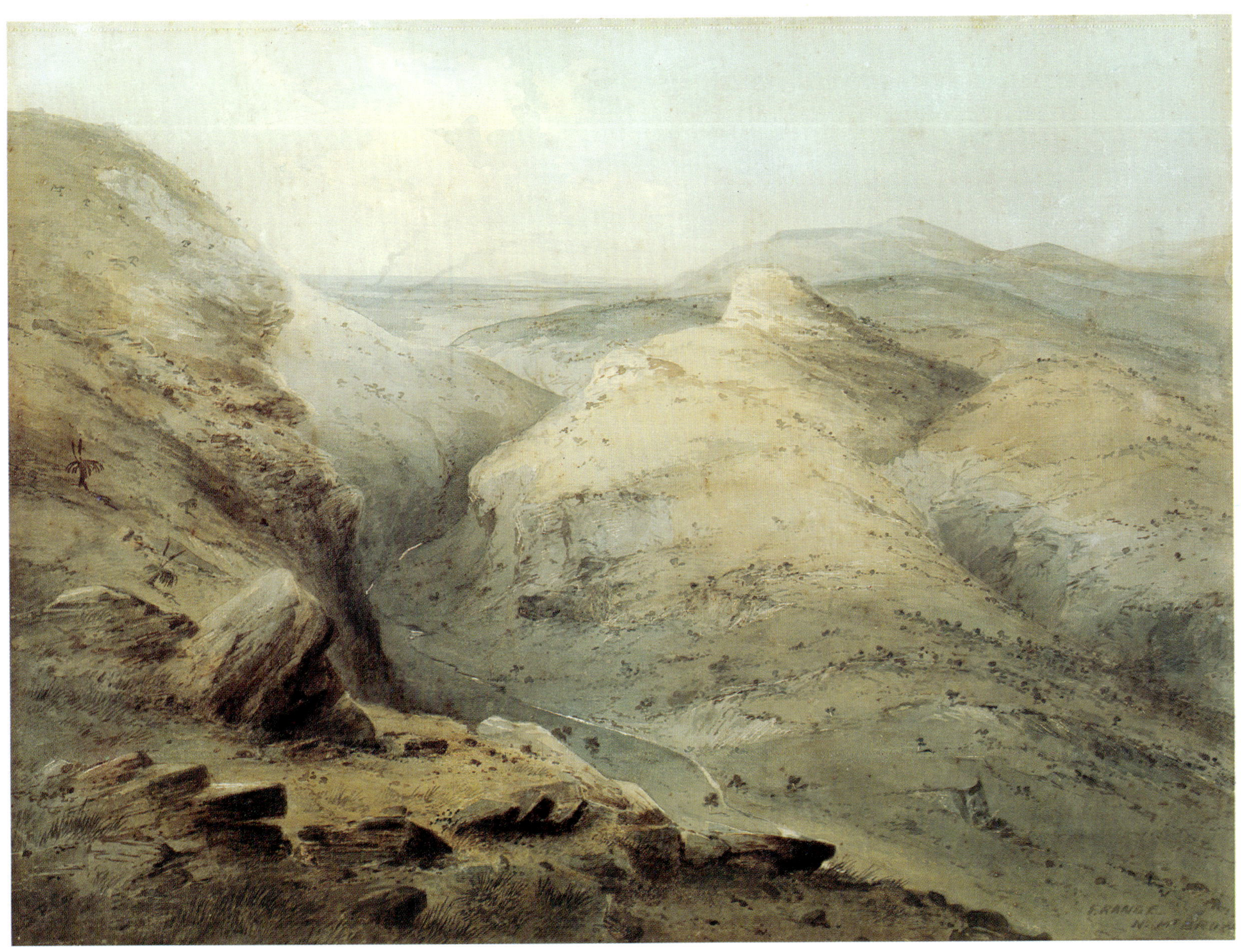

101 *Flinders Range, North of Mount Brown*, watercolour on paper, 32.8 x 44.8 cm, Art Gallery of South Australia.

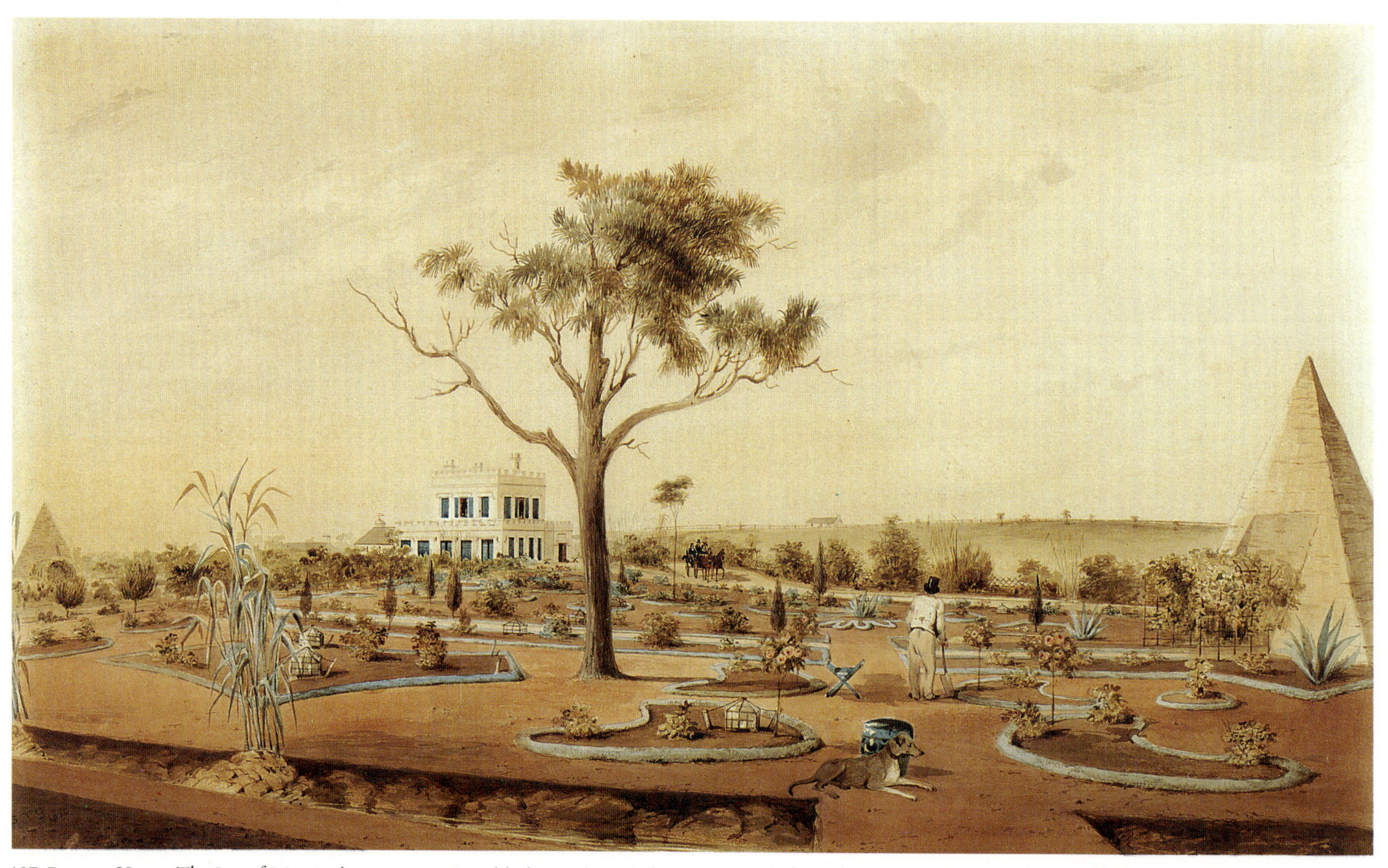

107 *Prospect House, The Seat of J.B. Graham, Esqr., near Adelaide, South Australia*, watercolour on paper, 40.5 x 68.6 (image), Art Gallery of South Australia.

Samuel Thomas Gill
A *biographical outline*

The scope of these biographical notes—compiled as far as possible from original sources such as official records, contemporary newspapers and family memorabilia—has been limited to the period from Gill's birth to his final departure from South Australia in about June 1853, with the exception of noting his move from Melbourne to Sydney in 1856 and return in 1864, and his death in 1880. A few facts about his activities in Melbourne, up to and just after his final visit to Adelaide during which he took possession of and mortgaged his property at Coromandel Valley on 13 May 1853, have been included to emphasise that the visit must have been brief because of his commitments in Melbourne, in particular his exhibition in February at the Exchange Rooms, Royal Hotel and the publication in June of the series of lithographs *Views in and around Melbourne*. Apart from this brief return there is no record of any further visit to South Australia.

1818, 21 May. Samuel Thomas Gill, first child of Reverend Samuel Gill[1] and his wife Winifred, born at the Baptist Manse, Perriton, Parish of Minehead, Somerset,[2] England.

1819 Reverend Samuel Gill moves to a living at Swansea, Glamorganshire, Wales.[3]

1821, 3 April. First brother, John Ryland Gill, born at Swansea.[4]

1822, 20 June. Second brother, William Carey Gill, born at Swansea.[5]

1823 Reverend Samuel Gill returns to England in charge of a Baptist Church at Millbrook, near Plymouth, Devon.[6]

25 October: sister, Winifred Mary Gill, born at Penzance, Cornwall.[7]

1824 The family moves to Stoke, near Devonport, Devon.[8]

1825, 25 October. Third brother Robert Richard Gill born at Navy Row, New Passage, Mount Devonport, Devon.[9]

1826 Samuel Thomas Gill and John Ryland Gill attend an infant school conducted by a widow.[10]

1826-27 Mrs Gill opens a large school on the third floor of a four-storey twelve-roomed house in Navy Row, Morice Town, near Devonport. The seminary was conducted for the reception of young gentlemen, the children of Captains, Colonels and other officers, intended for a classical education and was equipped with masters in language, drawing, painting, music, dancing and drill.[11]

1828 Samuel Thomas Gill and John Ryland Gill receive tuition from their mother and her assistants.[12]

Reverend Samuel Gill dissents from the Baptist Church and joins the Plymouth Brethren. He opens a warehouse, in partnership with a Mr Parker from India, for the sale of teas imported from India. The business prospers.[13]

1830-31 Parker returns to India and Reverend Gill concentrates on wholesale orders, travelling in a light gig to North Devon and sometimes to London. John Ryland Gill and no doubt Samuel Thomas Gill often travel with their father.[14]

1833 At about this time Samuel Thomas Gill completes his formal education at Dr Seabrook's Academy[15] and, having shown a talent for drawing, commences his art training. During this period, in response to his wish, a position is found for him with a carver and gilder in Plymouth so that he might study the works of the old masters brought in for framing.[16]

An outbreak of smallpox strikes first John Ryland Gill then Samuel Thomas Gill, Winifred Mary Gill and the two younger brothers, William Carey Gill and Robert Richard Gill who both die on 30 January and 5 February 1833 respectively.[17] As a result, the school closes and the family moves to a row of villas in Caroline Place, Stonehouse, looking across Mill Bay to Plymouth Sound and not far from Admirals Hard, which was a ferry terminal frequented by ferrymen's boats.[18] Samuel Thomas Gill is provided with many lively marine subjects, some of which appear later in his Sketchbook (cat. 1).

Reverend Samuel Gill relinquishes his tea warehouse to become Principal of a large school for the sons of sailors and soldiers, which is said to have accommodated 400 boys and was built by subscriptions from Naval and Military Officers.[19]

1834? Mrs Gill converts the drawing room of the villa in Caroline Place into a school for young gentlemen.[20]

1835, 21 February. Samuel Thomas Gill paints a *Self-portrait* in oils, aged 16 years 9 months[21]. (see p.viii)

1835–38 Samuel Thomas Gill and his father, Reverend Samuel Gill together fill a sketchbook with drawings, watercolours and poetry (cat. 1).[22]

During this period Samuel Thomas Gill is said to have studied under leading masters in London.[23] He was also a 'Draftsman and Water Color Painter to the Hubard Profile Gallery of London'[24] (see p.9).

1839, 28 June. The Colonization Commissioners for South Australia issue Land Order 1035 for 80 acres to Reverend Samuel Gill, of Stonehouse.[25]

24 June. Samuel Thomas Gill, Admirals Hard, Stonehouse, applies to his father the Reverend Samuel Gill for a free passage to South Australia giving his trade as 'Carver and Gilder'. His brother and sister, a female servant and two carpenters also apply.[26]

17 July. *Caroline*, 450 tons, sails from Plymouth (from London 28 June, Cape of Good Hope 19 October). 'Mr. and Mrs. Gill, Thos. Gill, J.R. Gill and W.M. Gill' are listed as Intermediate Passengers, the servant and carpenters are in Steerage.[27] The artist was possibly known as Thomas within his family.

17 December. *Caroline* arrives and disembarks passengers at Glenelg, South Australia.[28] The Gill family moves into a brick house at the corner of Gilles and Hanson Streets, Adelaide, the property of Osmond Gilles.[29]

1840, 7 March. Samuel Thomas Gill launches his artistic career with an announcement in the *South Australian Register* (see p.9) that he has opened rooms in Gawler Place and is available for commissions.

11 April. Samuel Thomas Gill's sister, Winifred Mary Gill, dies.[30]

21 October. Reverend Samuel Gill, described as 'Samuel Gill, Gentleman of Adelaide', receives a Land Grant of 80 acres at Coromandel Valley (earliest name, Sturt Vale), Section 863, Survey B pursuant to Land Order 1035,[31] where he builds a stone house with school attached.[32]

27 November. Samuel Thomas Gill's mother, Winifred Gill, dies, aged 54.[33]

1842 Samuel Thomas Gill is said to have visited Edward John Eyre at Moorundie.[34]

Reverend Samuel Gill marries Elizabeth Murray,[35] and a daughter, Eliza Jane, is born 23 August 1843.[36]

1844, 10 August. Samuel Thomas Gill sketches the departure of Captain Sturt's Expedition into Central Australia and develops a number of important watercolours of this historic event.[37]

October-November. Samuel Thomas Gill visits the Barossa to paint a group of watercolours for John Howard Angas, who records in his diary 29 October 1844 'Out with Mr. Gill the artist who has come from town to take some sketches — took Angaston, "Wheal Sally", sheep washing and flat below Mr. Evans'.[38] Two of the works which undoubtedly formed part of this commission were *The Gawler River* and *Rhodes's Cattle Station on the Gawler, Section 471, November 1844* (cat. 22 and 23).[39]

1845 Address: 'Gill, S.T., artist, Carrington Street'.[40]

19 June. Adelaide's first (one-man) exhibition, a group of watercolours by George French Angas of South Australian and New Zealand scenes, natives and artefacts is held in the Legislative Council Chamber[41] accompanied by some pre-publicity for *South Australia Illustrated*.[42] The event draws criticism of Angas's work and the first public commentary about the life-style of Samuel Thomas Gill

and his standing and technique as an artist. Frederick Robert Nixon,[43] criticises the work of Angas in favour of Gill in a letter to the *South Australian* which brings a response in the *South Australian Register* abusing Nixon, but praising Gill for his modesty and retiring disposition.[44]

November. Samuel Thomas Gill completes a large group of watercolours of Adelaide streets, buildings and events, Port Adelaide, country views and mines, mostly commissioned by James Allen (former Proprietor and Editor of the *South Australian Register*, see Appendix A) who sails for England in December, where, during 1846-7, by an arrangement with the South Australian Company he gives a series of illustrated Lectures on South Australia in London and a number of provincial centres designed to encourage emigration to and investment in the Province.[45]

November. The *South Australian Register* announces that 'A daguerreotype has been sent to the Colony and is in the hands of Mr. Gill, the artist' who 'will soon be prepared to show us as we are'.[46]

November. Samuel Thomas Gill is included in an exhibition *South Australia as it is*, taken to Scotland by Alexander Murray[47] and displayed during November and December at the Dilletanti Rooms, 52 Buchanan Street, Glasgow.[48] The press advises 'The views are 75 in number and with the exception of a few by Mr. S. Gill, Adelaide, have been all taken by Mr. Murray, the proprietor'.[49] Gill is represented by 'A Corroborie and other Drawings'.[50] The exhibition is 'on view' and offered for sale in London in May 1846.[51]

1846 Address: Gill, S.T., artist, Tavistock Street, Rundle Street.[52]

10 July. Samuel Thomas Gill joins John Ainsworth Horrocks's North West Expedition as an 'unremunerated' member 'for the purpose of filling his note book' and gives a parting supper to a few of his friends on the eve of the departure of the expedition from Adelaide.[53]

10 October. Samuel Thomas Gill's daily notes of the ill-fated Horrocks Expedition, covering the period 8 August to 24 September, are published in *The South Australian Gazette and Colonial Register*.[54]

1847 Address: Gill, S.T., artist, Leigh Street.[55]

5 January. The press announces that 'Mr. Gill has politely favoured us with an inspection of his series of no less than thirty-three views', 'depicting the most remarkable scenes met with by the [Horrocks] expedition'. Five of the works are described and it is reported that 'This interesting series of pictures is to be raffled for in the course of a few days'.[56]

6 January. Raffle of scenes from Horrocks expedition takes place in the Government Offices among 'thirty members at one guinea each'.[57]

23 January. Samuel Thomas Gill assists the Committee appointed to arrange the first general exhibition of paintings and drawings by 'South Australian artists — professional and amateur' by receiving 'at his rooms in Leigh Street, such paintings as are desired to be exhibited'.[58]

10 February. Samuel Thomas Gill displays 62 paintings and drawings, of which at least 33 are related to the Horrocks Expedition,[59] in the *Exhibition of Pictures, the Works of Colonial Artists*, held in the Council Room, North Terrace, Adelaide from 10 to 17 February 1847. A catalogue[60] was published (sixpence) and admission charged (one shilling) and surplus proceeds were set aside to 'aid in the formation of a Society for the encouragement of Art in the Colony'.[61] The exhibition is reviewed in the local press.[62]

12 April. Samuel Thomas Gill visits Kooringa to paint a series of watercolours of the town and the Burra Burra mining operations for the South Australian Mining Association.[63] In August the press lists seven works which adorn 'the walls of the Directors' Room' and reports that several sets of copies have been ordered by the proprietors.[64]

1848 Address: Gill, S.F. [*sic*], artist, Grenfell Street.[65]

10 February. Samuel Thomas Gill shows six Burra watercolours and four other pictures in the second *Exhibition of Pictures*, Adelaide, 1848, 'principally the works of artists residing in South Australia', which opens in the Council Room, North Terrace on 10 February, the day of

the Agricultural and Horticultural Show.⁶⁶ The exhibition includes works by foreign 'masters both ancient and modern' which the press complains makes it less interesting than the previous year 'as it does not entirely consist of the works of colonial artists'.⁶⁷ The exhibition closes 19 February.

1849, 11 May. Samuel Thomas Gill appears in the Police Court charged with keeping a ferocious dog which flew at and wounded a lubra in Leigh Street. He denies ownership and the charge is dismissed.⁶⁸

16 May. Samuel Thomas Gill makes his first venture into lithography and portraiture with *Heads of the People*, drawing directly on the stone a series of half-length portraits of well known colonists. The first set of three sheets with four portraits on each sheet, printed by Penman & Co., Lithographers, Adelaide, is published 16 May and available from Platts Library at three shillings, or five shillings on proof paper. This series is well received in the local press as 'admirable likenesses . . . with a spice of caricature' which 'will form a favourite article of exportation to friends "at home" '.⁶⁹ A second set of five *Heads of the People* on one sheet is published on 18 July⁷⁰ and the third set of 'bunches of fives' appears on 1 September.⁷¹

August. Samuel Thomas Gill and the painter J.M. Skipper and his wife prepare diagrams of the ear to illustrate a lecture given by Dr Eades at the quarterly conversazione of the Mechanics' Institute.⁷²

December. Samuel Thomas Gill produces his first lithograph of a topical event, a fete at Prospect House to celebrate the consecration of Christ Church, North Adelaide, which he dedicates as 'their obedient and humble servant' to the 'Lord Bishop and Clergy of South Australia'.⁷³

1850 February. Samuel Thomas Gill paints three watercolours of the Burra Burra copper mines and five views of Prospect House probably as a commission from J.B. Graham.⁷⁴

March: Samuel Thomas Gill's 'fine Newfoundland dog'

is poisoned and he offers a reward of five pounds to discover the perpetrator.⁷⁵

25 May. Samuel Thomas Gill is commissioned to draw a portrait of an accused murderer, James Johnson, as an illustration for a local newspaper.⁷⁶

October–December. Samuel Thomas Gill is laid up for the last three months of the year with a severe inflammation of the wrist, palm and fingers of the right hand, according to a press report dated 7 January 1851 which advises he is 'likely soon to recover the use of the affected member'.⁷⁷

November. Reverend Samuel Gill receives a Land Grant of a further 53 acres at Coromandel Valley.⁷⁸

1851 January. Samuel Thomas Gill places 'A Card' in several newspapers, advertising his studio in Pirie Street, opposite the Freemasons' Tavern. No doubt Gill wished his clients to know that he had recovered the use of his hand and was awaiting further commissions, because these 'cards' appeared regularly between January and April.⁷⁹

February. Samuel Thomas Gill's paintings of Mr Vansittart's horses, Merry Monarch, Lucifer, Kyeta and Jack attract considerable local attention.⁸⁰

March. Samuel Thomas Gill draws a lithograph of the Old Colonists' Festival Dinner, which was attended by 600 men to celebrate the first sale of city land on 27 March 1837. Printed and published by Penman & Galbraith, the print sells at five shillings per copy.⁸¹

21 June. Samuel Thomas Gill's landlord, Abraham Fordham places a notice in the paper 'To S.T. Gill, Esq., Artist. If he does not call and pay the undersigned £48. 8s. for Board and Lodging, and take away his Portraits and other Pictures, they will be sold to pay the expenses of advertisements'.⁸²

July: The first of a series of lithographs drawn on stone by S.T. Gill and printed by Penman & Galbraith is announced, *Views in Adelaide no. 1, Hindley Street from King William Street* 'gives a true and vivid idea of that bustling locality'.⁸³

At about this time Gill also drew two small lithographs *No. 1 The Auction Mart* and *No. 2 The Bank of Australasia* which were printed at the head of and sold as Illustrated Letter Paper by Platts' Book Warehouse (*South Australian Register*, 26 July 1851, p.2a).

August. Samuel Thomas Gill donates one guinea to a Testimonial to James Hurtle Fisher.[84]

September. Samuel Thomas Gill, artist, files a petition in the Supreme Court declaring himself insolvent and unable to meet his engagements.[85]

October: Gill produces two more lithographs *Views in Adelaide no. 2, Hindley Street* and *Views in Adelaide no. 3, Rundle Street looking East*.[86]

December. Samuel Thomas Gill paints watercolours of four of the crack steeple-chasers of the colony, one of which 'would do credit to Herring himself'. The pictures are to be raffled and are displayed at Schmidt's Exchange Hotel, Hindley Street.[87]

1852 January/March. Samuel Thomas Gill sets off for the Victorian goldfields early in 1852, probably between January and March. There is no evidence of his remaining in Adelaide during this period nor of the method of his travel, whether by sea[88] or overland.[89] It seems unlikely that he was accompanied by his brother as has been stated by a number of authorities.[90]

April/May. Samuel Thomas Gill undertakes the prodigious task of sketching life on the goldfields and then drawing on stone and proofing the series of 48 lithographs *Victoria Gold Diggings and Diggers as they are*, the first part of 24 plates of which are advertised for sale by Macartney and Galbraith on 20 August 1852 in the Melbourne *Argus*. Three of these plates are dated on the stone 10 and 27 June and 1 July.[91]

16 September. John Ryland Gill and his fiancee's brother James Thompson sail for Melbourne in the *Hero*, possibly joining Samuel Thomas Gill there and proceeding with him to the goldfields.[92]

16 December. Reverend Samuel Gill dies, aged 60, leaving behind 'a beloved wife, two sons and an only daughter'.[93] The two sons, Samuel Thomas and John Ryland are still in Victoria, probably at the goldfields, as late as 3 January 1853, when the widow, Mrs Elizabeth Gill, applies for Letters of Administration of the estate of her late husband.[94]

1853, 4 February. The Melbourne *Argus* reports an exhibition of watercolours by Samuel Thomas Gill of South Australian scenes and of the goldfields, held at the Exchange Rooms, Royal Hotel.[95]

13 May. Samuel Thomas Gill 'late of Melbourne . . . and now of Adelaide' returns briefly[96] and as eldest son and heir at law of Reverend Gill, who died intestate, inherits two sections of land and improvements, 70 acres and 53 acres, at Coromandel Valley which he mortgages for £500 to Robert Macgeorge, Timber Merchant of Bank Street (cat. 112) at the same time granting Macgeorge Power of Attorney. By 1856 all this property is sold at Gill's direction to satisfy the loan and accrued interest.[97]

21 June. Samuel Thomas Gill produces the first of a series of lithographs *Views in and around Melbourne*, published by Macartney and Galbraith.[98]

1856, 20 May. Samuel Thomas Gill and a Mrs Gill arrive in Sydney as saloon passengers in the *London*.[99]

1864 Samuel Thomas Gill returns to Melbourne, probably very early in 1864 because his name does not appear in the Sydney directory in this year. Mrs Gill remains in Sydney.[100] He lives in Melbourne until his death.

1880, 27 October. Samuel Thomas Gill collapses and dies on the steps of the Post Office in Bourke Street, Melbourne.[101]

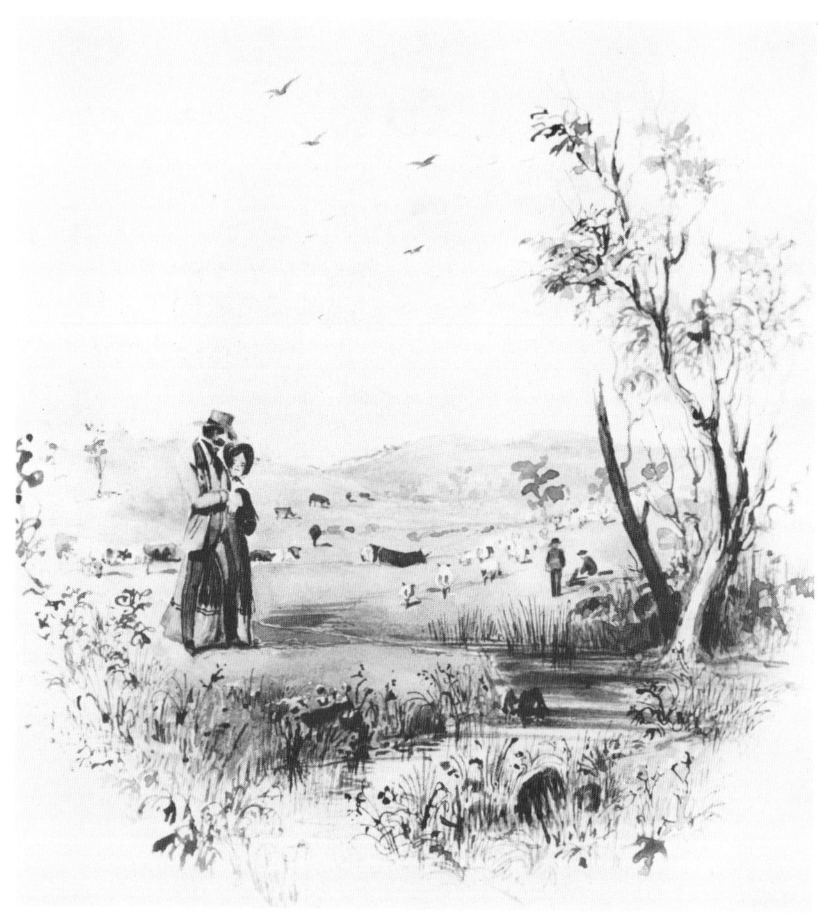

6 *May*, watercolour on paper, 21.9 x 18.2 cm, National Library of Australia.

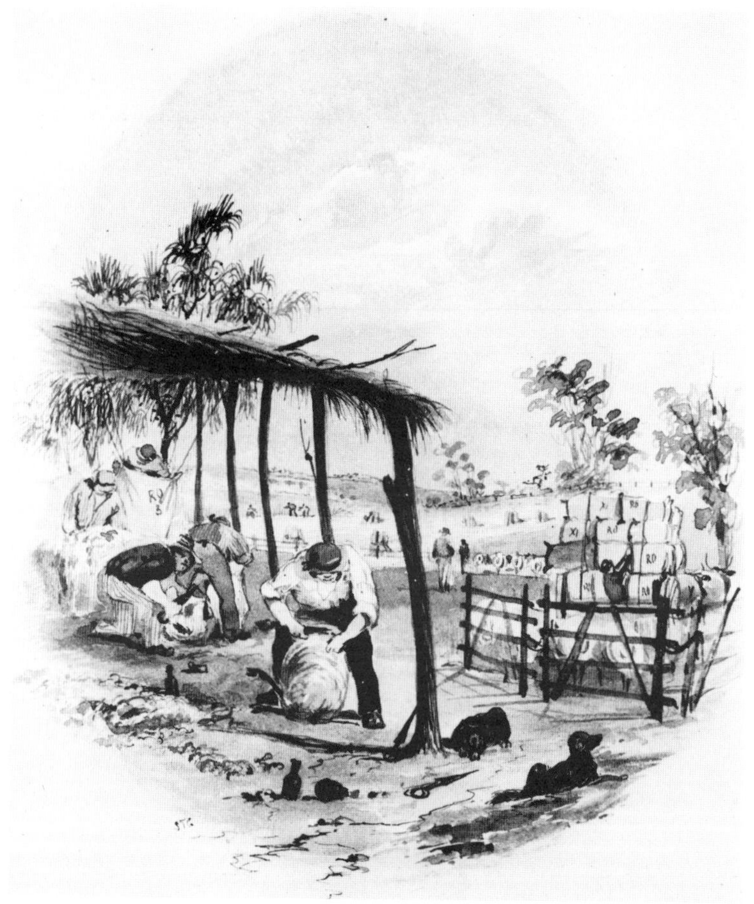

11 *November*, watercolour on paper, 21.8 x 18.3 cm, National Library of Australia.

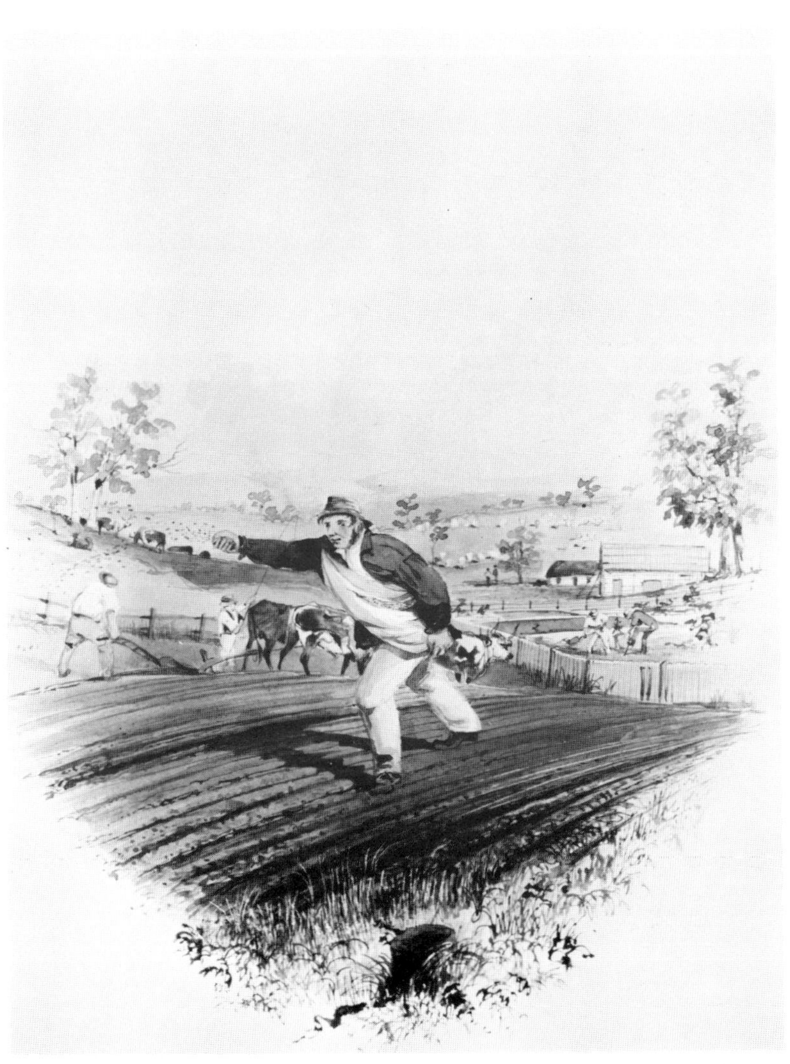

15 *Autumn*, watercolour on paper, 29.3 x 21.9 cm, National Library of Australia.

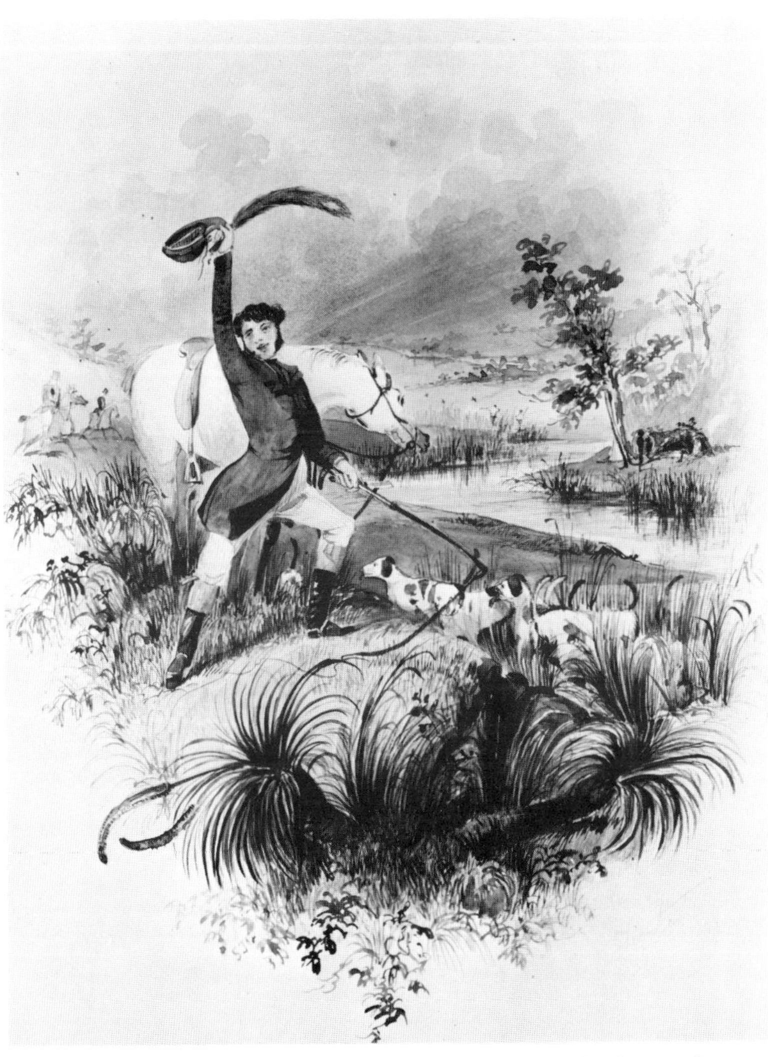

16 *Winter*, watercolour on paper, 29.6 x 21.8 cm, National Library of Australia.

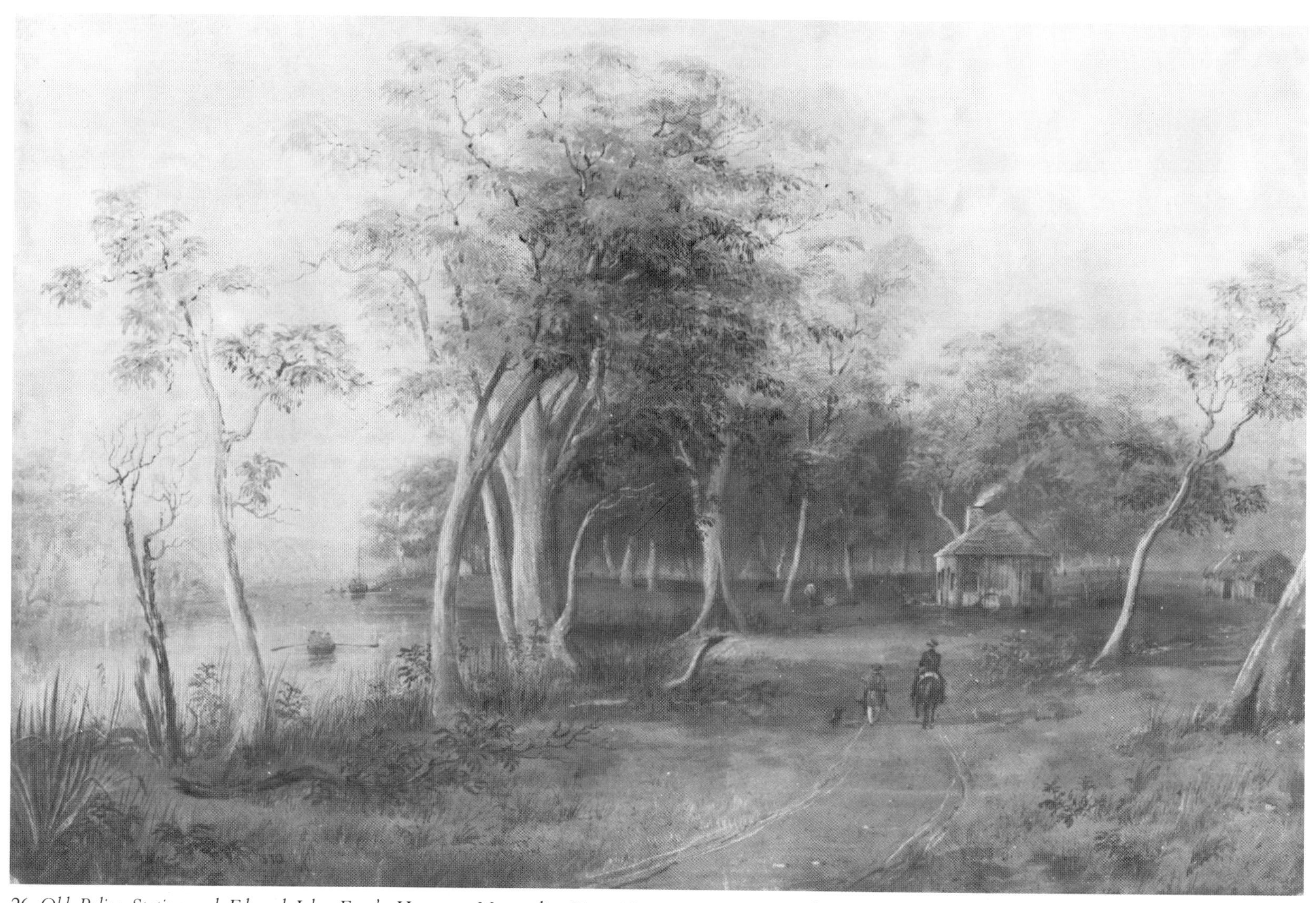

26 *Old Police Station and Edward John Eyre's House at Moorundie, River Murray, 1842,* watercolour on paper, 43.5 x 66.5 cm, Art Gallery of South Australia.

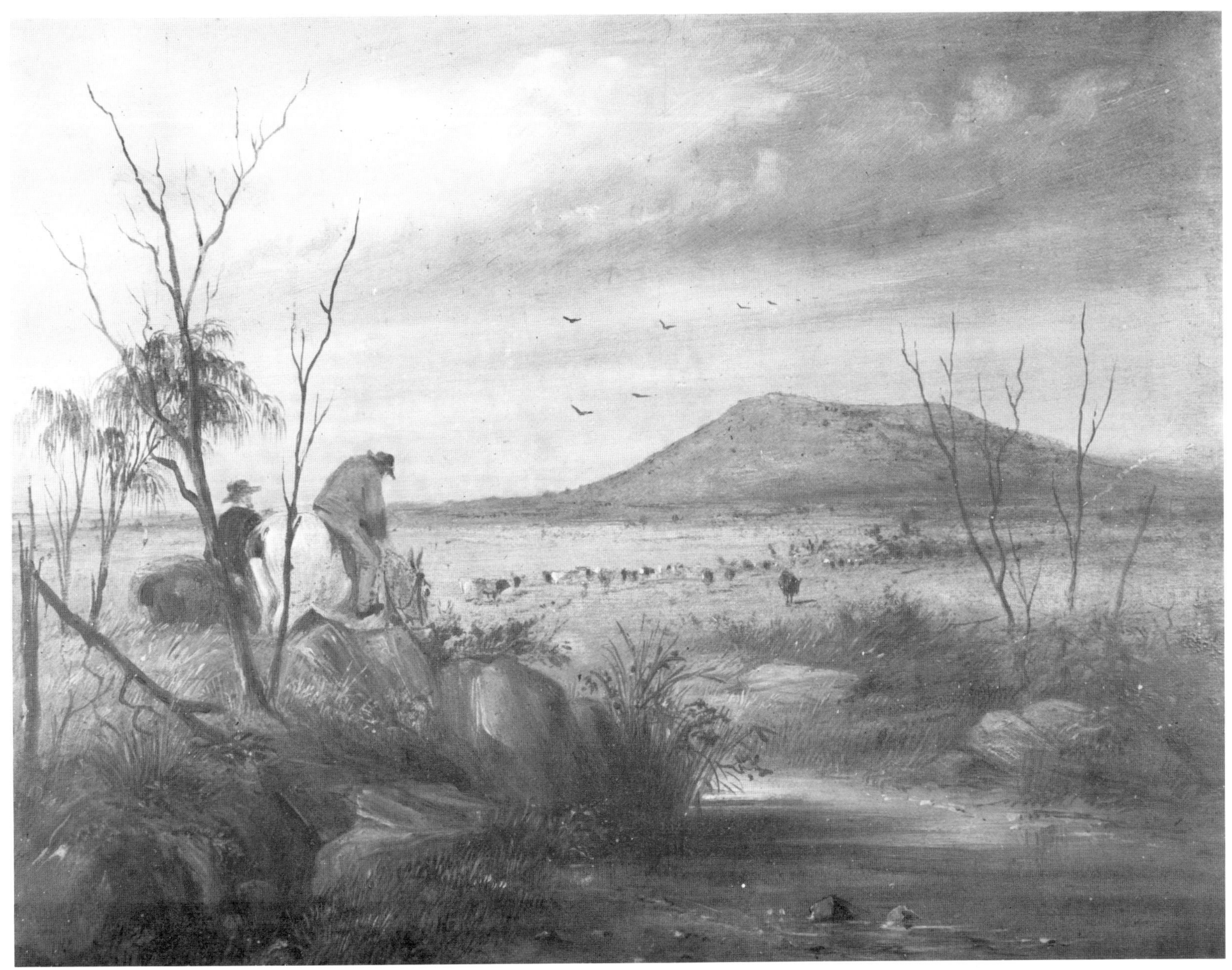

30 *Mount Gambier, South Australia, 1852*, oil on cardboard, 22.5 x 30.3 cm, National Gallery of Victoria.

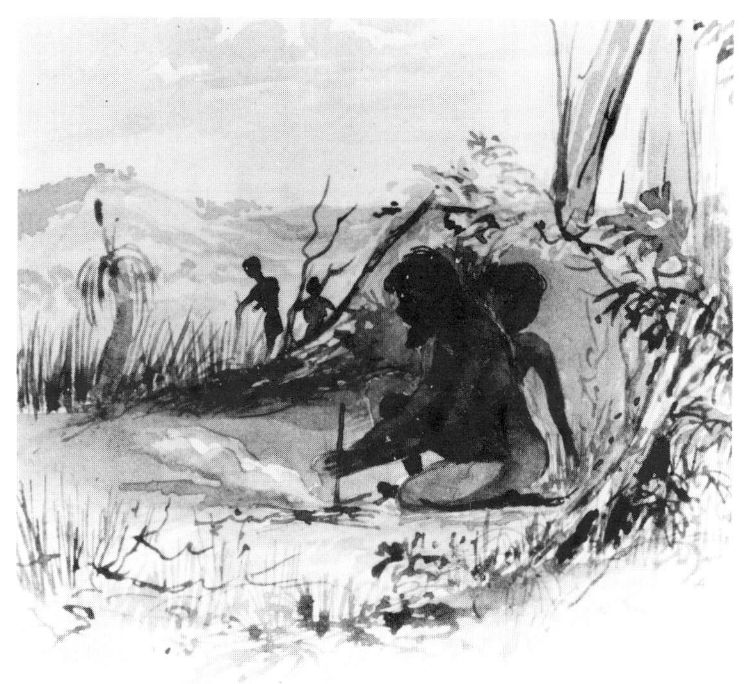

31 *Natives lighting a fire with the shaft of the grass tree*, watercolour on paper, 8.9 x 10.8 cm, National Library of Australia.

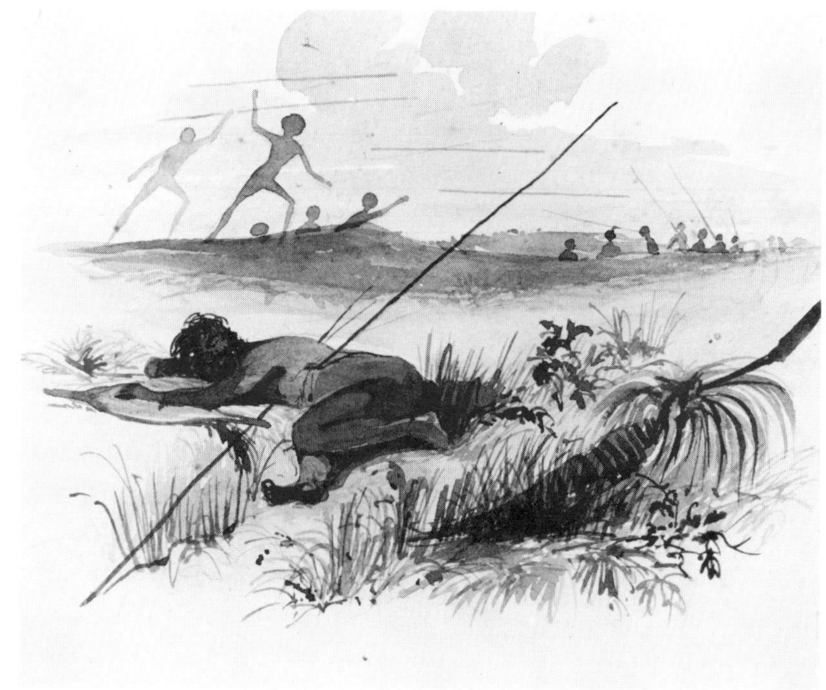

33 *Native speared in a skirmish*, watercolour on paper, 9.0 x 10.9 cm, National Library of Australia.

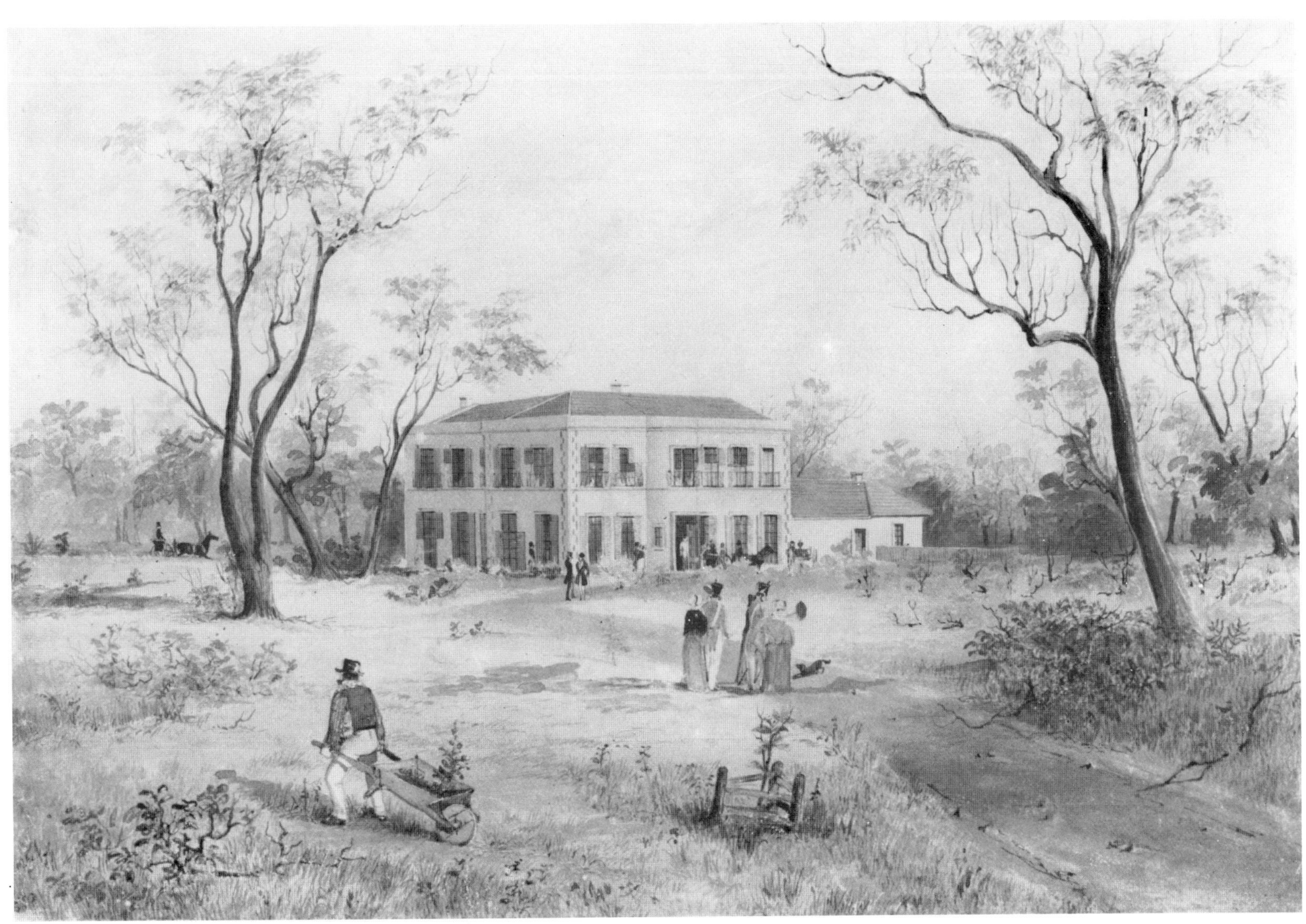

42 *Government House, North Terrace, Adelaide*, watercolour on paper, 27.1 x 39.7 cm, Art Gallery of South Australia.

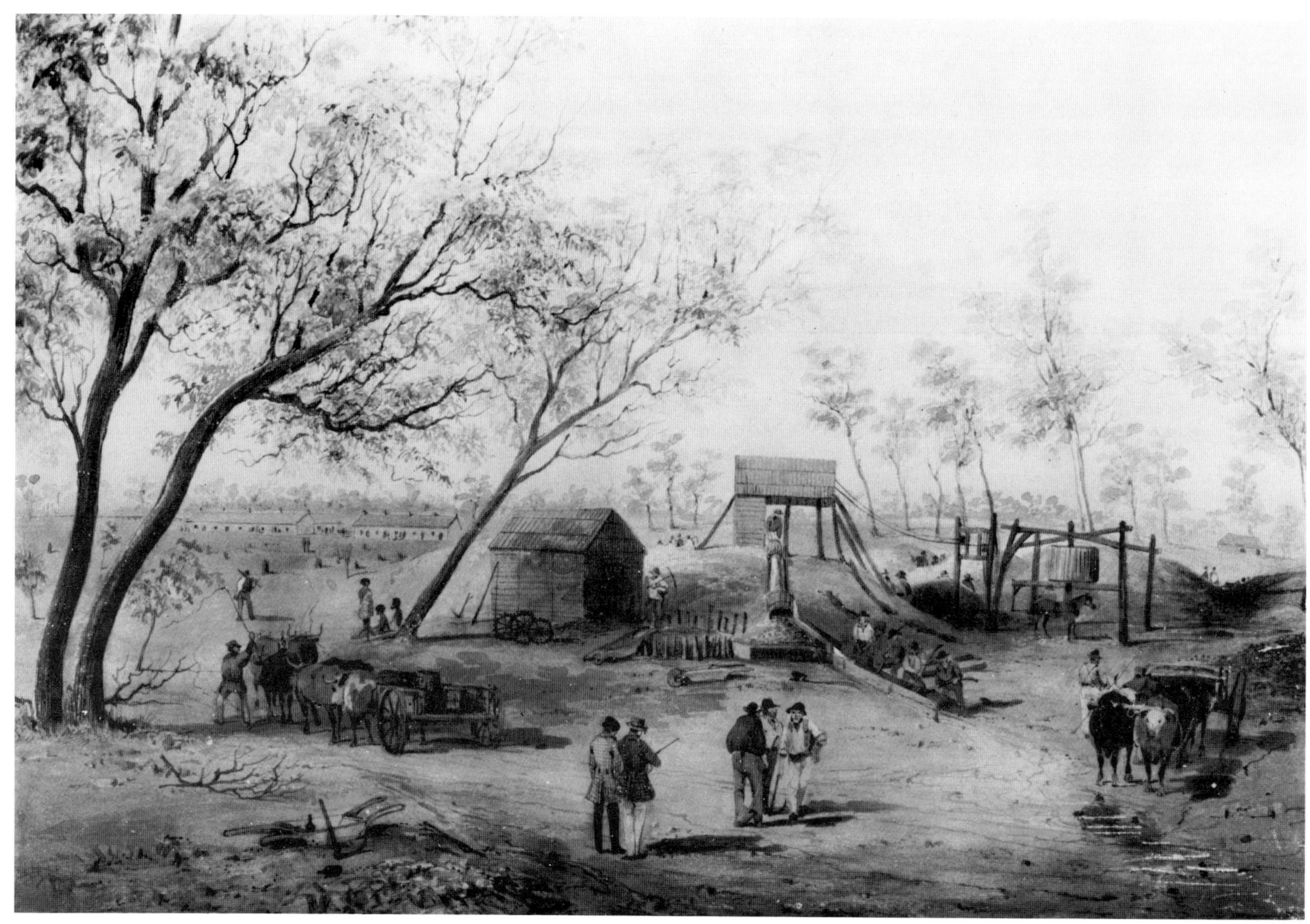

57 *Kapunda Mine*, watercolour on paper, 27.5 x 40.0 cm, Art Gallery of South Australia.

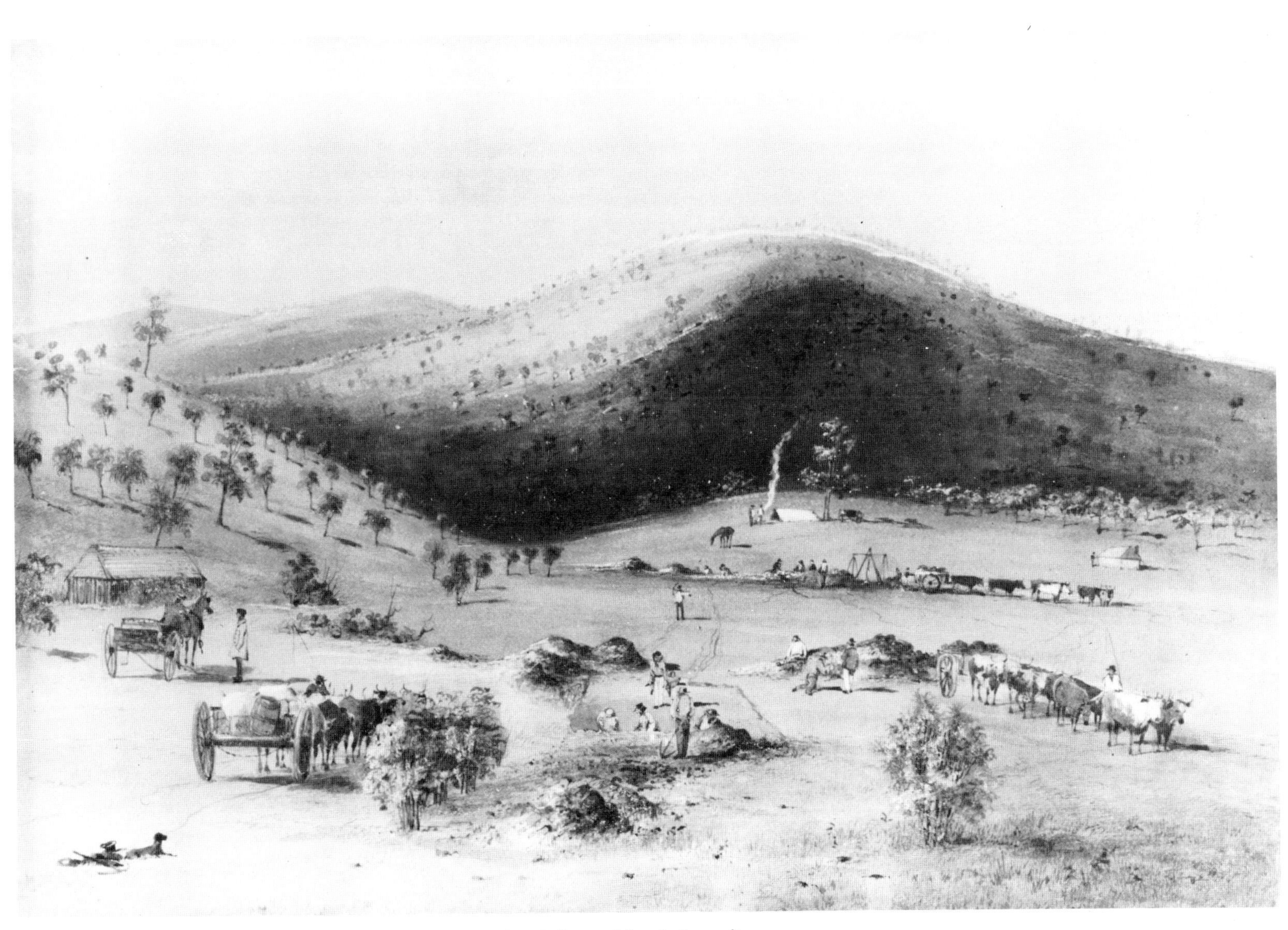

58 *Burra Burra Mine*, watercolour on paper, 27.3 x 39.7 cm, Art Gallery of South Australia.

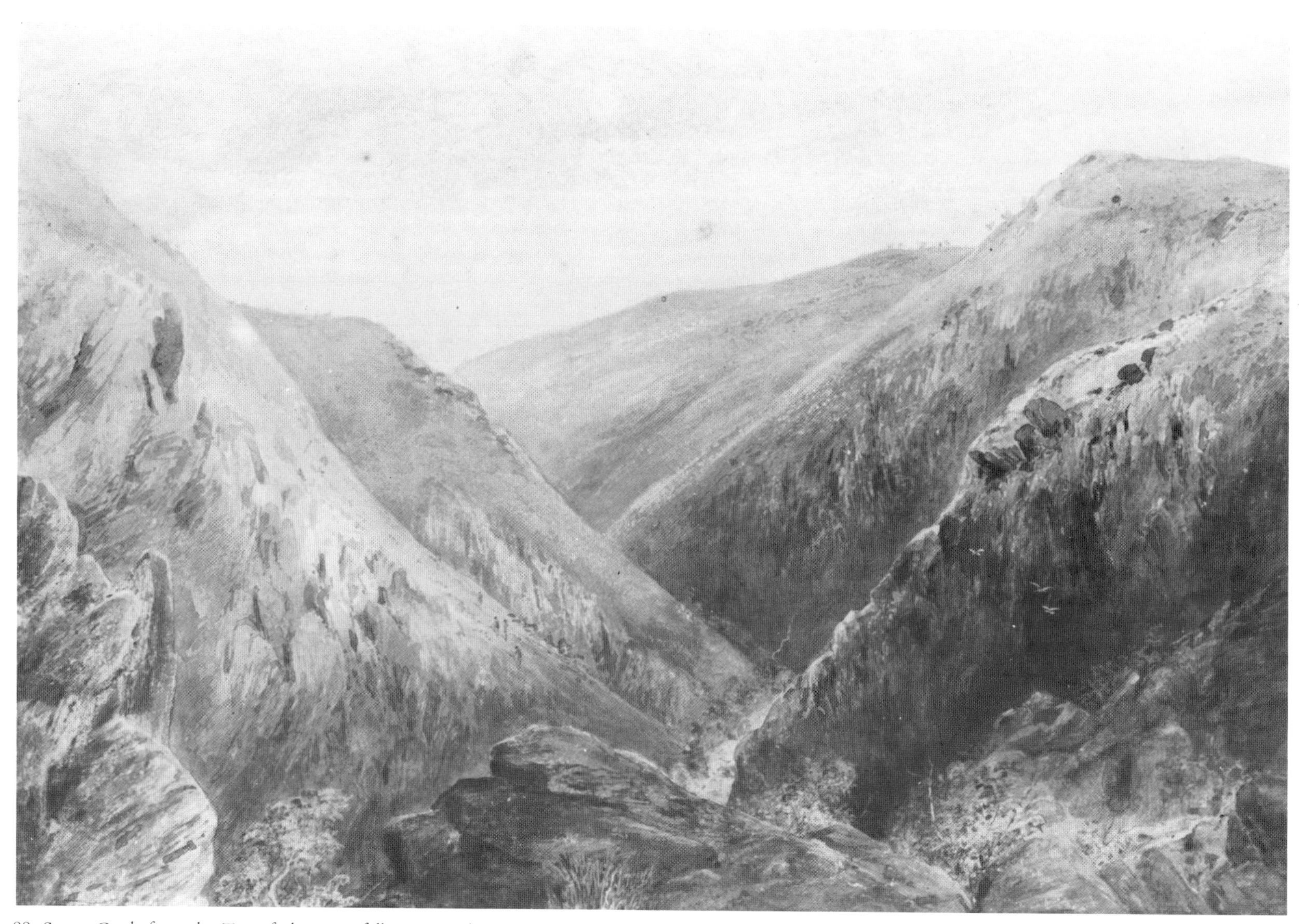

88 *Stony Creek from the Top of the Waterfall*, watercolour on paper, 27.5 x 40.2 cm, Art Gallery of South Australia.

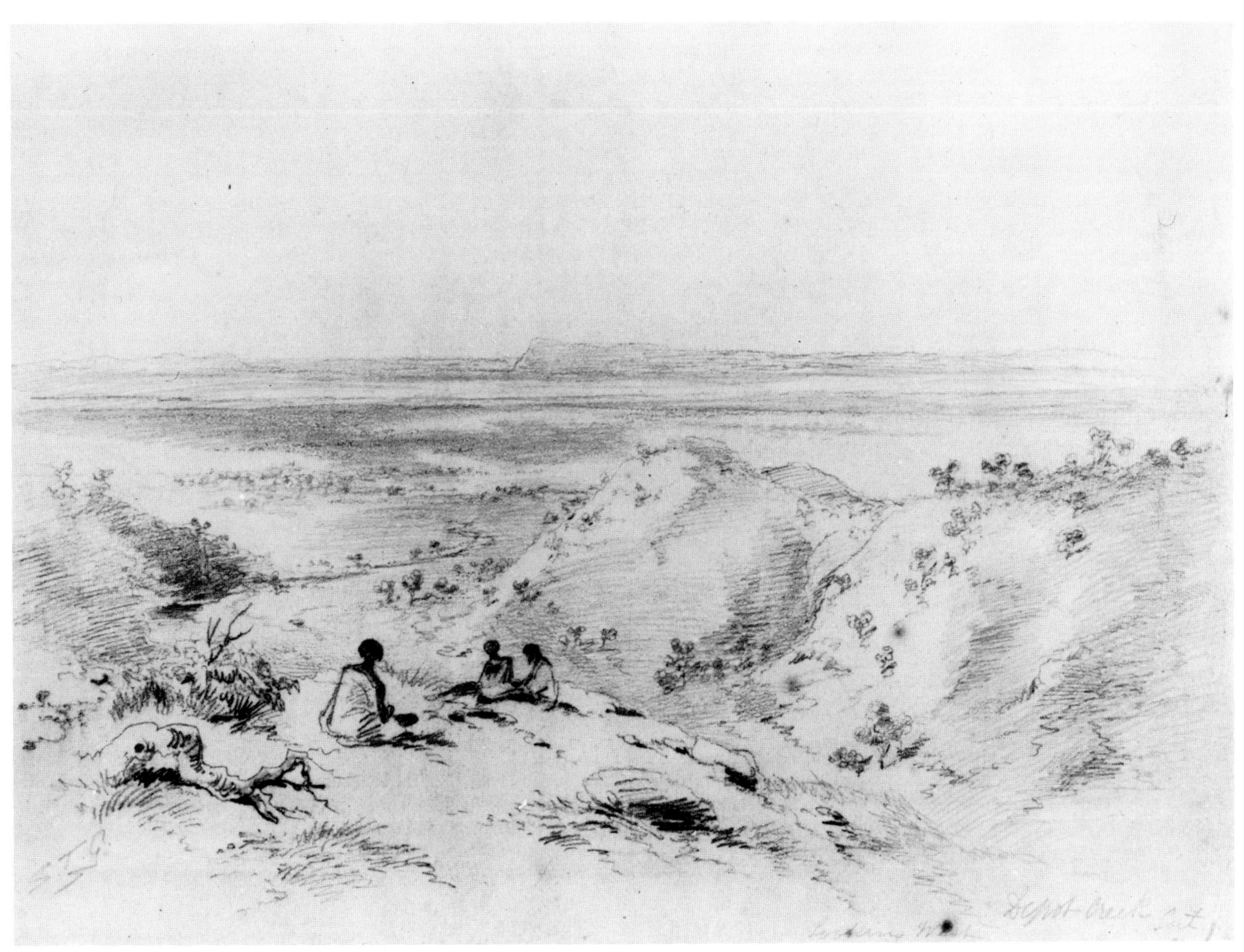

94 *Depot Creek, South Australia, looking west,* pencil on paper, 20.6 x 29.0 cm, Art Gallery of South Australia.

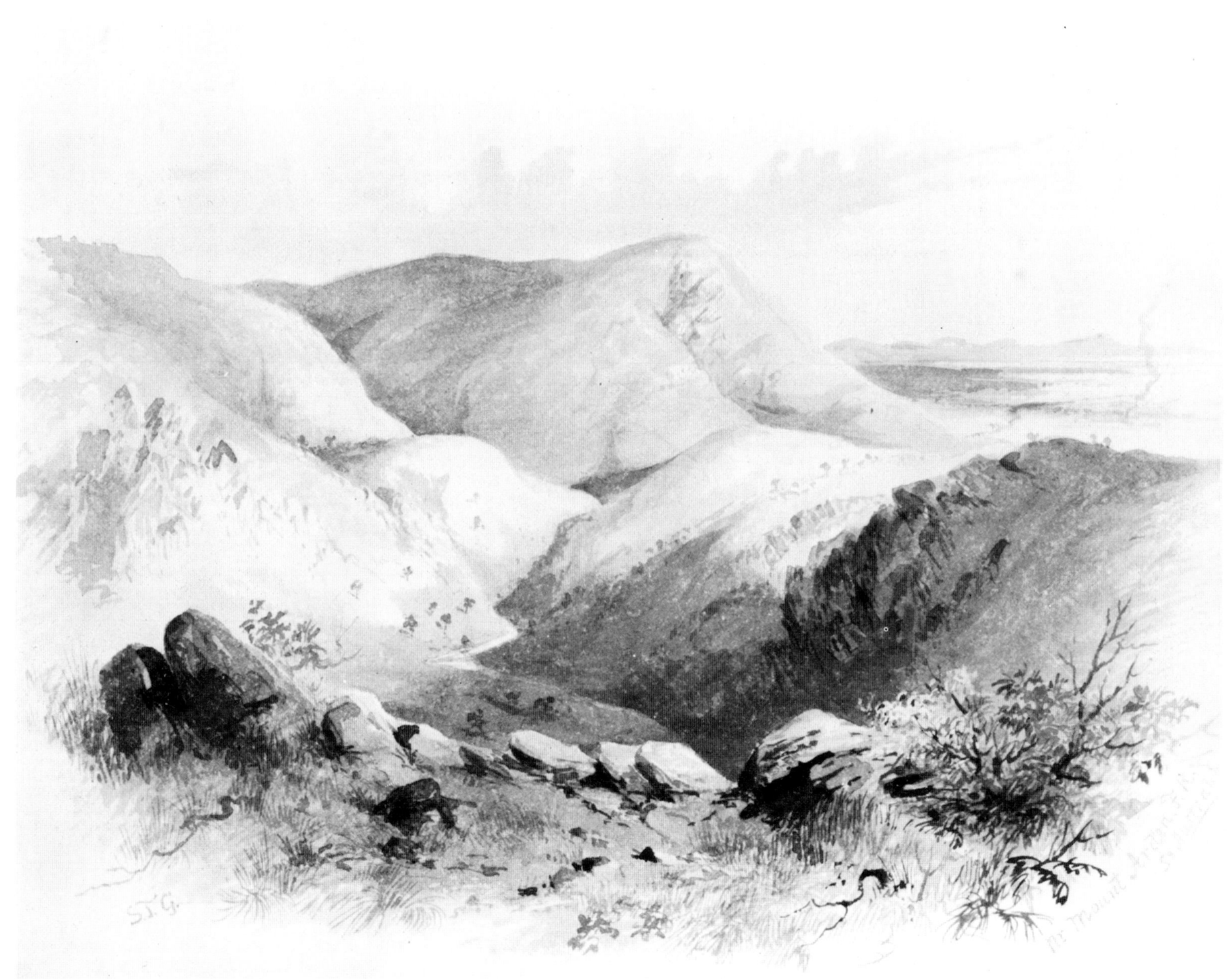

100 *Near Mount Arden, Flinders Range, South Australia*, grey wash drawing on paper, 16.8 x 21.6 cm, Art Gallery of South Australia.

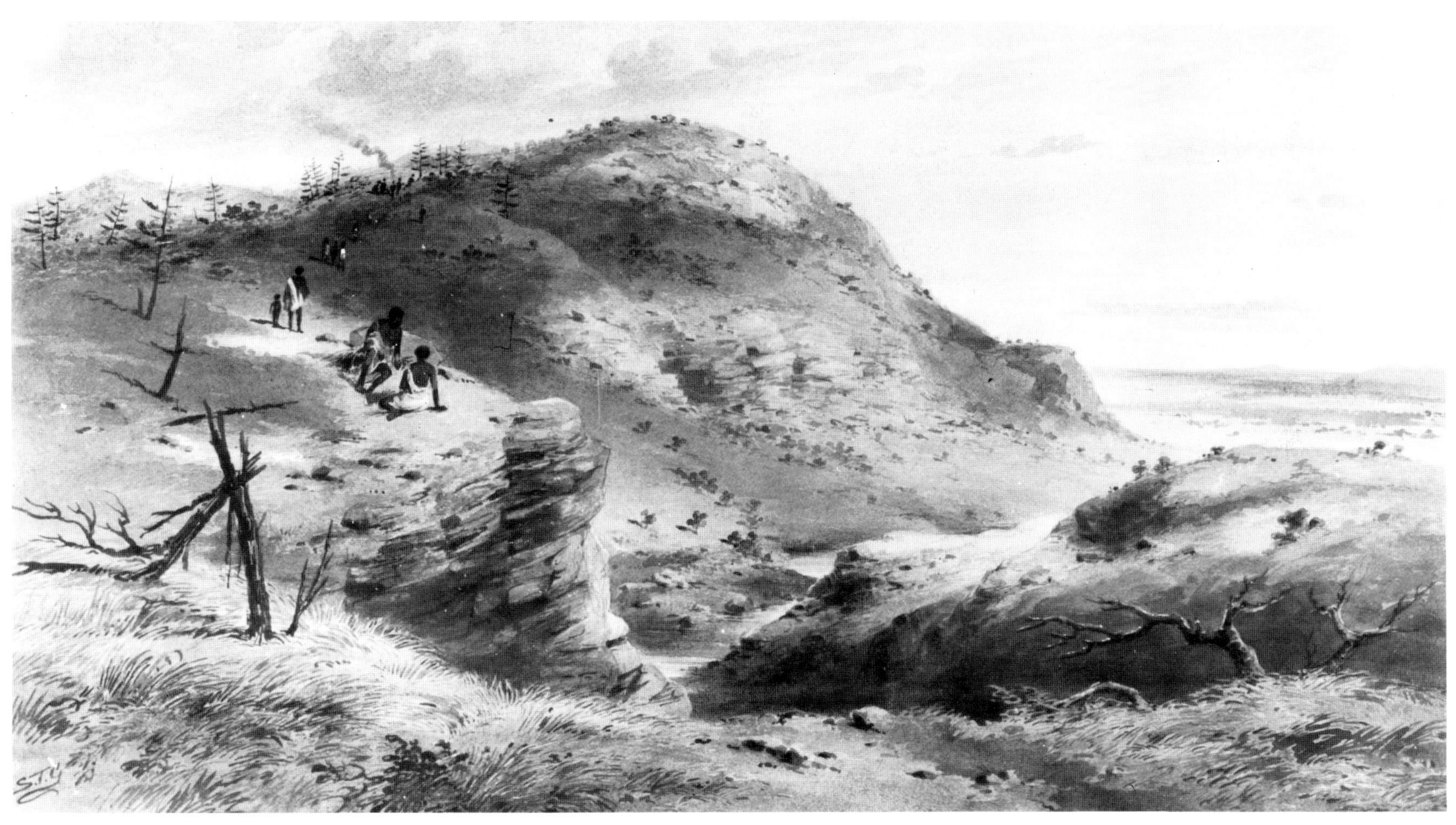

103 *The Flinders Range*, watercolour on paper, 36.5 x 68.0 cm, Art Gallery of South Australia.

S.T. Gill's Watercolour Materials and Techniques

S.T. Gill was one of the most prolific watercolour painters working in Australia in the nineteenth century. He was an artist who was often out in the field in the Adelaide Hills or the Flinders Ranges, and on the spot at mine sites, in city streets, at Port Adelaide, the races or at the Agricultural and Horticultural Society's annual show. The portability of watercolour paints and a sketchbook suited the immediacy of his style.

Watercolour is a deceptive word. In oil painting the oil binds the pigment to the canvas, but in watercolour it is finely ground gum arabic which binds the pigment to the paper. The water simply serves to spread the colour in transparent washes allowing the brilliance of the white paper to show through and give a quality of light and delicacy which oil painting never achieves.

S.T. Gill left no inventory of his materials, but it would have been possible to obtain artists' supplies in the new Colony of South Australia, in addition to what he must have brought with him when he first arrived in 1839, and confidently set up his studio in Gawler Place in 1840. Watercolour materials were readily available for watercolour painting was at the height of popularity in the early nineteenth century. He would have had access to excellent paints imported from England, probably made by William Winsor and H.C. Newton whose moist colours in small china pans were selling commercially from 1830 onwards, and were a great convenience compared with earlier methods of hand-ground pigment and gum.

Sable brushes were made in all sizes and a close examination of Gill's method of applying paint shows that he could lay broad washes in open skies such as *Sturt's Overland Expedition leaving Adelaide, 10th August, 1844* (cat. 80) or in the same painting develop fine detail in the legs of the cavalcade of horses and in the crowd of people watching. Grass and foliage in *The Gawler River* (cat. 22), and foreground detail in early works such as *May* (cat. 6) and *Winter* (cat. 16) show his skill and dexterity with a brush used as a drawing tool.

Gill used a fairly smooth watercolour paper for most of his work in South Australia, frequently using a sheet size of 10½ inches x 14½ inches (26.5 x 36.0 cm), which could have been from a sketchbook. For the large bravura work *Sturt's Overland Expedition leaving Adelaide, 10th August, 1844* he uses a very large sheet 16¼ inches x 28½ inches (41.0 x 72.2 cm). A clear watermark 'J WHATMAN 1845' on *Port Adelaide 1847* (cat. 53) proves that he used that brand of paper. An artist's folder belonging to Gill appears leaning against a garden seat in *Prospect House, the Seat of J.B. Graham Esqr. near Adelaide South Australia* (cat. 106), and later strapped to the saddle of the ill-fated camel Harry on the Horrocks Expedition (cat. 96).

His range of colours was simple but well used and probably consisted of yellow ochre, gamboge, vermilion, indian lake, terre verte, ultramarine, indigo, umber, raw sienna, burnt sienna and ivory black. This was a standard list recommended in books of instruction, and may have been used by other artists working in South Australia as well as Gill.

The demand for these well prepared and easily used materials was high, and while professional artists went in search of the picturesque on tours of English beauty spots, and further afield on the Grand Tour of Europe, drawing masters were teaching drawing and watercolour as genteel accomplishments for the fashionable lady as well as a necessary requirement for gentlemen soldiers who would be required to 'render a view' while surveying a newly discovered coastline or a potential site for a harbour or city. Both Colonel William Light and Captain E.C. Frome as successive Surveyors in South Australia left watercolour paintings of quality as testimony to skills acquired at military academies. Gill knew Frome and even worked from some of his field sketches.

Books of instruction in drawing and watercolour became popular, often using engravings after Claude Lorrain and Gaspard Poussin as examples of the perfect landscape, and students were encouraged to keep small sketchbooks of drawings and ideas for further development. Gill kept such a sketchbook (see p.44) and it appears that his father or tutors at his father's schools may have instructed him in his early years, though he did move to London to be employed at Hubard's Profile Gallery, after a period of apprenticeship with a carver and gilder in Plymouth in 1833.

Gill's work in South Australia was varied in size and subject. He often worked in delicate grey washes for a field sketch such as *Near Mount Arden, Flinders Range, South Australia* (cat. 100), but in some of his large, formal, fully developed watercolours of the 1840s and 1850s, such as those commissioned by James Allen (see Appendix A) and those of the Burra Burra Mines, he began to use a final addition of what appears to be varnish on dark foreground areas to give intensity and richness of tone and colour. This has proved a problem for conservation. The shiny surface congeals, cracks and flakes away and is difficult to restore satisfactorily. Recent scientific tests have shown that S.T. Gill used Gum Tragacanth or Karaya Gum to achieve this slightly varnished effect, probably using several layers where the surface is particularly shiny and the colour intense. In his later South Australian works he used bodycolour or gouache for occasional highlights.

Gill worked with fluidity and dexterity, using techniques he acquired in England in his youth and developed during his years in Australia. The immediacy of approach and freshness of colour that are typical of watercolour painting were ideally suited to the style of an artist who loved life and enjoyed recording it.

S.T. Gill's Sketchbook

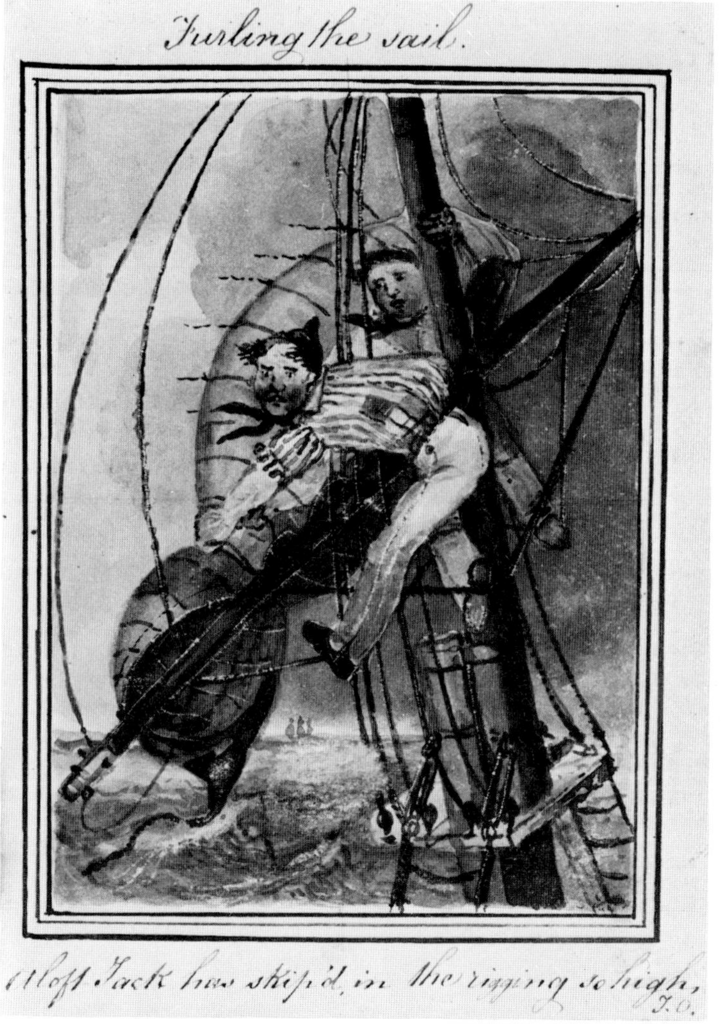

1 *Furling the sail*, (Sketchbook No.2) watercolour on paper, 14.7 x 11.5 cm, Art Gallery of Australia.

S.T. Gill's only known sketchbook is a small leather-bound, pocket-sized book of variously coloured papers containing drawings and watercolours which are the earliest known works by Gill. He was seventeen in 1835 when most of the work was executed, with intermittent entries in the following years up to 21 February 1838. It is the only work known to have been done by Gill in England apart from the youthful self-portrait in oils, since destroyed by fire (see p.viii). In the sketchbook there are seventy pen and ink sketches, one pencil drawing and seven watercolours by Gill. In addition there are four pen and ink drawings by his father, the Reverend Samuel Gill, who also contributed fifty-seven of the fifty-nine handwritten poems.

While the poems are over-moralistic and sentimental, the drawings show great strength and vigour, if occasional adolescent clumsiness. Their everyday subjects range from seascapes, winding country lanes and village life to more dramatic scenes such as the survivor of a wreck washed up on the shore, the furling of wind-lashed sails in a storm at sea or a serious portrait of Richard I in full armour.

This portable *aide-memoire* appears to enshrine the teachings of a loving father to his son. The Reverend Samuel Gill ran several educational establishments in England and soon after settling in South Australia he set up a school at Coromandel Valley in the Adelaide Hills. Drawing and painting in watercolours were part of the curriculum, so the subjects seen in this small book may well have been similar subjects to those set by the artist's schoolmaster father or by the drawing masters at his various schools.

It is not difficult to trace these recurring themes in the watercolours painted by S.T. Gill in South Australia. Many of the idyllic rural landscapes seen in the series *The Seasons* and *The Months* are hinted at in the delicate pen and ink vignettes of the sketchbook. Foreground detail, wooden fences and labourers in the fields are all to be found even though Gill's observant eye later added the essentially Australian details he saw before him.

Elegantly dressed groups of men seen in sketchbook drawings such as *Young men and women* and *The Duel* (Sketchbook 16 and 32) reappear as foreground figures in well developed watercolours such as *Kapunda Mine* (cat. 57) and *Rundle Street, Adelaide* (cat. 46).

Many of the fine sketchbook drawings have maritime subjects. The striped shirts and knitted caps of sailors and the sails, rigging and seashore paraphernalia recorded in England by the seventeen-year-old Gill become the basis for the series on Port Adelaide painted ten years later in South Australia.

The verses, with their moral tone and quaint use of English, have perhaps become less important to a modern reader, though it is interesting to read some of the more satirical of them such as *The Lawyer and the Client*:

From law and from physic preserve me I pray,
In health and in quiet I'd live the long day;
No good ever springs from commotion and strife,
'Tis a blight that destroys the comforts of life.
My neighbours and I in full harmony live
We've enough for ourselves and little to give;
We rack not our brains, or employ invention,
To serve some by ends — a bone of contention.
Each others kind word, we take in good part,
And no root of bitterness springs from the heart.
We throw a protection around a good name,
And where charity burns we fan the pure flame.
When scandal stalks round, with her forehead so bold;
We heed not her tale 'til the other is told.
'Tis thus that we live far from law's littigation
A thief to the pocket, a curse to the nation.
The way to avoid its mental anxiety,
Will be to walk in the path of propriety.
We know very well by others undoing
Such course often ends in direful ruin;
The winer and looser, engaged in this strife,
Oft hazard their all, and endanger their life.
The winer for sooth, can gain naught for his pains,

The lawyer not client, doth pocket the gains.
As the sheep of his wool, gets torn among bryers
So clients are mangled, by lawyers dub'd squires.
S.G. Jany. 6/36.

The Reverend Gill's stern exhortation to his son in the last pages of the sketchbook reflects the strong religious beliefs of the day and is worth recording:

Well if with all their misspent leisure,
Men valued peace before their pleasure,
And while they other good persue,
Sought God and his Salvation too,
Be this my boy thy chief concern,
For this thy soul with ardour burn,
Some others may be needful too
But this most needful keep in view.

While the sketchbook could be seen purely as a reflection of the life and times of early Victorian England, its importance lies in the embryonic vision of possible topics which Gill explored later as themes and compositions. As a source book of ideas, it is a precursor to much of the best work Gill did in Australia.

1 *Sketch Book*   1835-38

216 pages comprising seven watercolours,
seventy pen and ink sketches and one pencil
drawing by S.T. Gill and four pen and ink
sketches by the Reverend Samuel Gill who
also wrote fifty-seven of the fifty-nine
handwritten poems.

Sheets of white, cream, yellow, pink,
purple, blue and green paper 5¾ inches x 4½
inches (14.5 x 11.5 cm) bound in dark green
leather, with marbled end-papers.

Art Gallery of South Australia, Adelaide;
South Australian Government Grant 1965

(AGSA 659D34)

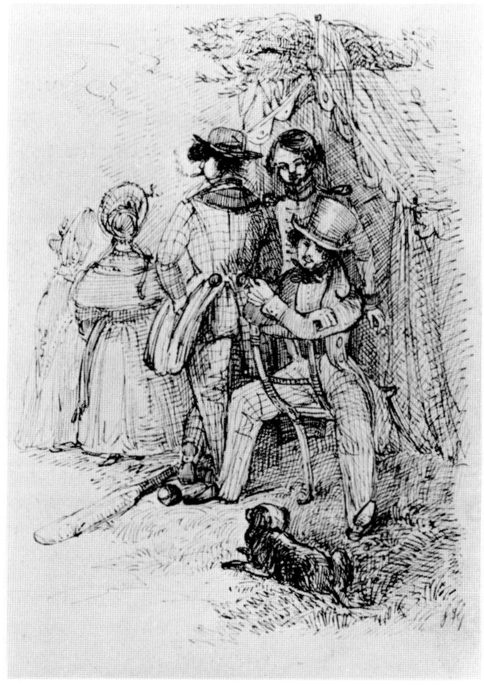

1 (*Young men and women*) (Sketchbook No. 16)
pen and ink on paper, 14.7 x 11.5 cm, Art
Gallery of South Australia.

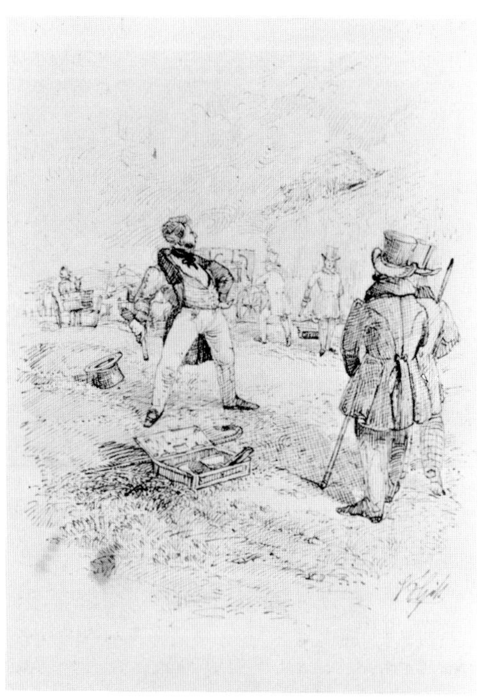

1 (*The duel*) (Sketchbook No. 32) pen and ink
on cream paper, 14.7 x 11.5 cm, Art Gallery of
South Australia.

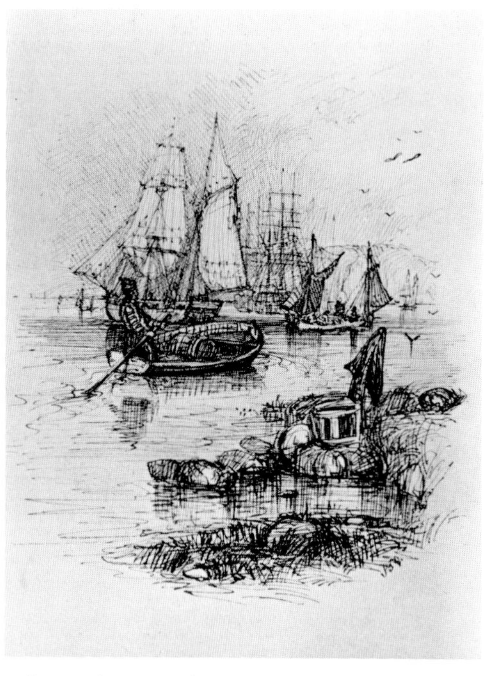

1 (*Coastal scene with ships at anchor and rowing boats*)
(Sketchbook No. 75) pen and ink on green
paper, 14.7 x 11.5 cm, Art Gallery of South
Australia.

The Seasons and The Months

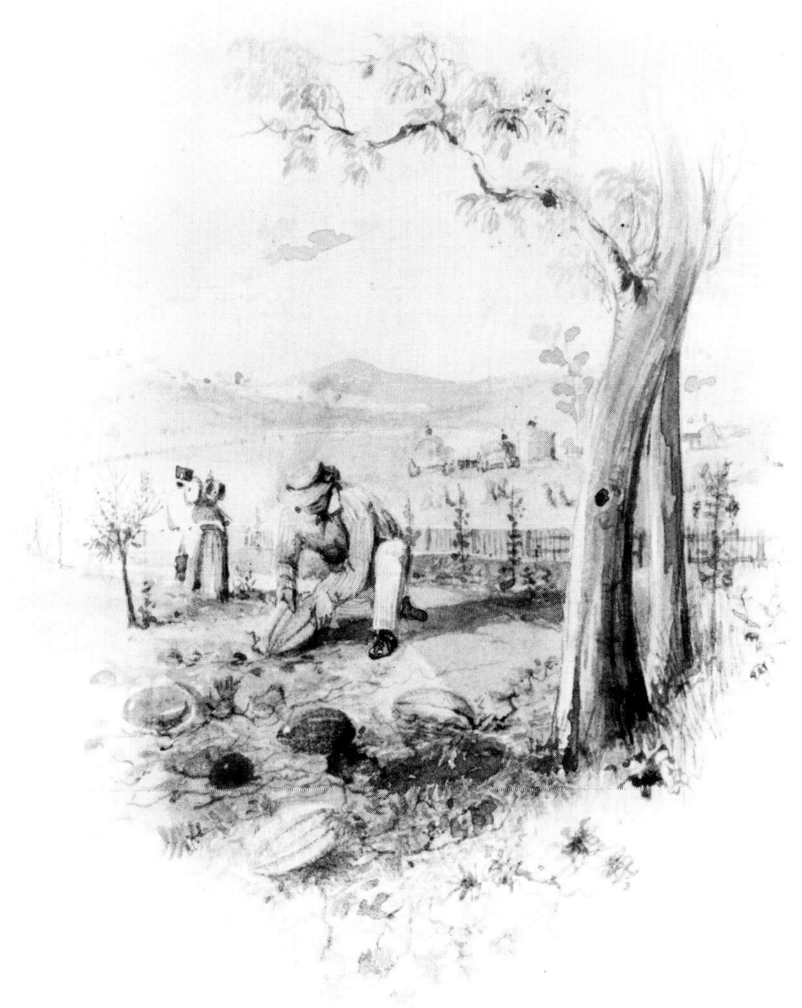

2 *January*, watercolour on paper, 21.8 x 18.3 cm, National Library of Australia.

The remarkable series of The Seasons and The Months are amongst the earliest watercolours painted by Gill in South Australia. They may have been painted with some feelings of nostalgia. The subject matter and its treatment in pretty vignette style is very English and is reminiscent of the pen illustrations in S.T. Gill's sketchbook.

The Seasons and The Months are themes often used in European and English art and here reflect the bounty of the new found colony. The colonists in writing home to England often commented on the wonderful climate, the rich earth and the crops and vegetables which thrived and were far superior in size and quality to anything produced in England.

Gill has nevertheless given The Seasons and The Months an Australian flavour. There is a feeling for the distance and atmosphere of the Australian landscape; the gum tree, the bush fire, the warmth of the sun, the blue sky and the Aborigines are all there. The set of paintings is unique and it is doubtful whether any other Australian artist has produced a series based on this theme.

The location and the date of execution of these views is not known. The two sets (July is lacking from *The Months*) were purchased in London by the National Library of Australia in 1933. At the time the vendor said that the paintings came to him through his mother-in-law who was related to a family named Rowe and that *The Seasons* had been in an album labelled 'John Rowe 1847'. He understood *The Months* had been executed in one locality, possibly on a pastoral property which may have belonged to John Rowe. However, no reference has been found to John Rowe as a pastoralist in South Australia, and it seems more likely that the sets were composed from sketches made at different times and places during Gill's travels in the settled areas of the colony.

The treatment of the compositions and the translucent watercolour, together with the methods of harvesting depicted, which pre-date the introduction of Ridley's stripper (see *Summer*, cat. 14) date the series to *c.* 1840-42. It is Gill's first major South Australian work.

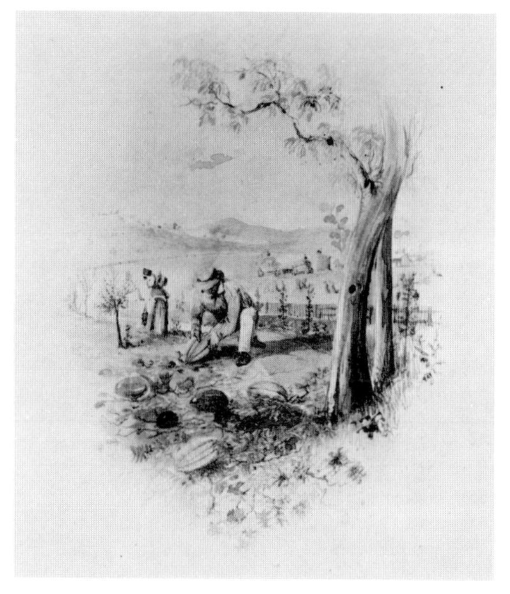 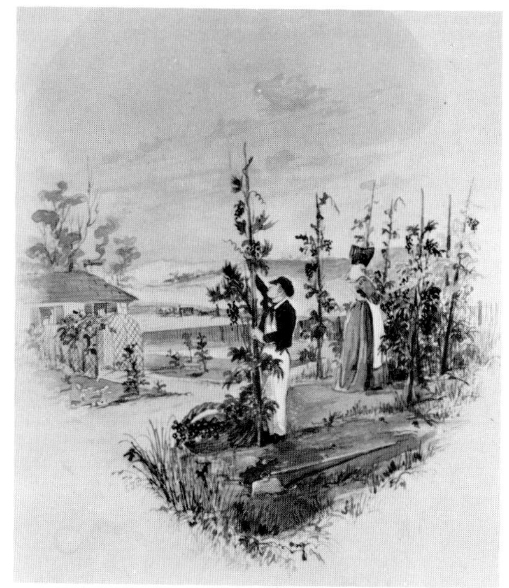 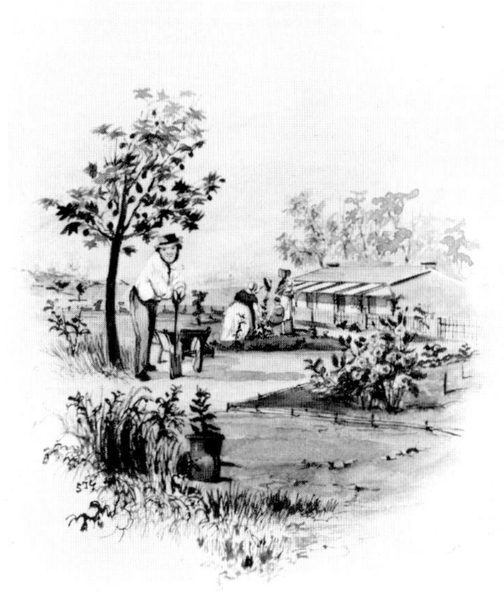

2 *January*   *c.* 1840–42

watercolour on paper 21.8 x 18.3 cm
Not signed. Not dated. Inscribed l.r.
corner diagonally in pencil *January*.

Early summer, the farmer and his wife
with poke bonnet and parasol, stand in the
vegetable garden, where a gardener is
picking a melon, and look across their
fields where farmhands are carting and
stacking hay.

National Library of Australia, Canberra;
Purchased 1933   (NLA R.3293)

3 *February*   *c.* 1840–42

watercolour on paper 21.8 x 18.3 cm
Signed l.l., brush and watercolour *S.T.G.*
Not dated. Inscribed l.r. diagonally in
pencil *Feby*.

Mid-summer, a gardener and maid are
harvesting grapes for the table or for wine
making. The garden is fenced and appears
to be formally laid out with paths and an
arbour leading to the shuttered, slate-
roofed cottage with its smoking chimney.

National Library of Australia, Canberra;
Purchased 1933   (NLA R.3294)

4 *March*   *c.* 1840–42

watercolour on paper 21.8 x 18.2 cm
Signed l.l., brush and watercolour *S.T.G*
Not dated. Inscribed l.r. corner diagonally
in pencil *March*.

Late summer, this tranquil domestic scene
shows a group of women, one with a
baby, in front of a typical colonial cottage
with slate roof and striped-roofed
verandah. Roses bloom nearby while the
gardener leans on his spade beneath an
English tree which contrasts with the gum
trees and rolling hills in the background.

National Library of Australia, Canberra;
Purchased 1933   (NLA R.3295)

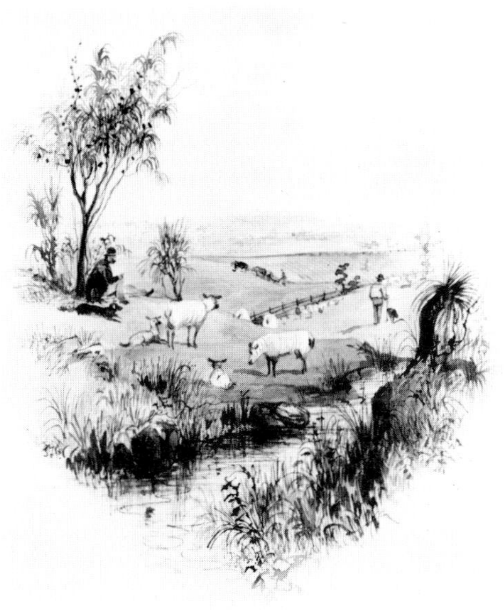

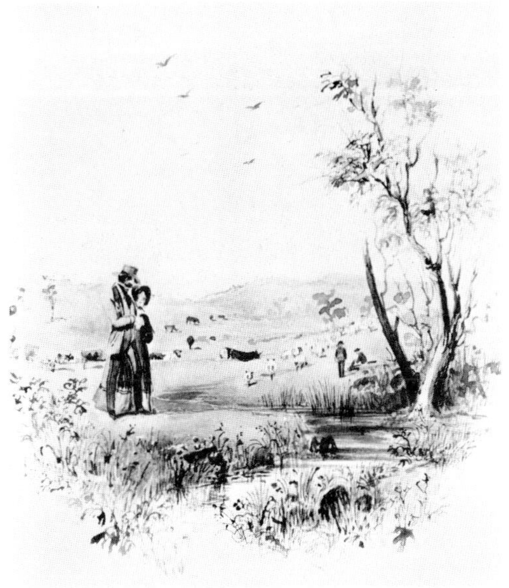

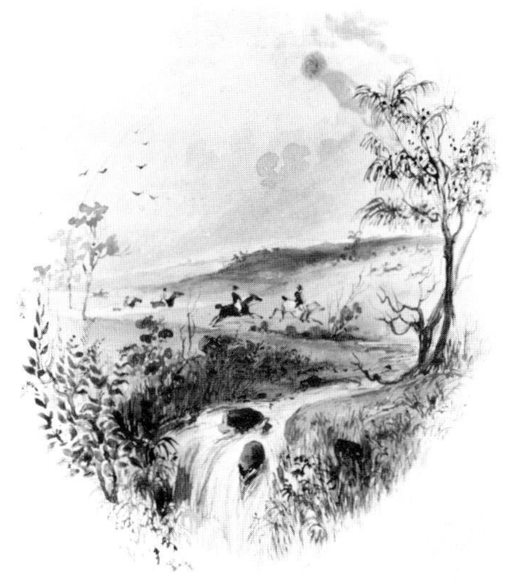

5 *April*   *c.* 1840–42

watercolour on paper 21.8 x 18.3 cm
Signed l.l., brush and watercolour *S T G*
Not dated. Inscribed l.r. corner diagonally
in pencil *April*.

Early rains and autumn weather encourage
the ploughman with his bullocks to
prepare for seeding, whilst the shepherds
and their dogs herd the sheep along the
grassy bank of the creek.

National Library of Australia, Canberra;
Purchased 1933   (NLA R.3296)

6 *May*   *c.* 1840–42

watercolour on paper 21.9 x 18.2 cm
Signed l.l., brush and watercolour *S T G*
Not dated. Inscribed l.r. corner diagonally
in pencil *May*.

The balmy days of autumn in South
Australia. The well dressed and apparently
prosperous farmer and his wife survey
cattle and sheep in the charge of
herdsmen. The well grassed and watered
property extends to rolling hills typical of
country close to Adelaide.

National Library of Australia, Canberra;
Purchased 1933   (NLA R.3297)

7 *June*   *c.* 1840–42

watercolour on paper 21.8 x 18.3 cm
Signed l.l., brush and watercolour *S T G*
Not dated. Inscribed l.r. corner diagonally
in pencil *June*.

Winter brings the relaxation of the hunt,
a subject which is featured in *The Seasons*.
Gill shows the hunt in full cry, possibly
after a kangaroo. The hunters are jumping
a creek and following the hounds uphill.
On the skyline two Aboriginal hunters can
be seen, probably intent on the more
serious aspect of hunting for food.

National Library of Australia, Canberra;
Purchased 1933   (NLA R.3298)

There is no known *July* in Gill's series of
The Months. It is presumed lost.

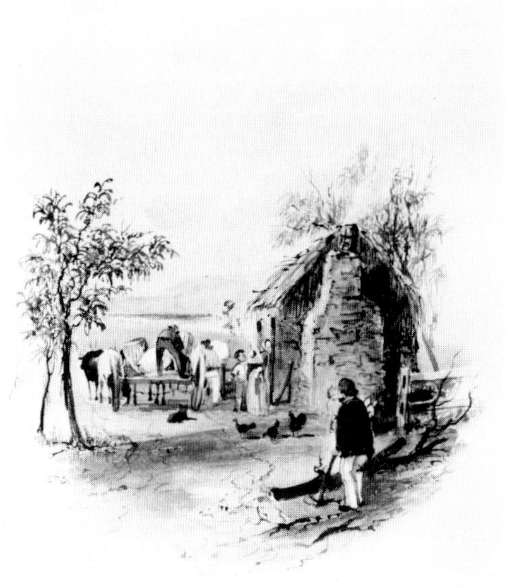

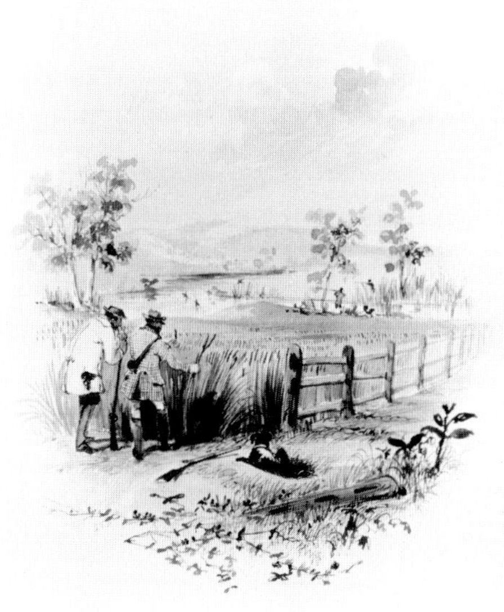

8   *August*   *c.* 1840-42
watercolour on paper 21.9 x 18.2 cm
Signed l.l., brush and watercolour *S.T.G.*
Not dated. Inscribed l.r. corner diagonally
in pencil *August*.

Late winter but a clear bright day with
two men loading a bullock dray, another
cutting wood and a group of people
watching near the cottage door. The
simple cottage with thatched roof and
stone chimney, together with its
surroundings gives the impression that this
is a group of the more humble colonists.

National Library of Australia, Canberra;
Purchased 1933   (NLA R.3299)

9   *September*   *c.* 1840-42
watercolour on paper 21.9 x 18.2 cm
Signed l.l., brush and watercolour *S T G*
Not dated. Inscribed l.r. corner diagonally
in pencil *September*.

The traditional month of spring in South
Australia. A group of colonists are duck-
shooting along the river banks watched by
two farmers and a dog. The wheat is fully
grown, and in ear, promising a good
season.

National Library of Australia, Canberra;
Purchased 1933   (NLA R.3300)

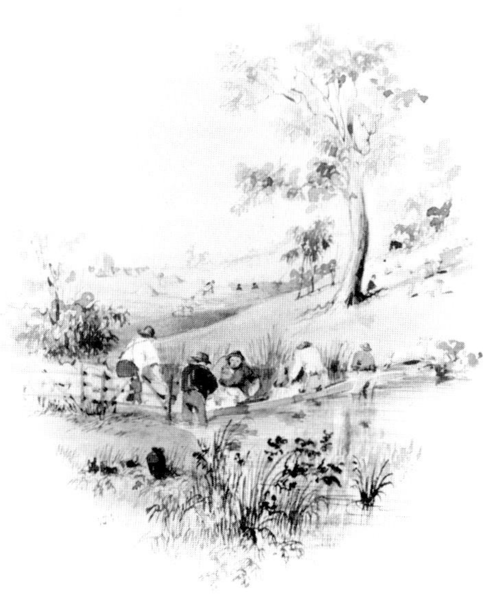

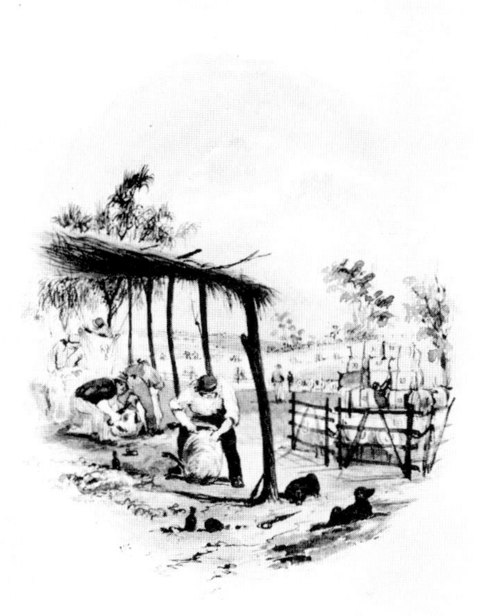

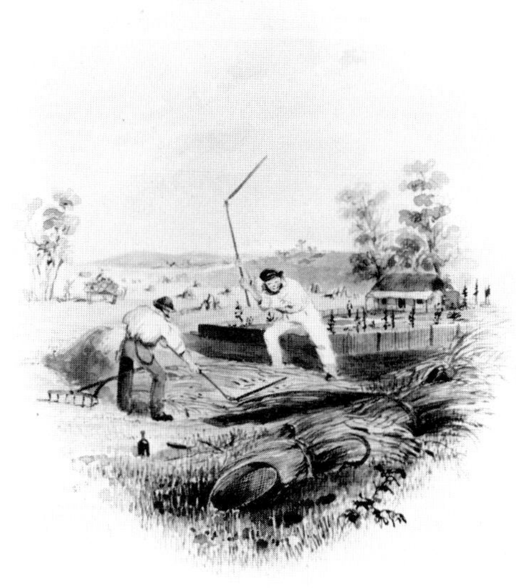

10 *October*   *c.* 1840-42
watercolour on paper 21.8 x 18.2 cm
Signed l.l., brush and watercolour *S T G*
Not dated. Inscribed l.r. corner diagonally
in pencil *October*.

A scene of bustling activity as the weather
improves. Sheepwashing was common
practice in the nineteenth century to
remove grease and clean the wool before
shearing and subsequent marketing. In the
background men are haymaking.

National Library of Australia, Canberra;
Purchased 1933   (NLA R.3301)

11 *November*   *c.* 1840-42
watercolour on paper 21.8 x 18.3 cm
Signed l.l., brush and watercolour *S T G*
Not dated. Inscribed l.r. corner diagonally
in pencil *November*.

As Geoffrey Dutton has said:* 'This must
be one of the earliest shearing scenes ever
painted in Australia. The shed is only a
bush lean-to; there is no floor, nor is
there a press, the bale being swung from
the rafters'. Bales are being loaded on a
bullock wagon whilst in the background
the wheat has ripened and harvest is in
progress.

*G. Dutton, *Paintings of S.T. Gill*, Adelaide:
Rigby, 1962

National Library of Australia, Canberra;
Purchased 1933   (NLA R.3302)

12 *December*   *c.* 1840-42
watercolour on paper 21.8 x 18.2 cm
Signed l.l., brush and watercolour *S T G*
Not dated. Inscribed l.r. corner diagonally
in pencil *December*.

The harvesting depicted in *October* and
November continues in the distant fields
whilst close to the cottage and fenced
garden two farmhands are threshing. The
sieve in the foreground would be used for
winnowing.

National Library of Australia, Canberra;
Purchased 1933   (NLA R.3303)

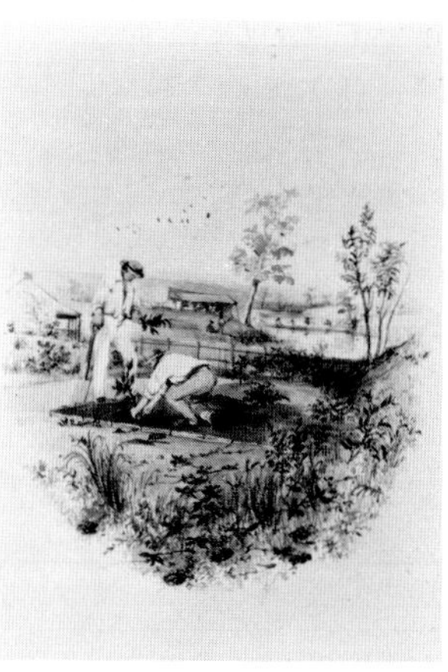

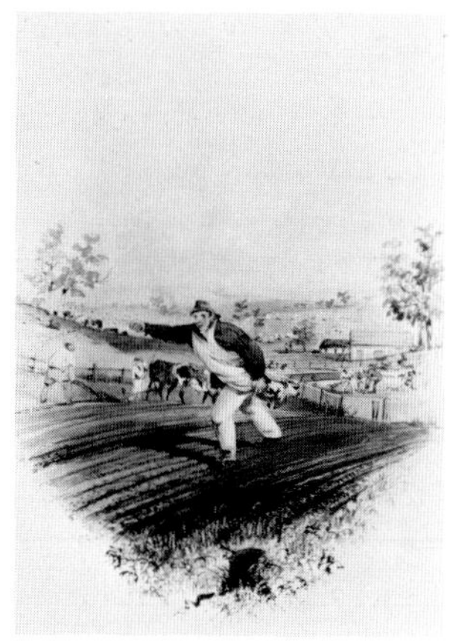

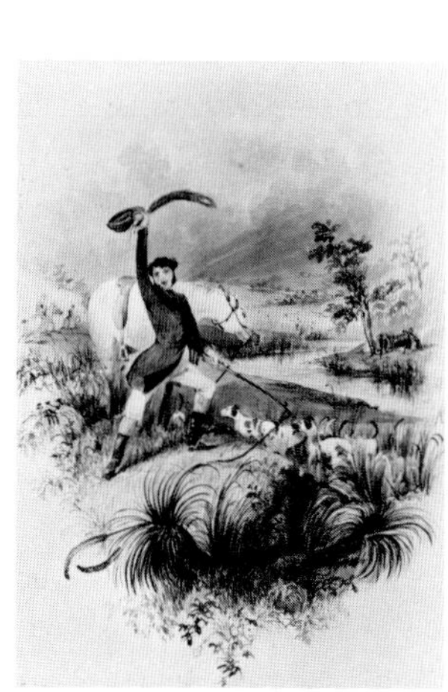

13 *Spring*   *c.* 1840–42

watercolour on paper 29.3 x 21.8 cm
Signed l.l., brush and watercolour *S T G*
Not dated. Inscribed l.r. corner diagonally
in pencil *Spring*.

Spring is a busy season in the garden and
on the farm. Gill shows two men planting
trees whilst in the background a large
group are sheepwashing—a scene shown in
detail in the month of *October*. Two
Aborigines watch by the river bank.

National Library of Australia, Canberra;
Purchased 1933   (NLA R.3304)

14 *Summer*   *c.* 1840–42

watercolour on paper 29.3 x 21.8 cm
Signed lower c., brush and watercolour
S T G. Not dated. Inscribed l.r. corner
diagonally in pencil *Summer*

In the summer of 1842–43 in South
Australia, the harvest was particularly
bountiful but there was a shortage of
labour to bring it in and a consequent
demand for high wages. A committee was
formed to consider the problem and
offered a reward for a solution. As a
result, in 1843–44 John Ridley built and
demonstrated a stripper which together
with a winnowing machine revolutionised
harvesting.

There seems to be no shortage of labour
on Gill's farm where men are reaping,
stooking, carting and threshing. The scene
is a variation of *December*, but in this
version smoke rises from a bushfire on the
distant hills.

National Library of Australia, Canberra;
Purchased 1933   (NLA R.3307)

15 *Autumn*   *c.* 1840–42

watercolour on paper 29.3 x 21.9 cm
Signed l.l., brush and watercolour *S T.G.*
Not dated. Inscribed l.r. corner diagonally
in pencil *Autumn*.

Gill has painted a typical South Australian
mixed farm where there is plenty of work
during the balmy autumn months in
preparing for the next season. Bullocks
with a teamster and ploughman are tilling
the soil whilst another farmhand casts the
seed. Two men are digging over the
vegetable garden close to the house, while
in the distance flocks graze peacefully.

National Library of Australia, Canberra;
Purchased 1933   (NLA R.3305)

16 *Winter*   *c.* 1840–42

watercolour on paper 29.6 x 21.8 cm
Signed l.l., brush and watercolour *S T G*
Not dated. Inscribed l.r. corner diagonally
in pencil *Winter*.

Winter was a time for leisure activities
and leading South Australian colonists
followed British customs of hunting and
shooting. By 1842 a pack of hounds had
been established and the Adelaide Hunt
Club held winter meets in traditional style
with pink jackets and champagne
breakfasts. The game, however, was
kangaroo or dingo which, according to
Francis Dutton,* gave good runs.

In this watercolour Gill portrays a
hunter in his pink coat and riding boots
with a fox's brush in hand. The
foreground grass, trees and hound's tail
form a busy pattern, while in the
background duck shooters and riders can
be seen. Gill also includes an Aboriginal
group with campfire in front of a wurley.

*Francis Dutton, *South Australia and its Mines*,
London: Boone, 1846, p.146.

National Library of Australia, Canberra;
Purchased 1933   (NLA R.3306)

Landscapes and Rural Scenes

When S.T. Gill arrived with his parents in South Australia in December 1839 the colony had been settled for just over three years and was struggling to develop as a rural economy. According to his niece, Gill made his first sketches of Adelaide and its surroundings soon after he landed to send to relatives in England by the next mail.

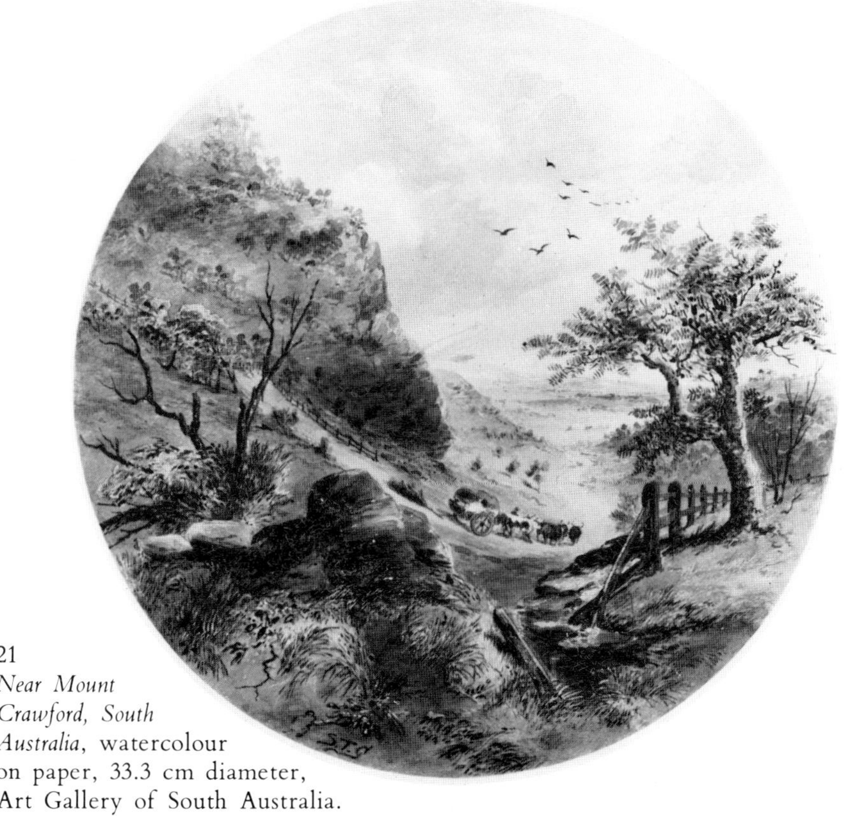

21
Near Mount Crawford, South Australia, watercolour on paper, 33.3 cm diameter, Art Gallery of South Australia.

He took long strolls with his brother, John Ryland Gill, through the country between Glenelg and the city, where the family made its first home, and often accompanied people who were driving or riding into the more distant parts of the settlement in order to procure sketches.[1]

Certainly within a few months of his arrival he confirmed an artistic career with an advertisement in the *South Australian Register*, 7 March 1840 (see p. 9), saying he had opened rooms in Gawler Place.

What kind of response this advertisement brought and how Gill fared in the early part of his career is difficult to discover. He did not begin to date his works until 1844 (see Appendix B) and he was not mentioned again in the press until June 1845. The first evidence of a commission appears in the diary of John Howard Angas, 29 October 1844, who records that 'Mr Gill . . . has come from town to take some sketches'.[2] Two of these works, *The Gawler River*, 1844, (cat. 22) and *Rhodes's Cattle Station on the Gawler, Section 471, November 1844*, (cat. 23) are also amongst the first Australian pictures by Gill to be either signed and dated or dated in the title.

Some of the earliest landscape watercolours are considered from their translucent style to date *c*.1842-43 and *c*.1844 and like *The Seasons* and *The Months* depict the impact of the colonists and their rural activities on the native landscape. Gill became a good horseman and the geographical spread of his subjects shows that he travelled widely throughout the colony in pursuit of his subjects and his commissions, at the same time developing an empathy with the colonist and the land.

These paintings illustrate the subtle changes in Gill's watercolour technique between *c*.1842 and 1847 and by the inclusion of *Near Mount Crawford, South Australia*, (cat. 21) painted *c*.1865-70, the dramatic change in style and technique in his later years is shown. There are also several pencil drawings, one of which, *Rankine's Station, Mount Crawford, Barossa Range, South Australia*, (cat. 19) with artist's notes, indicates that Gill may have painted many of his watercolours in the studio from pencil or wash drawings made in the field.

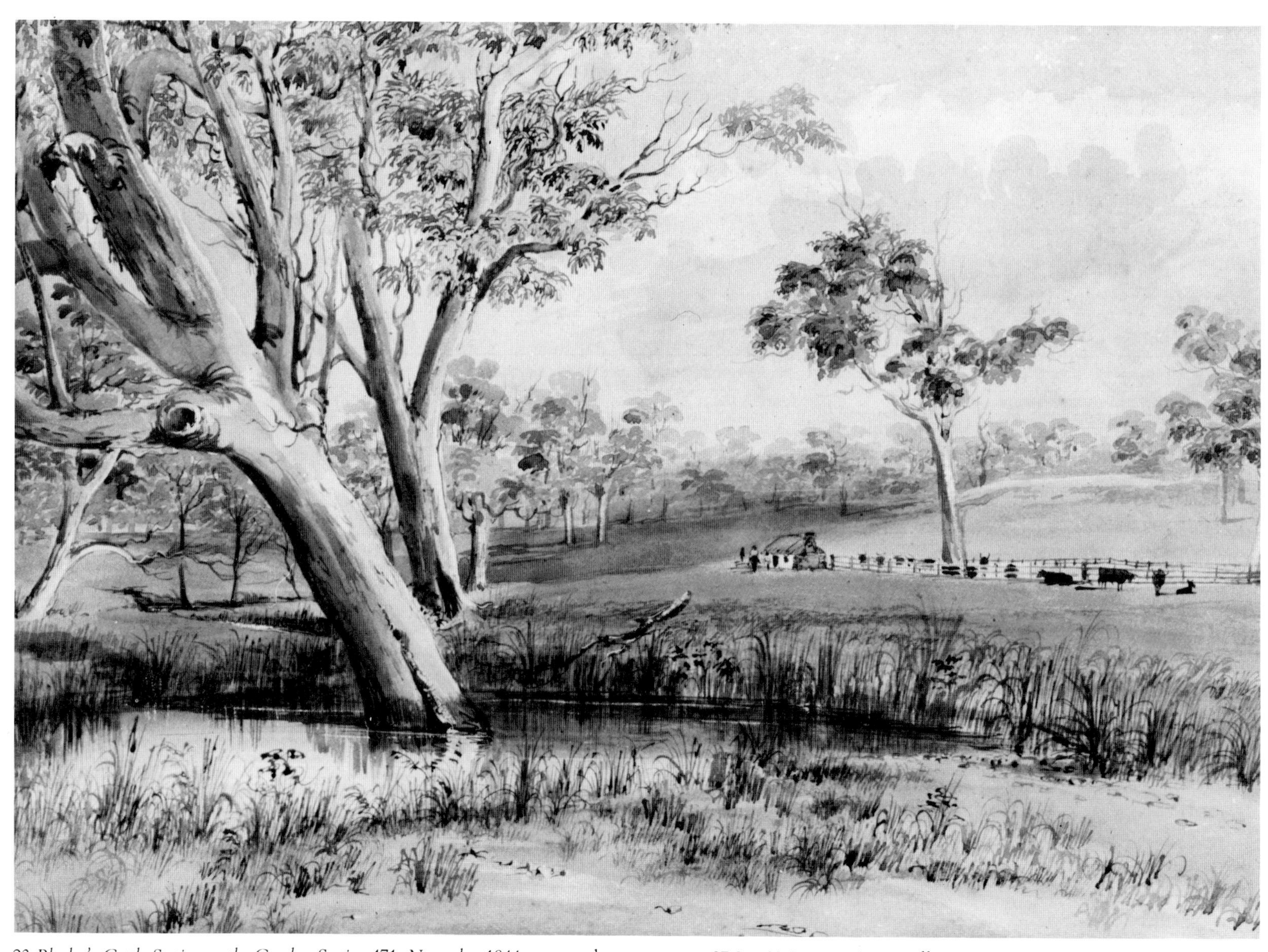

23 *Rhodes's Cattle Station on the Gawler, Section 471, November 1844*, watercolour on paper, 27.0 x 38.0 cm, private collection.

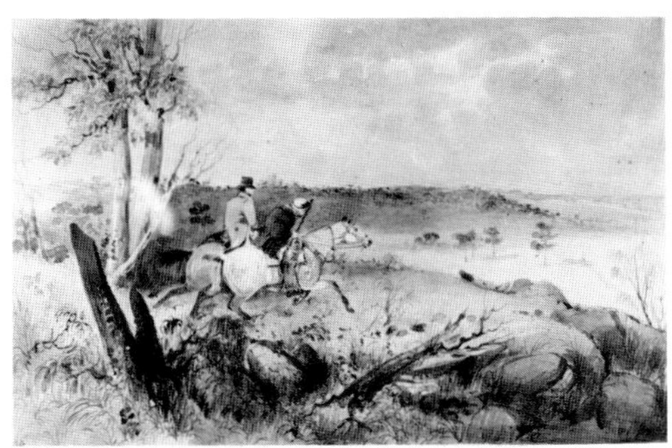

17   (*Two riders*)   *c*.1842-43
watercolour on paper mounted on linen
22.7 x 34.2 cm
Signed l.l. corner, brush and watercolour
S T G. Not dated.

A fine example of Gill's early translucent watercolour style depicting two men hunting or travelling. There were few hotels and travellers relied on the old English style of hospitality; '. . . a person may get on his horse in Adelaide, and ride north or south or east, and leave his purse behind him; for he will be able to traverse the whole colony, without expense, and find a hearty welcome, with comfortable accommodation for himself and beast.'[3]

National Library of Australia, Canberra

(NLA R.34)

18   *Mounted Police chasing Bushrangers overland from Port Phillip to Lake Albert, South Australia*   *c*.1842-43
watercolour on paper 25.3 x 34.7 cm
Signed l.l. corner, brush and watercolour
S T G. Not dated.
Inscribed in pencil below image, [*illeg*] *to Lake Albert/ South Australia/ Mounted Police chasing Bushrangers* [*illeg*] *overland from Port Philip* [*sic*]'. (The manner in which this inscription has been set out cannot be accurately recorded with the usual

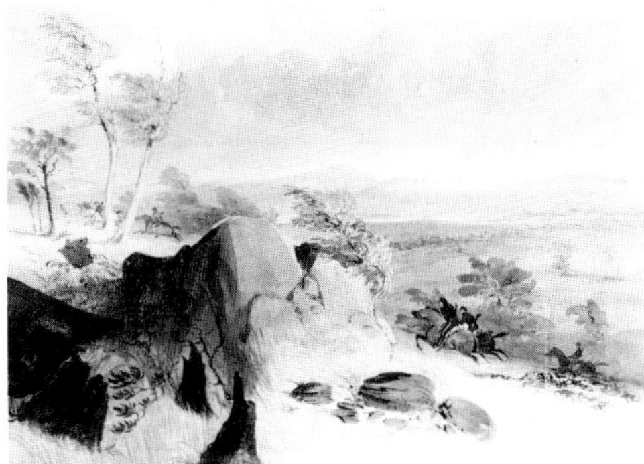

conventions. Logic suggests that the title should commence with the words 'Mounted Police')

Another fine example of Gill's early translucent watercolour style, full of atmosphere and action. The event cannot be identified; however the South Australian Mounted Police were constantly on the alert for bushrangers from New South Wales, some of them convicts who crossed the border into the Mount Gambier district and then the River Murray at Wellington, ranging as far as Lyndoch Valley, raiding shepherds' huts and outlying stations. Several of the bushrangers captured in South Australia in the 1840s were sentenced to death.

Rex Nan Kivell Collection;
National Library of Australia, Canberra

(NLA NK.2043)

19   *Rankine's Station, Mount Crawford, Barossa Range, South Australia.*   *c*.1842-43
pencil on paper 19.5 x 27.0 cm
Signed l.l. corner, pencil *S.T.G.* Not dated.
Inscribed l.r. corner, pencil *Rankin's* [*sic*] *Station/ Mount Crawford Barrossa* [*sic*] *Range/ So Aust*, c.l., *Flat*, upper c., *Thick*.

A field sketch with artist's notes for later development as a watercolour such as (*Approach to Mount Crawford*) (cat. 20)

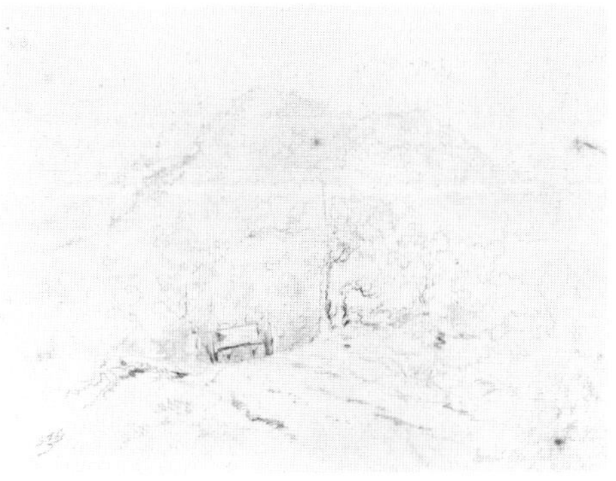

which is a slightly closer view. This drawing datable to *c*.1842-43 was signed many years later in Melbourne (see Appendix B).

Art Gallery of South Australia, Adelaide;
South Australian Government Grant 1969

(AGSA 697HP9)

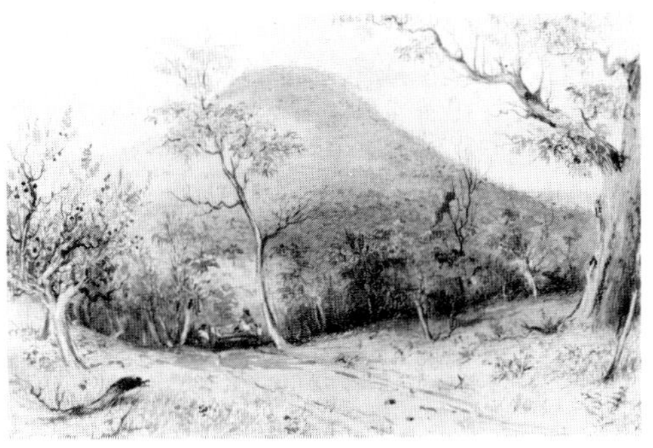

20   (*Approach to Mount Crawford*)
                                       c.1842-43
watercolour on paper 20.1 x 31.4 cm
Signed l.l. corner, brush and grey watercolour *S T G*. Not dated.

This watercolour, which was acquired from the Royal Commonwealth Society, London, in 1974 with the title *View in South Australia near Mount Crawford* was originally in the possession of Captain

E.C. Frome, Surveyor General of South Australia, 1839-49.[4] Another version of the subject with the bullock cart in a different position and other minor variations, titled *Mount Crawford S.A.* is in the National Library of Australia (NLA NK.2042)

Art Gallery of South Australia, Adelaide;
Elder Bequest Fund 1974   (AGSA 744HP4)

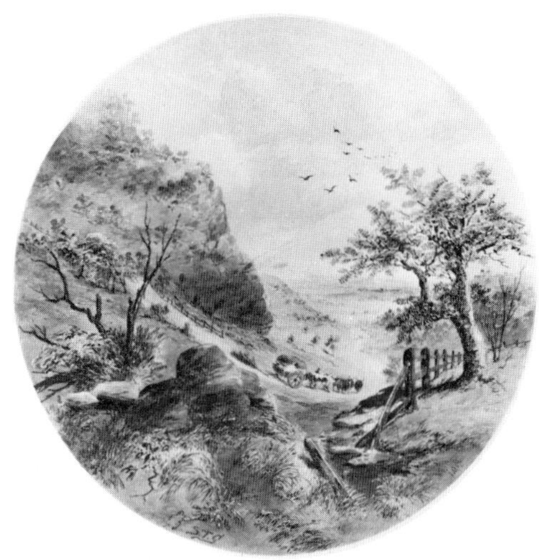

21   *Near Mount Crawford, South Australia*   *c.*1865-70
watercolour on paper, circular sheet 33.3 cm diameter, mounted on cardboard
Signed l.l. corner brush and grey watercolour *S.T.G.* Not dated. Inscribed on cardboard l.r. corner, pencil *Near Mt Crawford So Australia.*

This watercolour was painted in Melbourne *c.*1865-70 from drawings such as *Rankine's Station, Mount Crawford, Barossa Range, South Australia*, (cat. 19) made during Gill's South Australian years.

Art Gallery of South Australia, Adelaide;
South Australian Government Grant 1969
(AGSA 0.1260)

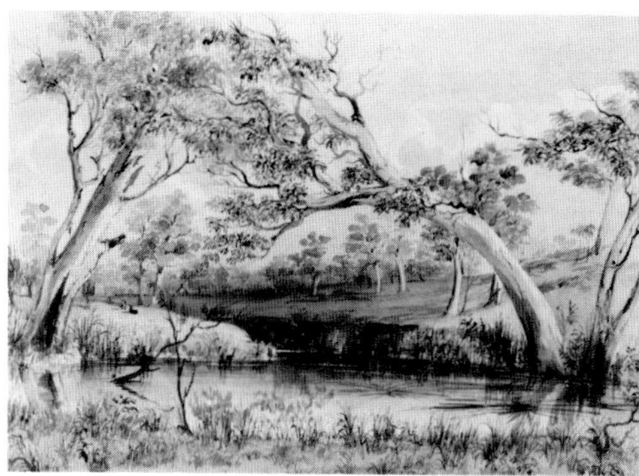

22   *(The Gawler River)*   1844
watercolour on paper 26.2 x 37.8 cm
Signed and dated, l.l. corner, pen and brown ink *S T G/ Nov// 44*

This watercolour and *Rhodes's Cattle Station on the Gawler, Section 471, November 1844*, (cat. 23) are views of the same out-station building, each from a different viewpoint and this one more distant. The Gawler River flows through section 471 which is upstream and four miles south of Terraworta, the home of John Howard Angas, who commissioned Gill to 'take some sketches' in the Barossa in October and November 1844.[5] This is one of the first known watercolours by Gill to be specifically dated in the signature (see Appendix B).

Art Gallery of South Australia, Adelaide;
South Australian Government Grant 1979
(AGSA 795HP30)

23   *Rhodes's Cattle Station on the Gawler, Section 471, November 1844*   1844
watercolour on paper 27.0 x 38.0 cm
Not signed. Dated in title.
Inscribed reverse u.l. corner, pen and brown ink *Rhodes's Cattle Station on the Gawler/ Section 471. . . November 1844,* diagonally u.r. corner, pencil *Rodes's [sic] Cattle Station/ Sec[n] 471.*

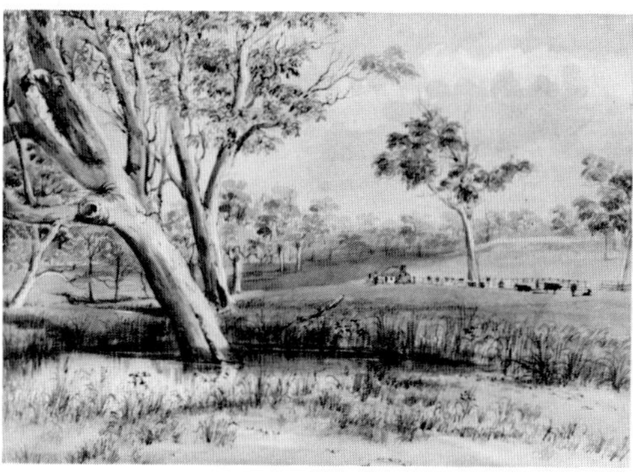

Section 471 was part of the Angas property on the Gawler in the Barossa,[6] and it is thought that Rhodes was an employee responsible for this particular 'run' or station.[7] John Howard Angas purchased shorthorn cattle from the South Australian Company soon after his arrival in 1843 and eventually established a shorthorn stud. This watercolour and *(The Gawler River)* (cat. 22) both feature the same out-station building, each from a different viewpoint, and both probably form part of the same commission.[8]

Private collection

24   *(Drove of cattle by pond in the bush)*   *c.*1844
watercolour on paper 21.8 x 34.6 cm
Signed l.l. corner, brush and watercolour *S T G.* Not dated.

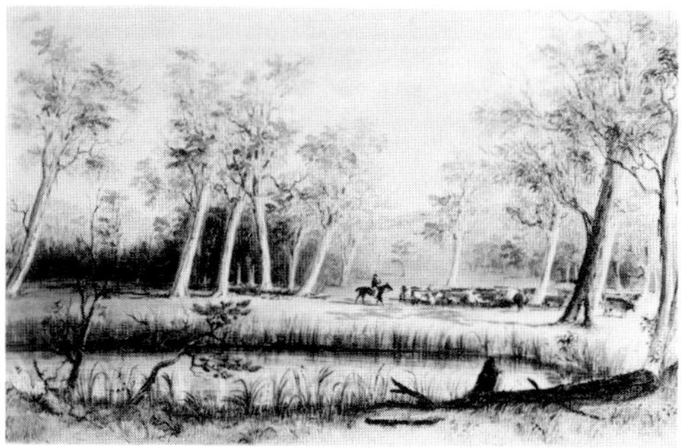

The style of this early watercolour and
the landscape is similar to the two
previous pictures (*The Gawler River*) and
*Rhodes's Cattle Station on the Gawler, Section
471, November 1844* and it is possible that
they are all related. In some places the
Gawler River resembles a series of ponds
and the cattle depicted are shorthorns,
which John Howard Angas was running on
properties connected with Terraworta.

Rex Nan Kivell Collection;
National Library of Australia, Canberra

(NLA NK. 286)

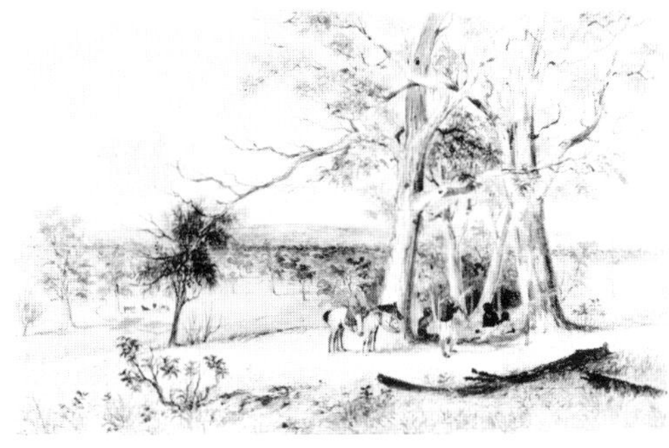

25   (*Cattlemen and natives by gum trees*)
c.1844

watercolour on paper 21.7 x 34.2 cm
Signed l.l. corner, brush and watercolour
S T G. Not dated.

The locality of this scene is unknown,
although it bears some resemblance to the
last three pictures. The signature and
technique date it to c.1844. The
watercolour is also known by the title
(*Stockmen and natives*).

Rex Nan Kivell Collection;
National Library of Australia, Canberra

(NLA NK.317)

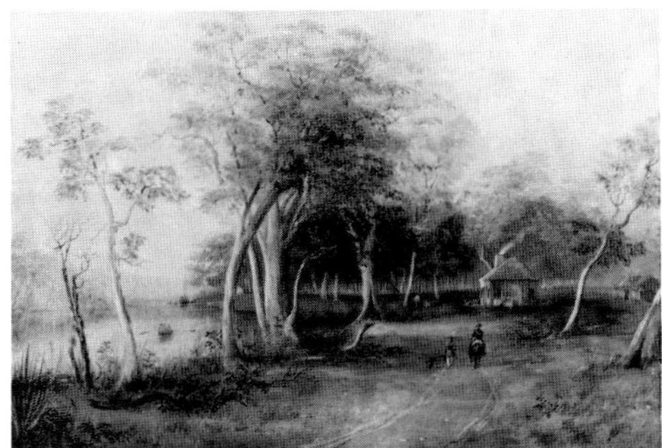

26   (*Old Police Station and Edward John
Eyre's House at Moorundie, River Murray,
1842*)   1844

watercolour on paper 43.5 x 66.5 cm
(original linen backing removed during
conservation)
Signed and dated, l.l. corner, brush and
black ink *S T G /44*. Inscribed, reverse, on
linen backing, pencil *Moorunde old Police
Station/ and Mr Eyres house from/ Sketch by
Hon*[ble] *Capt Frome.*

This watercolour was developed by Gill
from a pen and ink sketch (AGSA
709HP74) *Eyre's first station on the Murray,
South Australia, March 1842*, one of several
drawings made by Captain Frome during a
visit to Eyre in 1842. Frome's sketch
identifies the central building as 'Police
Hut' and the one on the right as 'Eyre's
Shanty'.[9] The Government cutter
Waterwitch is moored at the left.

Eyre discovered Moorundie, with its
remarkable natural avenue of trees, in June
1839 when returning from his first
northern expedition. He subsequently
applied for and was granted 1141 acres
there and in September 1841 was
appointed Resident Magistrate and
Protector of Aborigines at Moorundie and
set about the establishment of his house, a
police station, barracks and other
buildings. In December 1844 he was given
leave and sailed for England. During the

voyage he prepared for publication his
journals in which he used two of Gill's
sketches as illustrations.[10]

Since this watercolour was painted by
Gill in 1844, it seems reasonable to assume
that it was a commission from Eyre[11] who
took it to England where it apparently
became the property of the South
Australian Company and in 1846 may have
been used by James Allen to illustrate his
Lectures on South Australia (see Appendix
A). When given to the Art Gallery of
South Australia by the South Australian
Company in 1931 this picture was titled
*Edward John Eyre's Home at Moorundie, River
Murray.*

There are two other watercolours of
Moorundie, (*Natural avenue of trees near
Eyre's station at Moorundie, River Murray*)
(cat. 34) and (*Australian Aborigines river
fishing from a canoe and from the river bank*)
(cat. 35).[12]

Art Gallery of South Australia, Adelaide;
Gift of the South Australian Company 1931

(AGSA 0.35)

27   (*Extinct Crater, North of Spencer
Gulf, South Australia*)   1845

watercolour on paper 17.8 x 28.5 cm
Signed and dated, l.l. corner, pen and
brown ink *S.T.G /45*. Inscribed l.r. corner,
pencil *Crater N. of Spencer's Gulf* (possibly
not by artist).

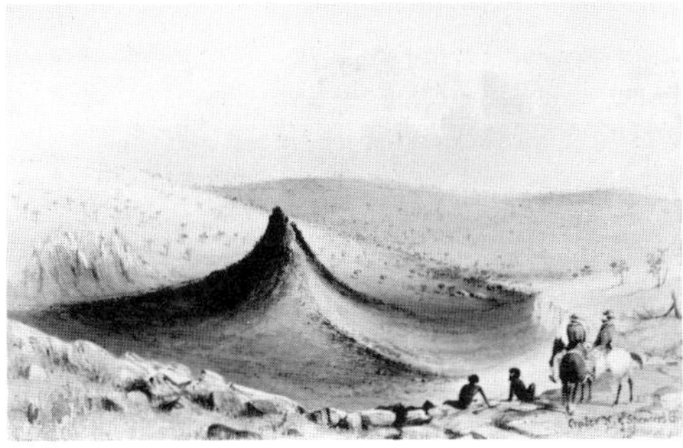

This rock formation, at the time thought to be an extinct volcano, was discovered by George Charles Hawker on 29 July 1843 during Captain E.C. Frome's second northern expedition. Next day both Captain Frome and James Henderson visited and sketched the feature.[13] Gill apparently never visited the scene, but made a number of watercolours, of which this is one, based on Frome's sketch. Two others and a pencil drawing are listed below. There was also another watercolour version, now lost, which was at one time in the possession of the Horrocks family.[14]

ML PX*D73 f5. *Crater of extinct Volcano. From Hon*[1] *Capt. Frome's northern Sketches.* The landscape only without the Aborigines and the horsemen. This watercolour is inscribed on the reverse in pencil by the artist '-Eyre Esqr-' which together with the signature and style suggest it was painted for Edward John Eyre, *c.*1844.

AGSA 697HP8 *Crater of Extinct Volcano Northward So. A. From original sketch by Capt. Frome.* The landscape forms have changed slightly and the disposition of the horsemen and Aborigines has also been changed. A pencil drawing, it is thought that the signature and date, which is incorrect, were added many years later in Melbourne, possibly after Gill painted the watercolour which is now in the Art Gallery of New South Wales.

AGNSW 214.1975 (*Landscape with crater and cone*) The signature and style of this watercolour indicate that it was painted in Melbourne *c.*1870 from the pencil drawing (AGSA 697HP8) because the placement of the horsemen and Aborigines is exactly the same.

Art Gallery of South Australia, Adelaide;
Bequest of J. Angas Johnson 1902   (AGSA 0.614)

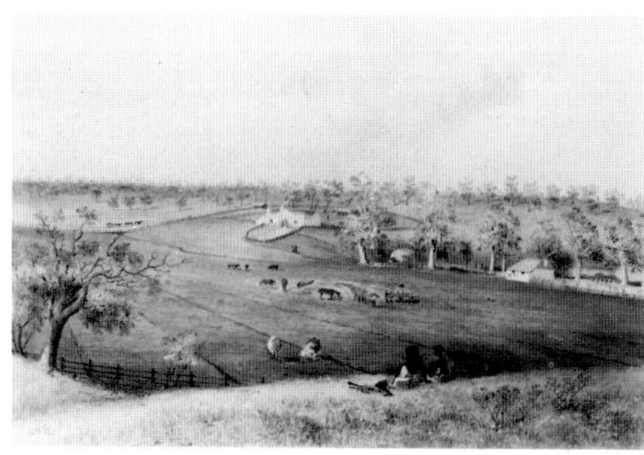

28   (*Floraville, property of Wm. Younghusband, Esq. near Gawler*)   1847
watercolour on paper 22.5 x 35.2 cm (image) 26.7 x 40.0 cm (original linen backing removed during conservation)
Signed and dated, l.l. corner, pen and brown watercolour *S T G/ /47.*
Inscribed, reverse, on removed linen backing, pencil *W. Younghusband Esq*[re] *July 9th/47.*

William Younghusband arrived in South Australia in 1842 and by 1844 had 2,000 sheep, 100 cattle, 6 horses and 25 pigs. He was associated with a number of pastoral ventures, established Messrs Younghusband and Co. and was a member of the Legislative Council 1857-1861. This watercolour of 1847 shows a well established fenced property with substantial house and garden, cottages and out-buildings.

Art Gallery of South Australia, Adelaide;
Gift of Mrs E.S. Levinson 1954   (AGSA 0.1546)

29   *On the River Onkaparinga, above Horseshoe Township, South Australia 1848*
*c.*1848
pencil drawing on paper 13.4 x 27.0 cm
Signed l.l. corner, pencil *S T G.* Inscribed reverse, pencil *On the River Onkaparinga/ Above Horseshoe Township/ So. Australia/*

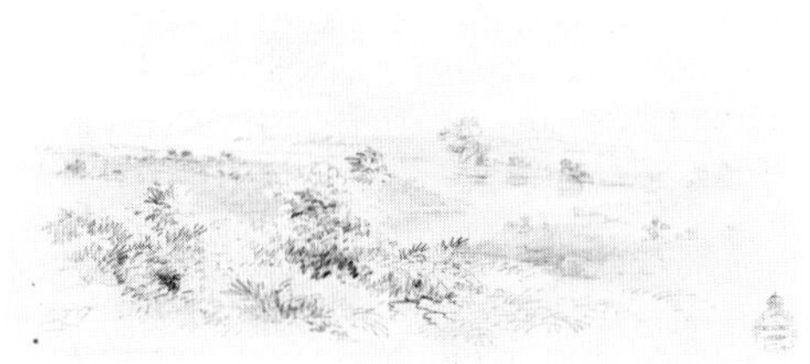

1848. The date below the inscription is written in a lighter pencil, similar to the signature, suggesting that the date may have been added at a later time when the work was also signed (see Appendix B).

Horseshoe, a name sometimes used for Noarlunga, derives from the curve in the river near the township. Land was first advertised 30 April 1840 under the heading 'Horse-Shoe section of No-orlunga Township'.

Mitchell Library,
State Library of New South Wales, Sydney
(ML PX*D383 f.4)

30   *Mount Gambier, South Australia, 1852*
*c.*1853-56
oil on cardboard 22.5 x 30.3 cm
Not signed. Inscribed, reverse, pen and ink *Mt Gambia* [*sic*], *So Australia /1852.*

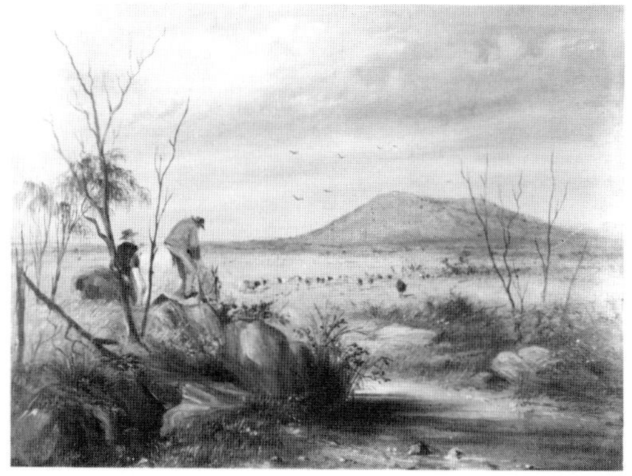

This rare example of an oil painting by
S.T. Gill has a reliable provenance, having
been given by the artist to Arthur H.S.
Piggin in 1876 as a wedding present.[15] The
picture was probably painted in Melbourne
c.1853-56.

The view, near Mount Gambier, is of
Mount Schank, probably from Mount
Schank Station which Robert and Edward
Leake purchased from the Arthur brothers
c.1844-45 for two shillings and sixpence
per head of sheep. The Mitchell Library,
Sydney has a pencil drawing by Gill
(PX*D383 f25) inscribed on the reverse in
pencil by the artist *On Leak's* [sic] *Station/*
Mt. Gambia [sic]*/ 1850*, which together
with several others establishes Gill's
presence in the area in the early 1850s.
The spelling of Mount Gambier should be
noted. The signatures, dates and
inscriptions on all of these works may
have been added later and cannot be
considered absolutely reliable. (See
Biographical Outline, note 89, also
Appendix B.)

National Gallery of Victoria, Melbourne;
Presented in memory of Arthur H.S. Piggin by his
family 1958   (NGV 84/5)

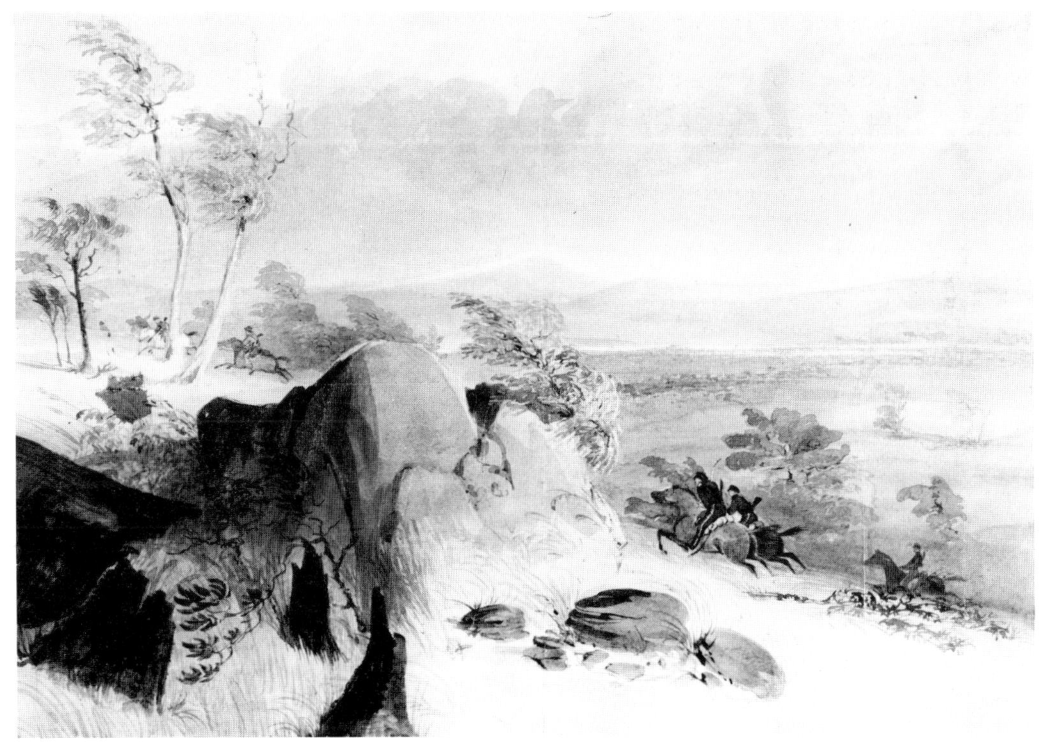

18 *Mounted Police chasing Bushrangers overland from Port Phillip to Lake Albert, South Australia,*
watercolour on paper, 25.3 x 34.7 cm, National Library of Australia.

Natives

At the time of Gill's arrival in South Australia at the end of 1839 the local Aboriginal tribes, which had never been great in number, were already depleted. The Adelaide tribes were allotted sections of the city's surrounding parklands and were employed to chop and carry wood and to undertake other menial tasks. The Aboriginal children were often unwillingly coerced into going to school. Adults and children were forbidden to go naked into the city of Adelaide and S.T. Gill has portrayed them in his Adelaide Streets series and the Port Adelaide series.

S.T. Gill's first known Australian works are *The Seasons,* executed within a year or so of his arrival and these include Aborigines seen in the distance. Natives assumed greater importance for Gill after he is believed to have visited Edward John Eyre at Moorundie on the River Murray in early 1842. As Geoffrey Dutton has claimed, Eyre was 'of all the great Australian explorers . . . the most knowledgeable about and sympathetic to the Aborigines.'

Eyre would have introduced Gill to their manners and customs. On stylistic grounds it would appear that the fresh paintings of *Natives Lighting a fire with the shaft of the grass tree* (cat. 31), *Native diving into a pool* (cat. 32) and *Native speared in a skirmish* (cat. 33) are probably his earliest works devoted to the subject of Aborigines and probably date from early 1842. His peculiar foreground brush doodles, which suggest native grasses and scrub, show a similar technique to that used in the vignettes in his early sketchbook. These early watercolours are rather circular like *The Seasons* and *The Months* series, but they are much smaller, more spontaneous and less formal. The Natives appear very much as part of their natural environment.

In larger landscapes of the interior, Gill depicted the Aborigines from a distance scampering like nimble ants over hills and cliff faces, their dark skins hardly discernible against the burnt landscape. He also energetically depicts them in inter-tribal warfare, in corroboree, and starkly in their unusual methods of burial.

Throughout Gill's career in South Australia, Victoria and New South Wales, he depicted the Aborigines in their natural state and in their corrupted displacement in the cities. They often appeared in his bush subjects and were sometimes used in his art to satirize the European's unquestioning claim on the new land.

Only once, in a small work now in the Mitchell Library, did Gill depict them as Angas did, as a species for objective, technical anthropology. In this small wash study the Natives, their habits, and individual studies of their weapons are illustrated together on one sheet.

In his depiction of the Aborigines he is full of understanding and compassion for their plight though, particularly in the later works, Gill often treats the subject with humour and wit.

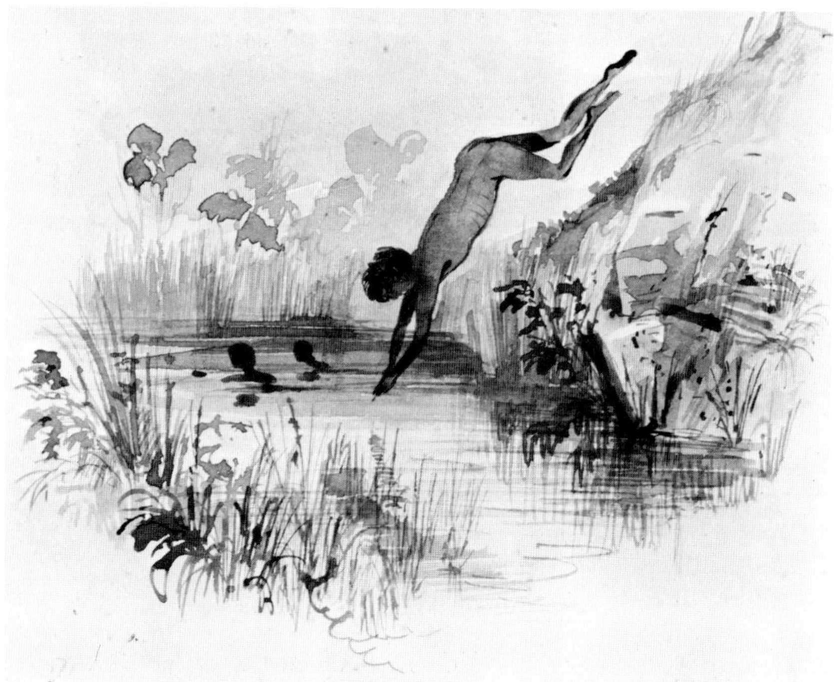

32 *Native diving into a pool,* watercolour on paper, 9.1 x 10.7 cm, National Library of Australia.

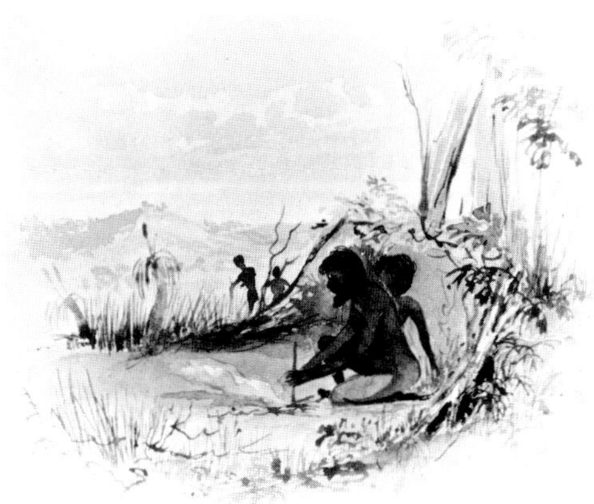

31 *(Natives lighting a fire with the shaft of the grass tree)* c.1842

watercolour on paper 8.9 x 10.8 cm
Not signed. Not dated. Inscribed on the reverse *Lighting a fire with the shaft of the grass tree (you can see the two shrubs in the distance)'*

Rex Nan Kivell Collection;
National Library of Australia, Canberra

(NLA NK.6897/C)

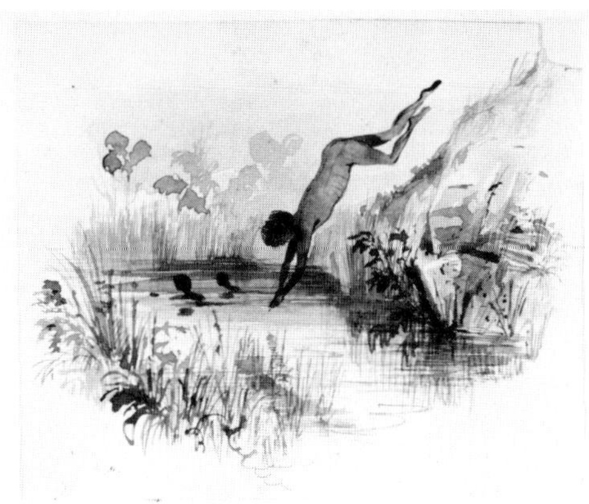

32 *(Native diving into a pool)* c.1842

watercolour on paper 9.1 x 10.7 cm
Not signed. Not dated.

As mentioned above this and the following two sketches were probably the first by Gill devoted to Aboriginal subjects and were almost certainly drawn on the spot.

Rex Nan Kivell Collection;
National Library of Australia, Canberra

(NLA NK.6897/B)

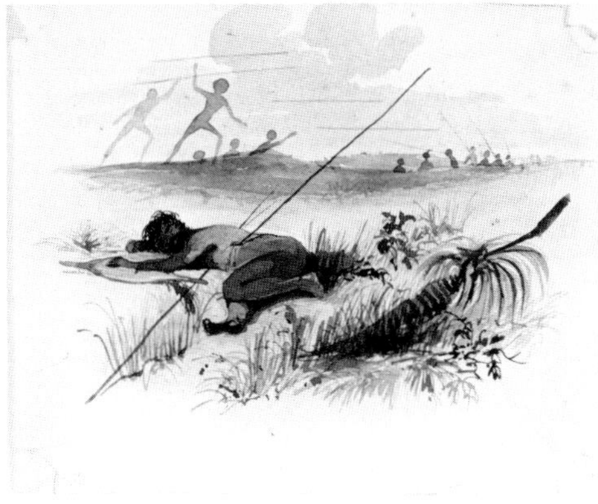

33 *(Native speared in a skirmish)* c.1842

watercolour on paper 9.0 x 10.9 cm
Not signed. Not dated.

Rex Nan Kivell Collection;
National Library of Australia, Canberra

(NLA NK.6897/E)

34 *(Natural avenue of trees near Eyre's station at Moorundie, River Murray)* c.1842-44

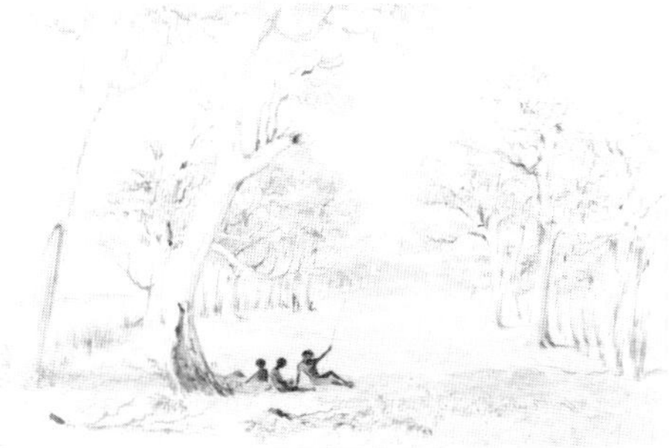

watercolour on paper 19.5 x 30.3 cm
Signed l.l. corner, brush and grey watercolour *S T G* (*S* partly cropped).
Not dated.

This work is catalogued by the Mitchell Library under the title (*Australian Aborigines resting beneath trees by a river, c.1845*). It has been dated from another work in the album in which it was acquired.

Eyre discovered Moorundie, a magnificent alluvial flat and its famous natural avenue of noble gum trees in June 1839 when returning from his first northern expedition. Frome also sketched this intriguing natural avenue of trees in 1842. It would seem that in this view Gill has allowed the natural avenue of trees to form a classical arcade for the noble savages.

Mitchell Library,
State Library of New South Wales, Sydney

(ML (Z)PX*D73 f.2)

35 *(Australian Aborigines river fishing from a canoe and from the river bank)* c.1842-44

watercolour on paper 19.6 x 30.3 cm
Signed l.l. corner, brush and grey watercolour *S T G* .Not dated.

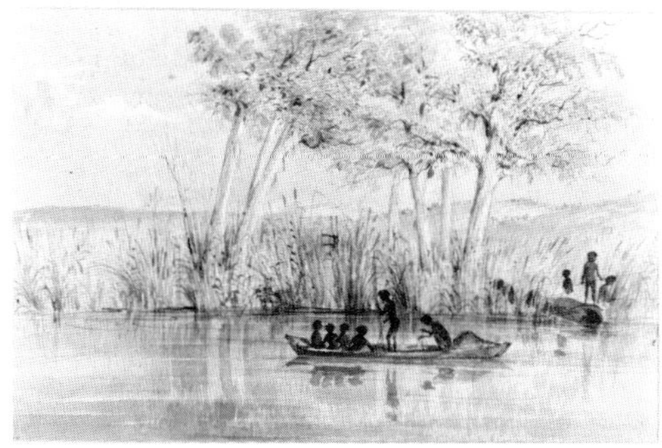

This is a companion to the previous picture painted at the same time at Moorundie. Fish was a major part of the diet of the powerful River Murray tribes. By the time this painting was executed they were using fish hooks supplied by Eyre. Murray cod was the largest and most common fish which was caught.

Mitchell Library,
State Library of New South Wales, Sydney
(ML (Z)PX*D73 f.1)

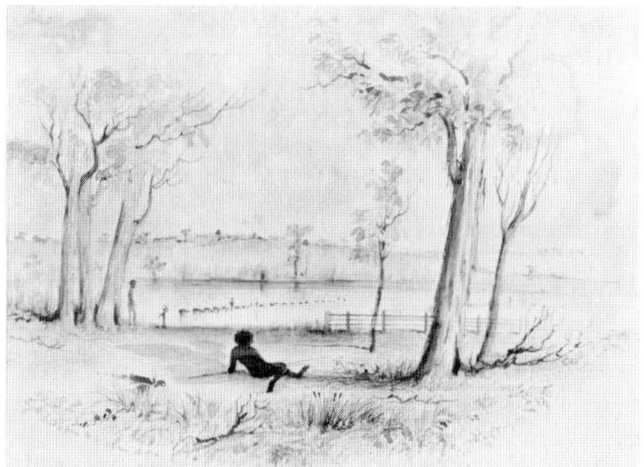

36   *Native Women fishing on the Murray*
                                    c.1842-44

watercolour on paper 14.5 x 20.2 cm
Signed l.l. corner, brush and watercolour *S T G from Mr. Hamilton's Sketch.* Inscribed bot.c., brush and brown watercolour *NATIVE WOMEN FISHING — on the MURRAY* followed by *for crayfish/ EUKODKO* in pencil in a different hand.

Crayfish formed another part of the Aborigines' fish diet, the women catching them in the manner seen in this illustration. Based on a sketch by George Hamilton, the painting is not an eye-witness work. When the need arose, Gill occasionally used sketches of other artists, as was general illustrative practice at the time. For instance, Gill was commissioned to do works after Sturt and Frome. George French Angas used Gill's (*Native Burial, Myponga*) (cat. 39) but did not acknowledge the source.

Rex Nan Kivell Collection;
National Library of Australia, Canberra
(NLA NK.2041)

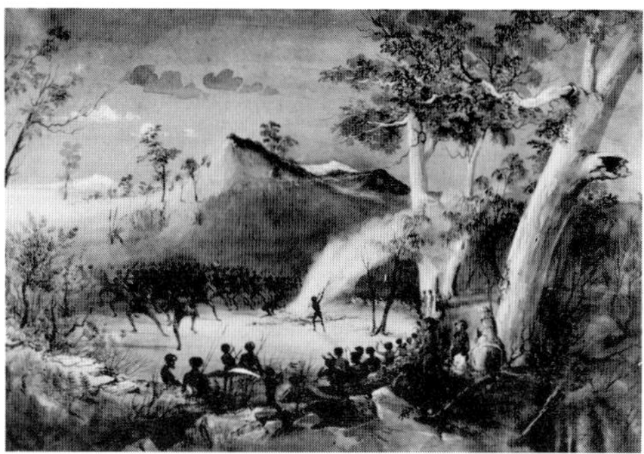

37   (*A native corroboree at night*)   *c*.1844

watercolour on paper 42.7 x 63.5 cm
Not signed . Not dated.

This work was originally titled (*A native corroboree at night*) by Rex Nan Kivell and has been more recently titled (*Corroboree, Mount Leura and Mount Sugarloaf, near Camperdown, Victoria*) *c*.1850 by the National Library. However, it is clearly a work executed in South Australia which can be dated on stylistic grounds to the first half of the 1840s.

It is one of Gill's largest landscapes executed in South Australia and certainly his largest corroboree subject painted in the colony. It is similar to a large oil painting of the very early 1840s by J.M. Skipper (see 'S.T. Gill An Appreciation' p.1) Geoffrey Dutton in his *S.T. Gill's Australia,* 1981, rightly questions a date of 1850 given for this corroboree by Gill and suggests the possibility that both artists witnessed the same corroboree, as it was unlikely that Gill would have copied Skipper. Dutton makes the point that Gill 'never needed to copy other artists' work'. However, Gill did in fact occasionally use other artists' work as a departure. There may have been a watercolour by Skipper which is the basis for both paintings, but one would certainly assume that Gill at some time had actually witnessed a corroboree.

Edward John Eyre, the explorer who was Resident Magistrate and Protector of the Aborigines at Moorundie, River Murray, from 1841 to 1844, probably introduced Gill to some of the native customs. Eyre commissioned Gill to provide illustrations for his Journals (see Biographical Outline note 34). Eyre states '... at nights, dances or plays are performed by the different tribes in turn, the figures and scenes in which are extensively varied, but all are accompanied by songs, and a rude kind of music produced by beating two sticks together, or by the action of the hand upon a cloak of skins rolled tightly together, so as to imitate the sound of a drum. In some of the dances only are the women allowed to take a part; but they have dances of their own, in which the men do not join.'

Rex Nan Kivell Collection;
National Library of Australia, Canberra
(NLA NK.2124)

38   *Australian warfare — Native Skirmish*   1845

brown wash drawing on paper 12.2 x 18.8 cm
Signed and dated l.l. corner, pen and brown wash *S.T.G./ /45.* Inscribed l.l. corner and bot. c., pen and red ink *Australian warfare,* l.r. corner, pencil *Native Skirmish.*

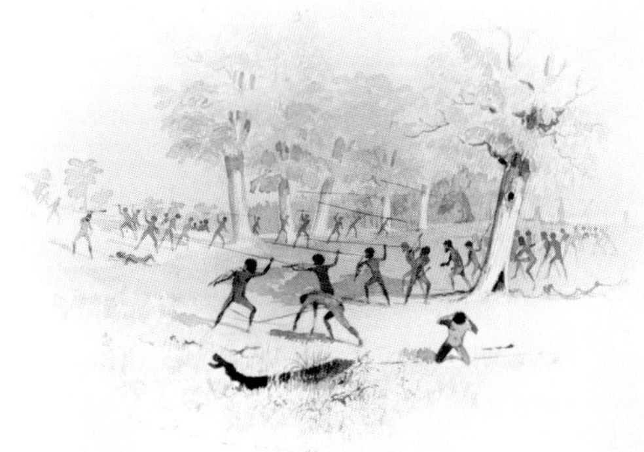

Gill executed a number of works on this theme. In them the Aborigines appear like a cross between embattled insects and Greek warriors and the movement and excitement have been caught aptly by Gill. Skirmishes were sometimes the result of the abduction by a member of one tribe of a lubra belonging to another tribe.

Rex Nan Kivell Collection;
National Library of Australia, Canberra

(NLA NK.6897/D)

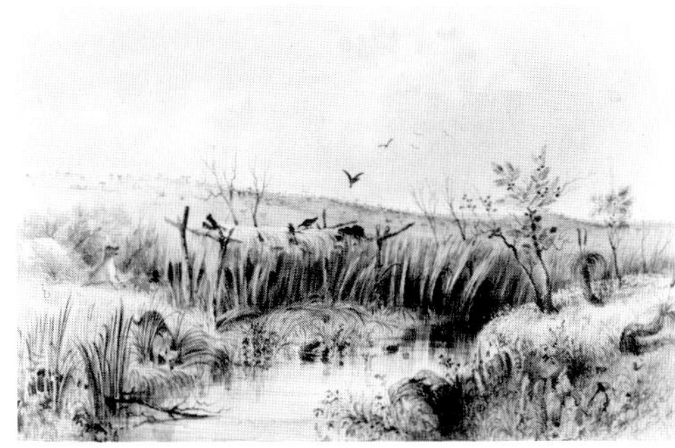

39　(*Native burial, Myponga*)　　　*c.*1845
watercolour on paper, mounted on cardboard 18.6 x 28.7 cm
Not signed. Not dated.
Inscribed l.r. corner, pencil *Native tomb/ Myponga/ T.S. Gill* [*sic*] and l.l. below image *G.F. Angas* (not by artist)

This is perhaps the finest and one of the earliest of all Gill's watercolours on the subject of elevated Native tombs, an unusual burial practice, here recorded at Myponga Vale, in the Fleurieu Peninsula, south of Adelaide. It was probably preceded by the small watercolour by Gill, dated by an unknown hand as 1842, which was until recently held by the Royal Commonwealth Society, London. Many artists, including Gill himself, were to use the image as a prototype; George French Angas, E.C. Frome and John Skinner Prout were three contemporaries who borrowed this stark subject.

The 1842 image was used as the basis for the illustration *Mode of disposing of the dead at the Lower Murray* in E.J. Eyre's *Journals of Expeditions of Discovery into Central Australia,* 1845. The later watercolour here was reproduced in *Savage Life and Scenes in Australia and New Zealand,* 1847, by George French Angas, with the title *Elevated Native Tomb, Myponga Vale, South Australia,* and wrongly labelled as being based on an original work by Angas, not Gill.

Eyre's *Journals* record 'Another method practised upon Lake Alexandrina is to construct a platform, or bier, upon high poles of pine, put upright in the ground upon which the body is placed, bandages being first put round the forehead, and over the eyes, and tied behind. A bone is stuck through the nose, the fingers are folded in the palm of the hand, and the fist is tied with nets, the end of which are fastened about a yard from the hands; the legs are put crossing each other'.

South Australian Museum, Adelaide;
Bequest of J. Angas Johnson 1902.

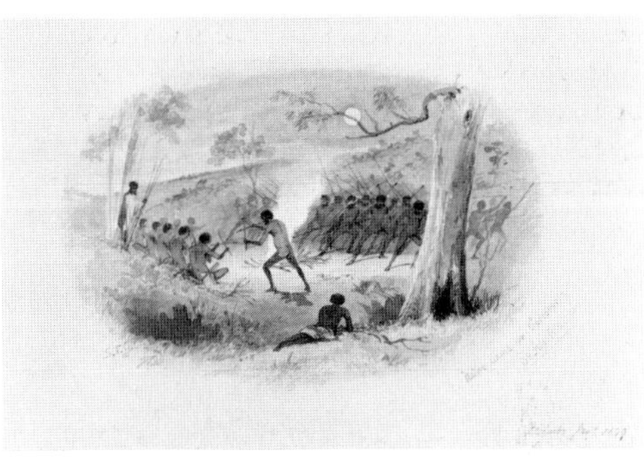

40　*Native dance or Corroberie, South Australia*　　　1849
grey wash drawing on paper 15.6 x 23.8 cm
Signed l.l. corner, brush and grey watercolour *S.T.G.* Inscribed l.r. corner diagonally, brush and grey watercolour *Native dance or Corroberie/ So Australia.* Inscribed l.r. corner *Adelaide Jan*[y] *1849.*

Rex Nan Kivell Collection;
National Library of Australia, Canberra

(NLA NK.7063/12)

Adelaide and Port Adelaide

Gill's paintings of the Adelaide streets painted in 1845 and the paintings of Sturt's 1844 expedition leaving the centre of the city, together with the paintings of Port Adelaide executed in the following years, are amongst the best known images of Adelaide in the mid-nineteenth century. They have been frequently reproduced and often used to illustrate historical discussion on the early days of the colony of South Australia. As a set of paintings they show Gill at his best.

Writing generously of Colonel Light's wisdom of choice in the siting of the city Captain Sturt says in his *Narrative of an Expedition into Central Australia* published in London in 1849,

The position and ground chosen by the first Surveyor-General of South Australia, as the site of its future capital is a remarkable instance of the quick intelligence of that officer.

Having given a description of the dreary flat wastes between Port Adelaide and the city in evidence in the background of some of Gill's paintings of Prospect House in 1850 (cat. 108 and 109), he goes on to say:

Established where it is, the City of Adelaide stands on the summit of the first elevated ground, between the coast and the mountain ranges.

He notes that the city is divided by the River Torrens, bridged in several places and that Government House and all public buildings and offices are in South Adelaide. As to the streets in the heart of the city, then as now,

the streets in the vicinity of North Terrace, have assumed a regularity and uniformity greater than any street in North Adelaide.

Remarking that Hindley and Rundle Streets are the equal to those in any secondary town in England he goes on to describe recent developments:

every shop and store that is now built is of a substantial and ornamental character, and those general improvements are being made which are the best proofs of increasing prosperity and opulence.

It was this increasing prosperity and opulence that led to James Allen's commission to Gill for these city paintings and others which were to be used to publicise the benefits South Australia could bestow on would-be colonists and investors. Though these works and James Allen's accompanying lectures were not the first propaganda campaign for immigrants they were intended to give an impression of activity and development in a new country. Captain Sturt also had observations to make about the development of the site of South Australia's largest port:

As regards Port Adelaide itself, I cannot imagine a securer or a more convenient harbour. Without having any broad expanse of water, it is of sufficient width for vessels to lie there in perfect safety ...

The choice of the sites for Adelaide and for Port Adelaide had been controversial from the beginning of settlement in South Australia, with arguments in favour of all sorts of other possible locations. The permanent site for Port Adelaide was not chosen until 1839, but once development began, the choice was seen to have been a good one. A two-mile road had been built by the South Australian Company at a cost of £12,000, and they also constructed a wharf and warehouse buildings. The Government had built a Custom House and line of sheds so that it was evident that the new colonists intended to set up for business in a permanent and orderly way.

Gill was asked to record these splendid developments, and produced several watercolours between 1845 and 1848 which capture the atmosphere of a busy port as well as the delicacy of a fresh morning with a sea breeze blowing.

Sturt's description of Port Adelaide as

... a bar harbour, about nine miles from Glenelg and situated on

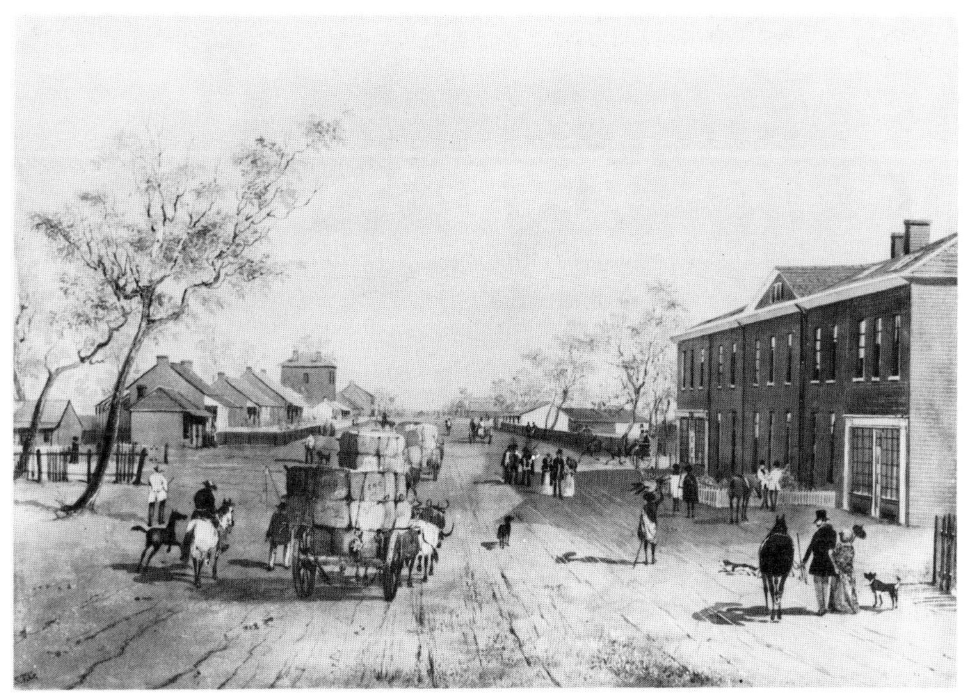

the eastern bank of a large creek, penetrating the mangrove swamp by which the shore of the Gulf is thereabouts fringed

sounds quite primitive and undeveloped compared with the aspects of the Port which Gill painted only a few years later. All arrivals and departures by sea and all imports of food and produce other than goods brought overland were organised here. The new port was a great improvement on what the first settlers had encountered arriving to summer heat, dust, flies and mosquitoes. They had dubbed that spot Port Misery, a site three miles further up the river and very difficult to negotiate. Gill has shown that by the mid-nineteenth century at least the basic buildings and facilities were completed or under construction, and the amount of rigging to be seen in the view of Port Adelaide in 1848 (cat. 55) testifies to the amount of trade both in goods and passengers. Comparisons have been made between some of

the delightful early drawings in S.T. Gill's English sketchbook and these well-developed watercolours made some ten years later (see p. 17). Gill is at his best when undertaking a subject of this kind with well observed buildings and ships placed in depth in the composition, giving him scope to populate the foreground with typical nautical figures such as net-mending sailors in conversation with a passing lady in a sun-bonnet, or yarning with another sailor in striped jumper and knitted cap.

Gill's use of anchors, fishbaskets, spars and nets as well as the smaller beached craft like rowing boats as design elements within a composition is one of his most delightful trademarks, seen to advantage in these Port Adelaide paintings. Two of the works, both painted in 1847 (cat. 52 and 53), are in remarkably fresh condition after conservation and may serve as a yardstick for measuring the delicacy of Gill's colour.

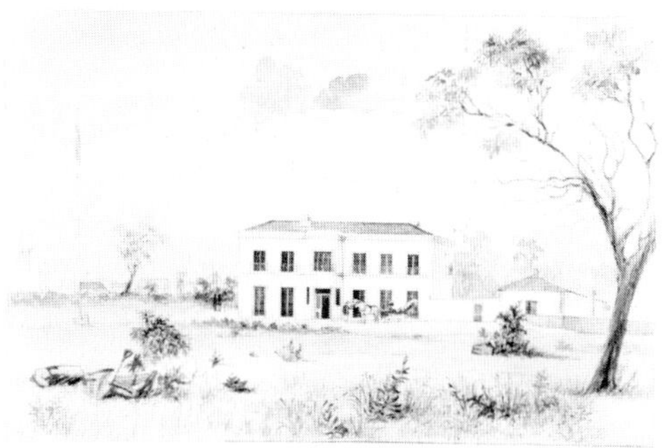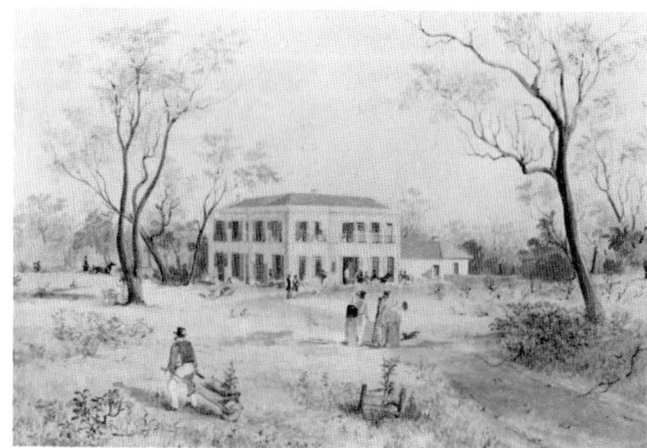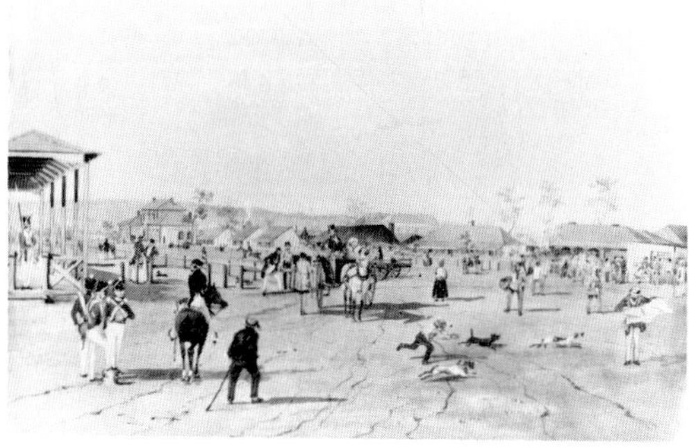

41 (*Government House, Adelaide, 1844*)
1844

watercolour on paper 20.0 x 31.3 cm (image), 26.3 x 39.3 cm
Signed and dated l.l. corner, brush and grey watercolour *S T G/ 44.* Inscribed reverse, pen and ink *Govt. House Front View/ from Park Lands/ nearly opposite/ Bank of Australasia* (probably not by artist)

Captain Sturt locates Government House in his *Narrative of an Expedition into Central Australia* '... King William Street divides Hindley from Rundle Street, and is immediately opposite to the gate of Government House, which is built on a portion of the Park lands, and is like a country gentleman's house in England'.

Mitchell Library,
State Library of New South Wales, Sydney
(ML PX*D383 f.1)

42 (*Government House, North Terrace, Adelaide*)
1845

watercolour on paper 27.1 x 39.7 cm (original linen backing removed during conservation)
Signed l.l. corner, brush and grey watercolour *S T G.* Not dated. Inscribed, reverse on removed linen backing, pencil *Government House,* also imprinted in black

in three places with oval stamp *South Australian Company* each inscribed in centre, pencil *No 12.*

Framed by two large delicately painted trees, Gill has placed Government House in the background. The sunlit foreground is occupied by chatting soldiers and a busy gardener with a young tree in a wheelbarrow. Government House was built during Governor Gawler's tenure under the supervision of the architect Sir George Kingston.

One of the paintings probably commissioned by James Allen (see Appendix A).

Art Gallery of South Australia, Adelaide;
Gift of the South Australian Company 1931
(AGSA 0.34)

43 (*North Terrace, Adelaide, looking south-east from Government House Guardhouse*)
1845

watercolour on paper 27.4 x 39.7 cm (original linen backing removed during conservation)
Signed l.l. corner, brush and black watercolour *S T G.* Not dated.
Inscribed reverse, on removed linen backing, imprinted in black in three places with oval stamp *South Australian Company* each inscribed in centre, pencil *No 3.*

A variety of domestic housing styles is shown in the background, but Gill has focused attention on the activity in the street in front of the guardhouse. Gill has used its shaded columns with sunlit hills seen through them, together with the strongly defined shadows of the soldiers in the street to give a sense of the brilliance of Australian sunlight.

One of the paintings probably commissioned by James Allen (see Appendix A).
Art Gallery of South Australia, Adelaide;
Gift of the South Australian Company 1931
(AGSA 0.939)

44 (*Hindley Street, Adelaide, looking west from King William Street*)
1845
watercolour on paper 27.3 x 39.8 cm (original linen backing removed during conservation)
Signed and dated, l.l. corner, brush and black watercolour *TG/45* (cropped).
Inscribed, reverse, on removed linen backing, pencil *Hindley Street,* also imprinted in black in three places with oval stamp *South Australian Company* each inscribed in centre, pencil *No 4.*

Gill has used his full repertoire of observed characters to populate his road and pavements.

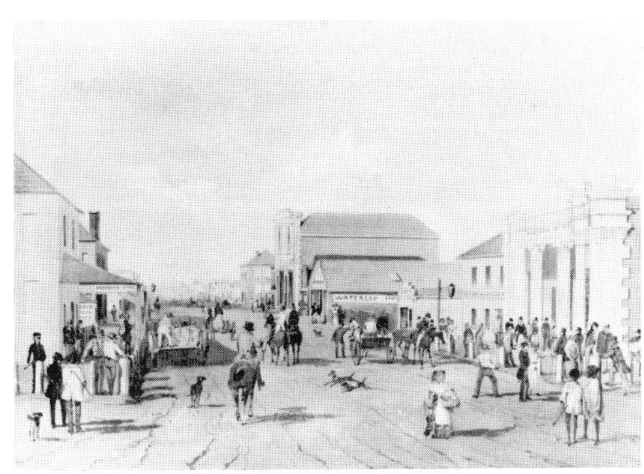

This watercolour was probably commissioned by James Allen (see Appendix A) and is also the original of the lithograph by J.W. Giles for plate 41 of George French Angas's *South Australia Illustrated* titled *Adelaide, Hindley Street from the Corner of King William Street* (see Biographical Outline note 42). Gill also produced a lithograph of this scene some five years later (see cat. 48).
Art Gallery of South Australia, Adelaide; Gift of the South Australian Company 1890
(AGSA 0.642)

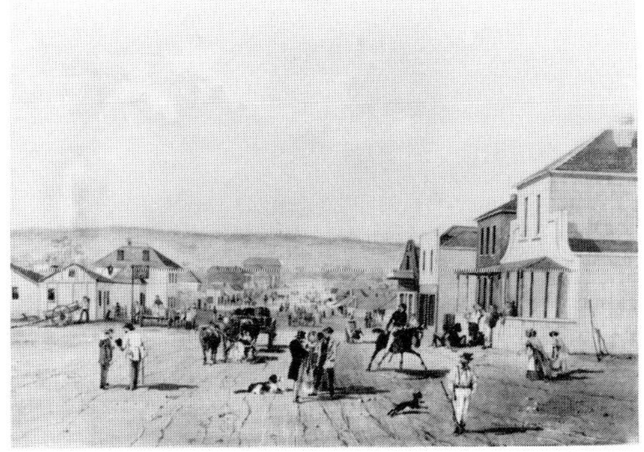

45 *(Hindley Street, Adelaide, looking east)*
1845

watercolour on paper 27.4 x 39.5 cm
(original linen backing removed during conservation)

Signed l.l. corner, brush and grey watercolour *S.T.G.* Not dated.

Hindley Street has always been the centre for entertainment and Gill gives that impression with the many hotels with their signs.

With deft small strokes and subtle lighter tones of watercolour he has suggested the receding buildings and diminishing figures in the distance.

One of the paintings probably commissioned by James Allen (see Appendix A).

Art Gallery of South Australia, Adelaide; Gift of the South Australian Company 1890
(AGSA 0.944)

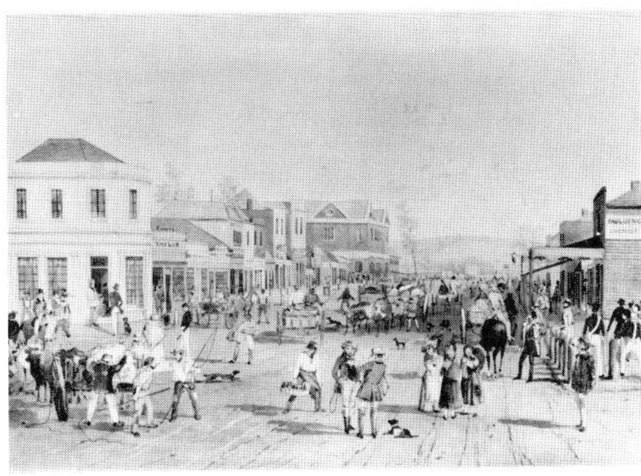

46 *(Rundle Street, Adelaide)*   1845
watercolour, body colour on paper
27.3 x 40.5 cm
(original linen backing removed during conservation)
Signed l.l. corner, brush and grey watercolour *S.T.G.* Not dated.
Inscribed, reverse, on removed linen backing, pencil *Rundle Street,* also imprinted in black in three places with oval stamp *South Australian Company* each inscribed in centre, pencil *No 11.*

The busiest of all the street scenes, then as now Rundle Street at the Beehive Corner is the hub of the city.

One of the paintings probably commissioned by James Allen (see Appendix A).

Art Gallery of South Australia, Adelaide; Gift of the South Australian Company 1890
(AGSA 0.647)

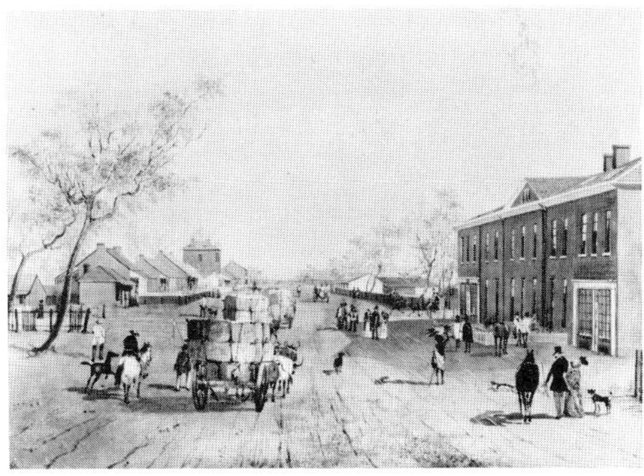

47 *(Rundle Street looking west across Frome Street, Adelaide)*   1845

watercolour on paper 27.3 x 39.7 cm
(original linen backing removed during conservation)
Signed l.l. corner, pen and ink *S.T.G.* Not dated. Removed linen backing, imprinted in black in three places with oval stamp *South Australian Company* each inscribed in centre, pencil *No 9.*

A warm atmosphere is created by the colour of the red brick buildings contrasted with the coolness of sky and foliage. A beautifully detailed bullock dray and mare with foal at foot pass busily by at the left while conversations continue quietly at the right in the shade.

'Tavistock Building', on the right, contained residential chambers, owned by the South Australian Company.

One of the paintings probably commissioned by James Allen (see Appendix A).

Art Gallery of South Australia, Adelaide;
Gift of the South Australian Company 1931
(AGSA 0.940)

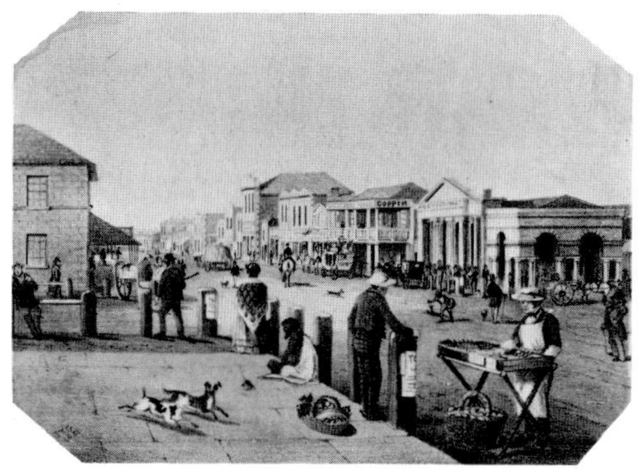

48   *Views in Adelaide no. 1: Hindley Street from King William Street*   1851

printed by Penman and Galbraith
lithograph, two stones 15.6 x 22.3 cm
(image), 16.5 x 23.2 cm
Signed l.l. on stone *S T G/ 1851*.

The *South Australian*, 15 July 1851, announced this lithograph as the first of a series of views in Adelaide, whilst the *Adelaide Times* 10 July 1851, commended the view from Waterhouse's Corner of the busy intersection of 'our chief streets'. Comparison with the earlier watercolour of Hindley Street (cat. 44) illustrates the development since 1845.

Art Gallery of South Australia, Adelaide;
Transferred from the South Australian Museum 1968

49   *Views in Adelaide no. 3: Rundle Street looking east*   1851

printed by Penman and Galbraith
lithograph, two stones 15.6 x 22.2 cm
(image), 16.5 x 23.2 cm

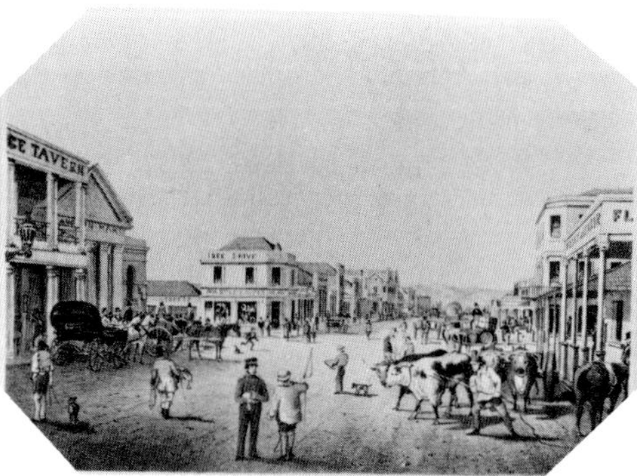

Signed l.l. on stone *S T G/ 1851* (the S reversed)

The third and final lithograph in the series *Views in Adelaide*, all of which were reviewed in the *South Australian Register*, 3 October 1851 which reported that the three views comprise '... the chief business sites in Adelaide'. Again, comparison with the watercolour of Rundle Street (cat. 46) shows the development since 1845, in particular the erection of Waterhouse's Building on the south-east corner of Rundle and King William Streets. This building still stands today as the Darrell Lea Chocolate Shop.

Art Gallery of South Australia, Adelaide;
South Australian Government Grant 1965

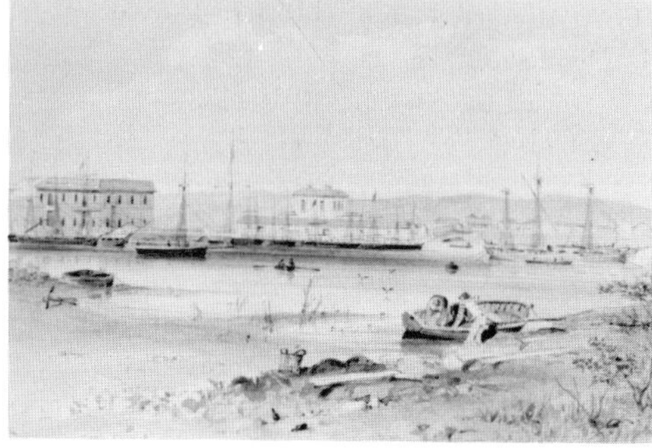

50   *(Port Adelaide, South Australia)*   1845

watercolour on paper, 10.2 x 17.6 cm
(image), 19.7 x 26 cm

Signed l.l. corner, brush and black watercolour *S T G* . Not dated.
Inscribed centrally below image, pencil *Port Adelaide. S A*.

The two tall buildings have been drawn in pencil in the lower margin approximately below each image at l.l. and centrally and inscribed, pencil *S A Comp*^(ys) *Store* and *Custom House* respectively.

Mitchell Library,
State Library of New South Wales, Sydney
(ML SSV*/Sp coll/Gill 3)

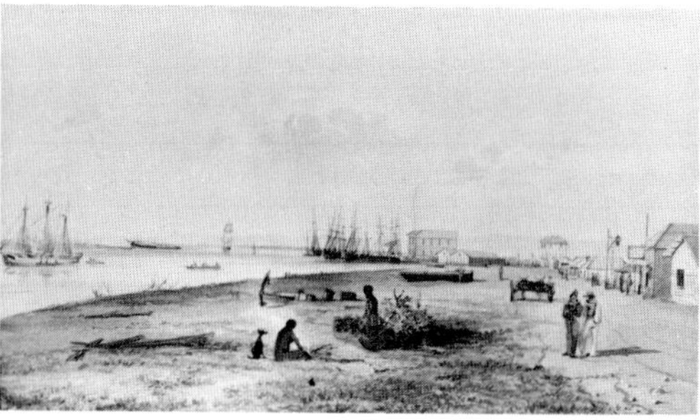

51   *(Port Adelaide looking east along North Parade)*   1846

watercolour on paper 15.6 x 27.0 cm
Signed and dated l.l. corner, pen and grey ink *S T G 1846*.

Cool colours and light tones make a harmonious whole in this watercolour. On the right the 'Hen and Chickens' hotel; in the distance tall ships, the South Australian Company's Store and the Custom House.

Art Gallery of South Australia, Adelaide;
Gift of B.W. Bagenal 1941   (AGSA 0.1181)

52   *(Port Adelaide looking across Gawler Reach)*   1847

watercolour on paper 19.7 x 32.4 cm
(image), 20.7 x 33.2 cm
Signed and dated l.l. corner, pen and brown ink *STG/47.*

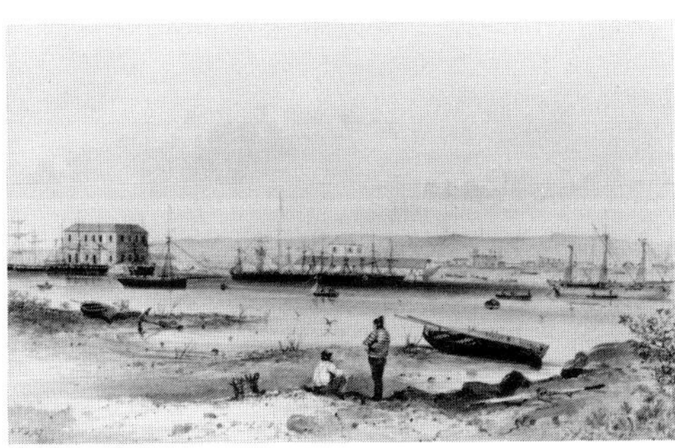

Distant hills behind the port buildings, some still under construction, and a harbour full of well-rigged ships reflected in the calm water are set in contrast to the two sailors deep in conversation on the shore amidst the clutter of anchors, baskets and spars. Gill is looking from Birkenhead towards No. 1 Wharf.

Art Gallery of South Australia, Adelaide; Morgan Thomas Bequest Fund 1923   (AGSA 0.655)

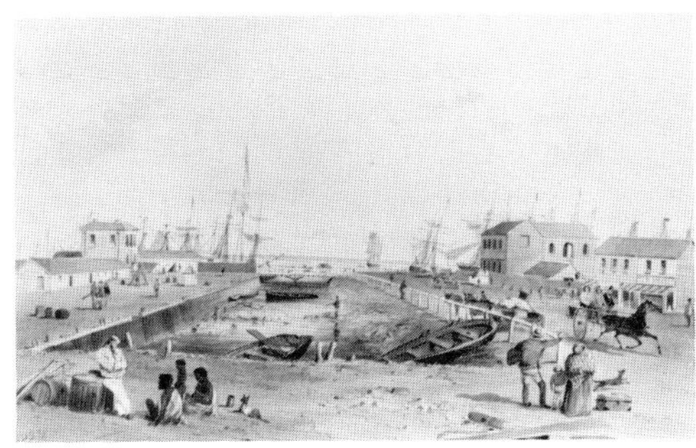

53 *(Port Adelaide looking north along Commercial Road)*   1847

watercolour on paper 20.3 x 32.0 cm (image), 21.1 x 32.7 cm
Signed and dated l.l. corner, pen and brown ink *STG/47.*

The paper, held to light, shows a clear watermark *J WHATMAN 1845.*

Gill is at the intersection of St Vincent Street and Commercial Road. The inlet was filled in the 1850s.

Art Gallery of South Australia, Adelaide; Morgan Thomas Bequest Fund 1923   (AGSA 0.656)

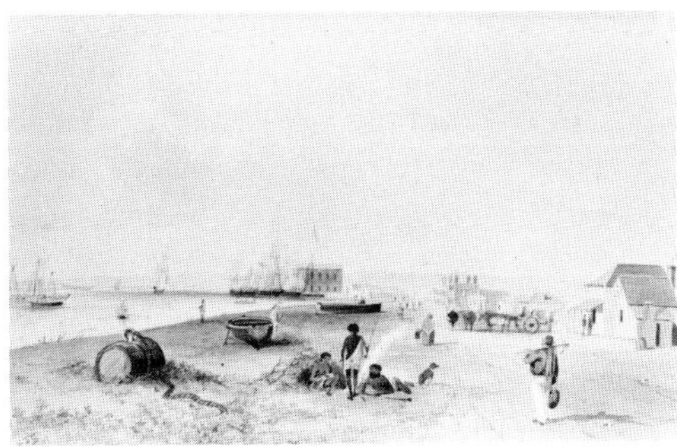

54 *(Port Adelaide looking east along North Parade)*   1847

watercolour on paper, mounted on cardboard 19.4 x 32.0 cm (image) 20.4 x 32.8 cm
Signed and dated l.l. corner, brush and brown watercolour *S T G/ /47.*

A subject and location similar to (cat.51) but with a change in the cast of characters in the foreground.

Art Gallery of South Australia, Adelaide; Morgan Thomas Bequest Fund 1923   (AGSA 0.657)

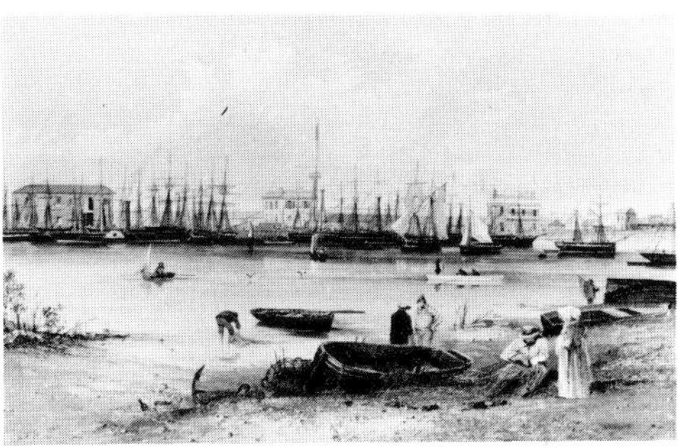

55 *(Port Adelaide looking across Gawler Reach)*   1848

watercolour, body colour on paper 28.2 x 46.1 cm
Signed and dated l.l. corner, pen and brown ink *S.T.G. 1848.*

This version shows the completed buildings that were under construction in *Port Adelaide 1847* (cat.52), and the foreground is populated more fully by people and paraphernalia. The port with its many ships looks the picture of prosperity.

Art Gallery of South Australia, Adelaide; Gift of the South Australian Company 1890
     (AGSA 0.646)

Mining

Australia's first metal mines were discovered and developed in South Australia, and S.T. Gill has left a unique record of an enterprise which helped to set the young colony on its feet. In fact, for a few short years, South Australia was hailed as the Copper Kingdom.[1]

In the early 1840s South Australia was severely depressed; Governor Grey had restricted Government expenditure, pastoralists and farmers were struggling to develop their properties, markets were poor and money was scarce.

Silver-lead was discovered at Glen Osmond on the outskirts of Adelaide where the Wheal Gawler mine[2] was opened in 1841, but it was the discovery of copper first at Kapunda in 1842 and then at Burra in 1845 which really ushered in Australia's earliest mining era.[3] The discovery brought new immigrants, more capital, and generally stimulated the economy and restored confidence to the community.

The three watercolours, *Glen Osmond Mine* (1845), *Kapunda Mine* (1845) and *Burra Burra Mine* (1845) (cat. 56, 57 and 58) were probably painted as a commission from James Allen (see Appendix A) who used three 'Views of the lead and copper mines of South Australia' to illustrate his lectures on South Australia in England in 1846.[4] One London lecture was specially devoted to 'the mines and mining capabilities of South Australia'.[5]

By late 1845, when *Glen Osmond Mine* was painted, another silver-lead mine adjacent to Wheal Gawler had been opened and activity in the area had been stepped up, whilst the Kapunda Mine had been working since January 1844 and its richest ore had sold as high as £35 per ton in London.[6] In December 1845, Ann Jacob wrote in her diary that the Colony was now making 'rapid progress' and that 'copper mines are the mania', mentioning the huge sums of money being paid for Special Surveys of land with 'copper visible on the surface'.[7]

During 1845, a 'Monster Mine' had been discovered at Burra, two promising outcrops, in fact, some miles apart. Two competing parties, the 'Nobs' and the 'Snobs', each raised £10,000 towards the cost of a Special Survey of 20,000 acres at £1 per acre. With the Governor's approval, they combined, then split the Survey into two sections of 10,000 acres and drew lots.

The Nobs who formed the Princess Royal Mining Company drew the southerly section, and Gill's watercolour *Burra Burra Mine* (cat. 58) shows the activity at the Princess Royal in October 1845, a few weeks after the opening of the mine. Rich ores were extracted but by 1851 the lode had failed, the capital was exhausted and the owners abandoned the mine and sold the land for pastoral purposes.

The northerly section fell to the Snobs, shareholders in the South Australian Mining Association whose Burra Burra Mine was opened in September 1845 and proved to be a bonanza for its shareholders. Annual dividends of 800% were being paid in 1847[8] when the South Australian Mining Association commissioned Gill to paint a series of seven watercolours at two guineas a painting.[9] They were to depict the township of Kooringa, two surface views and 'four sketches of the subterranean excavations and the mining operations therein'[10] (cat. 59–65). The press reported that the 'drawings form very appropriate adornments for the walls of the Directors' room' and that 'several sets of copies have been ordered from the artist by the Burra Burra proprietors' among whom was J.B. Graham.[11]

For the proprietors, the four remarkable underground sketches dramatically illustrated the life of the miner:

. . . you descend and find it is only twenty fathoms; you follow on through galleries dotted with copper, down little shafts and into great vaults and chambers, and caverns like Vulcan's forge, where men are seen with candles in their hats or stuck on rocks, hewing away at the most splendid copper ores that eyes have ever beheld.[12]

The Burra Burra mine continued to prosper and in February 1850 Gill was again commissioned by the South Australian Mining Association to paint a view of the township of Kooringa and two views of the surface operations showing the extensive development that had taken place in just under three years.[13] By this time there were nearly 5000 people living in the townships and villages in the vicinity of the mine.[14]

The activity was short-lived, however, as the discovery of gold in the neighbouring colony of Victoria in July 1851 attracted most of the male population of South Australia to the diggings during 1851 and 1852 and by the end of the latter year mining operations had been suspended at Kapunda and at Burra.

Gill joined the exodus, leaving behind a remarkable record of the days when 'Copper was King' in South Australia. He was soon to earn a reputation as the 'Artist of the Goldfields'.

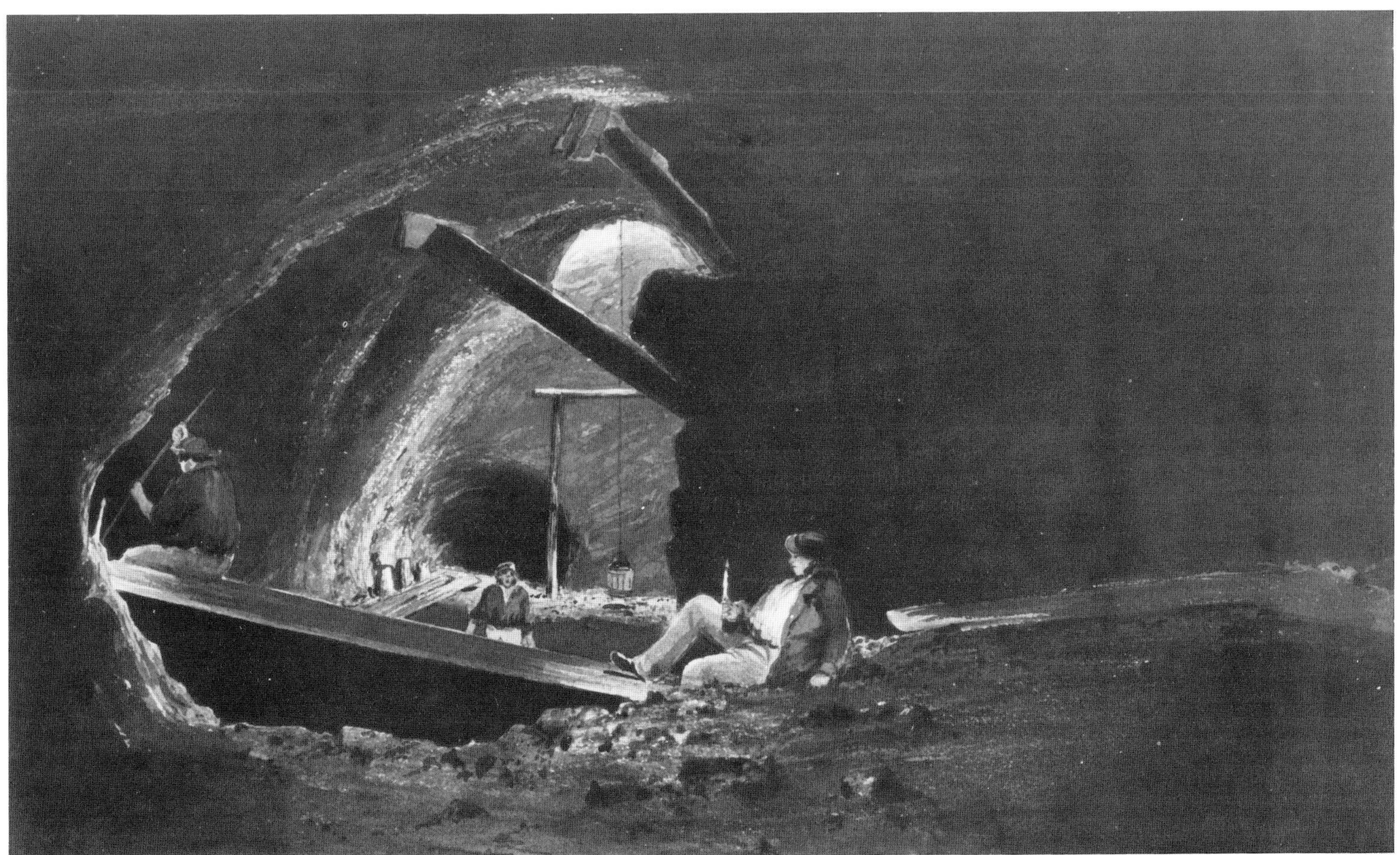

62 *Penny's Stopes, Burra Burra Mine, April 12th 1847*, watercolour on paper, 26.7 x 36.0 cm, Art Gallery of South Australia.

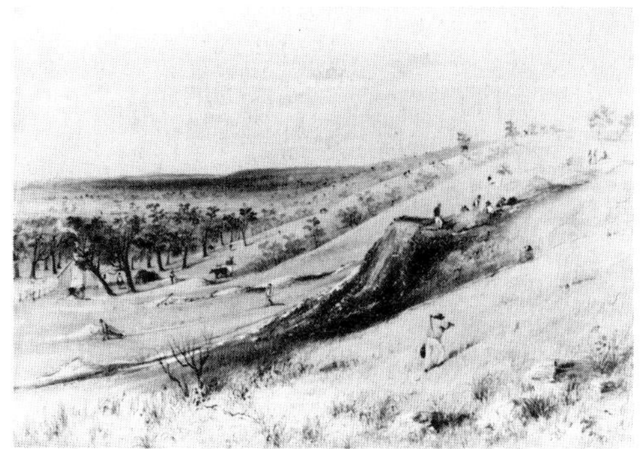

56 Glen Osmond Mine   1845

watercolour on paper 27.3 x 39.7 cm
(original linen backing removed during
conservation)
Not signed. Not dated. Inscribed, reverse
on removed linen backing, pencil, *Glen
Osmond Mine*, also imprinted in black in
three places with oval stamp *South
Australian Company* each inscribed in centre,
pencil *No 15*.

Known as Wheal Gawler, this silver-lead
mine was opened in May 1841 to become
Australia's first metal mine. It languished
until 1844 when Wheal Watkins, an
adjacent silver-lead mine came into
operation and Glen Osmond became a
busy mining area on the outskirts of
Adelaide. This painting was probably
commissioned by James Allen for his
lectures in England in 1846.

Art Gallery of South Australia, Adelaide;
Gift of the South Australian Company 1931

(AGSA 0.943)

57 Kapunda Mine   1845

watercolour on paper 27.5 x 40.0 cm
(original linen backing removed during
conservation)
Not signed. Not dated. Inscribed, reverse,
on removed linen backing, pencil *Kapunda
Mine*, also imprinted in black in three
places with oval stamp *South Australian*

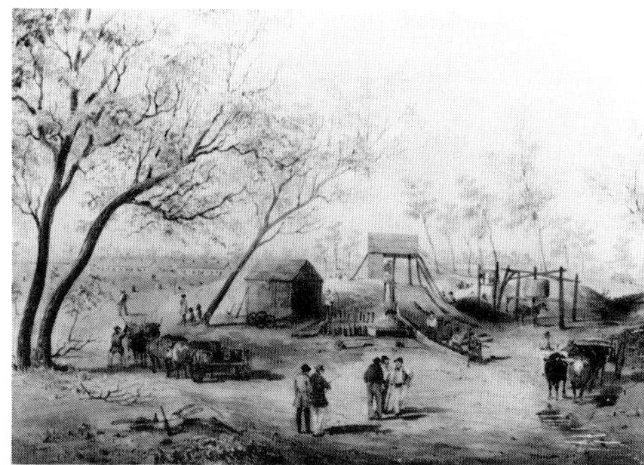

Company each inscribed in centre, pencil
No 1.

Australia's first copper mine was
discovered in 1842 by Francis Dutton and
Captain Bagot's youngest son, Charles
Samuel. Proving to be a rich deposit,
operations commenced in January 1844 and
the mine was well developed by the
second half of 1845. This painting was
probably commissioned by James Allen for
his lectures in England in 1846.

Art Gallery of South Australia, Adelaide;
Gift of the South Australian Company 1931

(AGSA 0.942)

58 Burra Burra Mine   1845

watercolour on paper 27.3 x 39.7 cm
(original linen backing removed during
conservation).

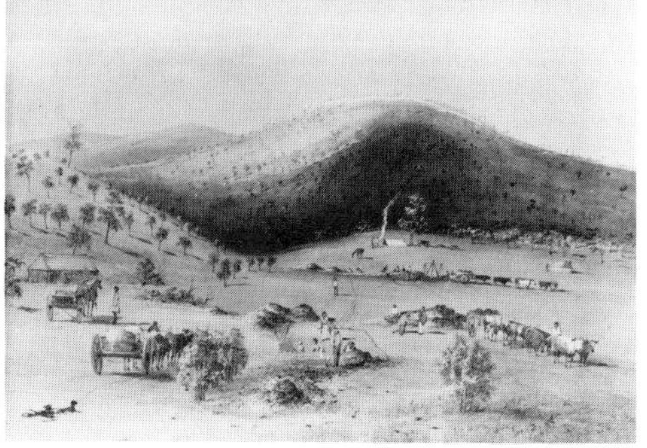

Not signed. Not dated. Inscribed, reverse, on
removed linen backing, pencil *Burra Burra
Mine*, also imprinted in black in three places
with oval stamp *South Australian Company* each
inscribed in centre, pencil *No 2*.

The opening of the Monster Copper Mine,
as the discoveries at Burra were first
known, took place at a number of sites
during September and October 1845. This
scene is thought to be at the site of the
Princess Royal mine. This painting was
probably commissioned by James Allen for
his lectures in England in 1846.

Art Gallery of South Australia, Adelaide;
Gift of the South Australian Company 1931

(AGSA 0.941)

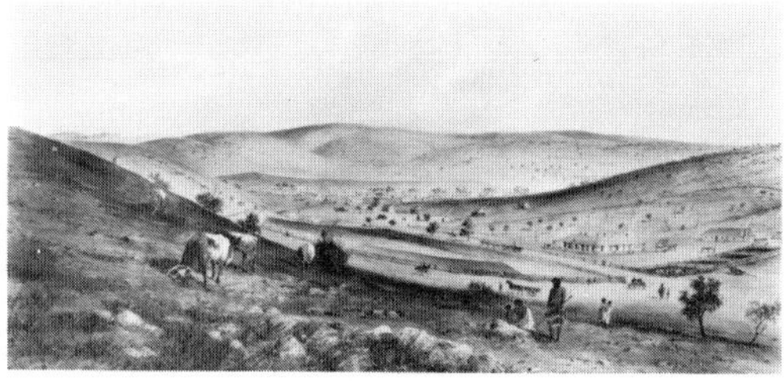

**59 Kooringa, the Burra Burra Township,
April 12th 1847**   1847

watercolour on paper, mounted on linen
33.0 x 68.4 cm (image), 40.3 x 73.8 cm
Signed l.l. corner, brush and brown ink,
S T G. Inscribed decorative label affixed to
sheet centrally below image, pen and
brush with brown, black and blue
watercolour *KOORINGA/ THE/ BURRA
BURRA TOWNSHIP/ APRIL 12th 1847*;
reverse, pencil *J.B. GRAHAM Esq*.

A version, produced for J.B. Graham, of
one of the seven watercolours
commissioned by the South Australian
Mining Association.[11] The original
commissioned work is AGSA 0.652 and is
signed *S T G ADELAIDE*. A wood-
engraving of this painting appeared in the

Illustrated London News, 2 December 1848, p.340, and in the *Mining Journal*, London, 30 December 1848, p.611.

Six Burra subjects were included in the *Exhibition of Pictures*, Adelaide 1848, this one probably as no. 15, *Township of Burra Burra*.

Art Gallery of South Australia, Adelaide; Gift of Mrs F.M. Graham and family, 1947.
(AGSA 0.1353)

60 *A General View of the Burra Burra Mine, April 12th 1847*   1847
watercolour on paper, mounted on linen 33.0 x 68.5 cm (image), 40.5 x 74.7 cm Signed l.l. corner, brush and brown

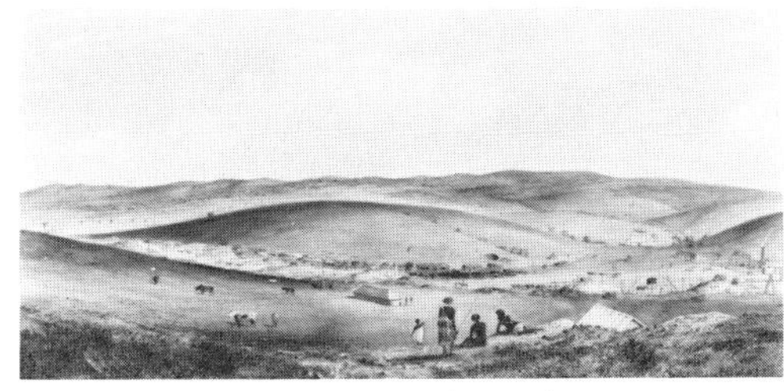

watercolour *S T G*. Inscribed decorative label affixed to sheet centrally below image, brown and blue watercolour *A GENERAL VIEW/ OF THE/ BURRA BURRA MINE/ LOOKING N.N.E. APR*[L] *12th 1847*; reverse, pencil *J.B. GRAHAM Esq.*

A version produced for J.B. Graham, of one of the seven watercolours commissioned by the South Australian Mining Association.[11] The original commissioned work is AGSA 0.651 and is signed *S T G/ ADELAIDE*.

Art Gallery of South Australia, Adelaide; Gift of Mrs F.M. Graham and family 1947
(AGSA 0.1351)

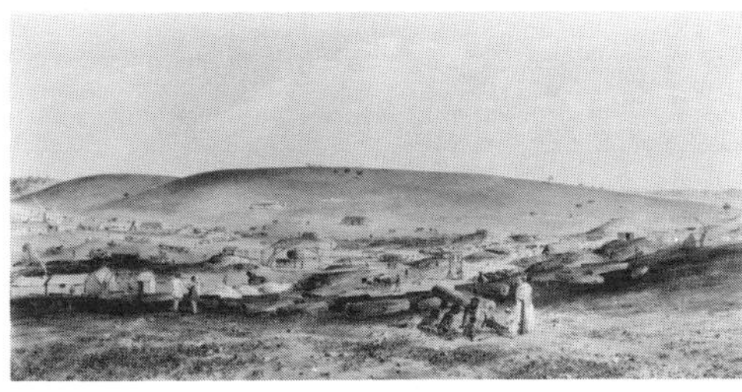

61 *Burra Burra Mine, Showing main portion of the Surface Operations, April 12th 1847*   1847
watercolour on paper, mounted on linen 33.2 x 68.5 cm (image), 40.5 x 74.6 cm Signed l.l. corner, brush and brown watercolour *S T G*. Inscribed decorative label affixed to sheet centrally below image, two shades of brown and blue watercolour *BURRA BURRA MINE/ Showing main portion of the/ SURFACE OPERATIONS/ APRIL 12th 1847*; reverse, pencil *J.B. GRAHAM Esq.*

A version produced for J.B. Graham, of one of the seven watercolours commissioned by the South Australian Mining Association.[11] The original commissioned work, a gift to the Burra Institute from the South Australian Mining Association, is on loan to the Art Gallery of South Australia, and is signed *S T G/ Adelaide*. A wood-engraving of this painting appeared in the *Illustrated London News*, 2 December 1848, p.340, and in the *Mining Journal*, London, 30 December 1848, p.611.

Six Burra subjects were included in the *Exhibition of Pictures*, Adelaide 1848, this one probably as no. 21, *View of the Principal Workings, Burra Burra*.

Art Gallery of South Australia, Adelaide; Gift of Mrs F.M. Graham and family 1947
(AGSA 0.1355)

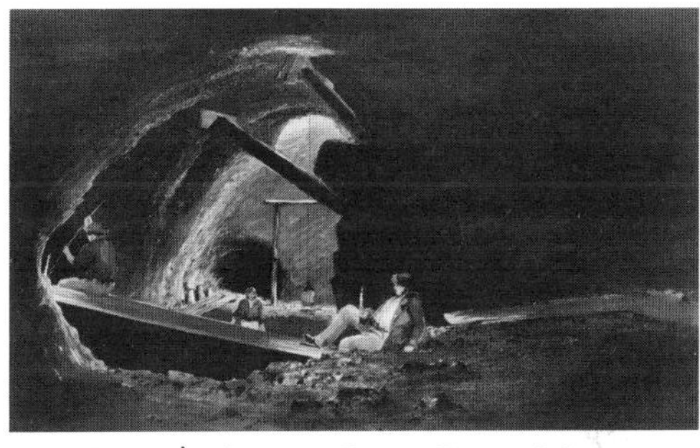

62 *Penny's Stopes, Burra Burra Mine, April 12th 1847*   1847
watercolour on paper, mounted on linen 18.3 x 30.7 cm (image), 26.7 x 36.0 cm Signed l.l. corner, pen and brick-red ink *Sam Thos Gill*. Inscribed decorative label affixed to sheet centrally below image, pen and brush and brick-red ink *PENNY'S STOPES. B.B. MINE./ April 12th 1847*.

One of the original seven watercolours commissioned by the South Australian Mining Association.[11] Another version is in the Nan Kivell Collection (NLA. NK 1411/C).

Six Burra subjects were included in the *Exhibition of Pictures*, Adelaide 1848, this one as no. 35, *Penny's Stopes, Burra Burra Mine*.

Art Gallery of South Australia, Adelaide; Gift of the South Australian Mining Association 1914
(AGSA 0.649)

63 *Neales's Stopes, Burra Burra Mine, April 12th 1847*   1847
watercolour on paper, mounted on linen, 19.5 x 31.3 cm (image), 26.7 x 37.4 cm Not signed. Inscribed decorative label affixed to sheet centrally below image, pen and brush and brick-red ink *NEALES'S STOPES. B.B. MINE/ April 12th 1847*.

Gill painting by candlelight, 'surrounded on every side with malachite, red oxide, green and blue carbonates, mingled in rich confusion'.[15]

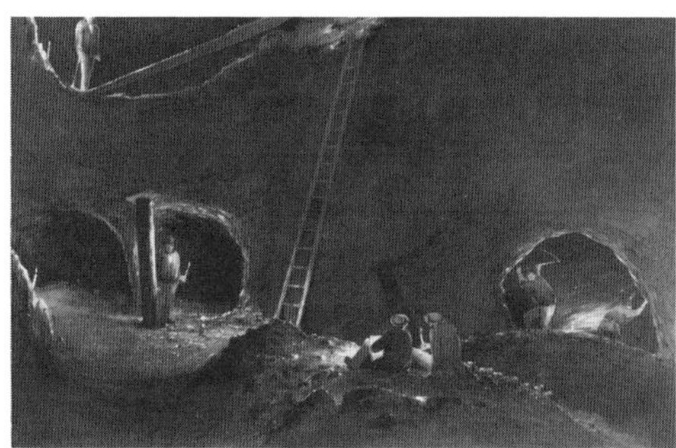

One of the original seven watercolours commissioned by the South Australian Mining Association.[11] Another version is in the Rex Nan Kivell Collection (NLA NK 1411/b). A wood-engraving of this subject wrongly titled *Opening of Lode in Stock's Air Hole, in the Mine*, appeared in the *Illustrated London News*, 2 December 1848, p. 340, and in the *Mining Journal*, London, 30 December 1848, p.611.

Six Burra subjects were included in the *Exhibition of Pictures*, Adelaide 1848, this one as no. 32, *Neale's Stopes, Burra Burra Mine*.

Art Gallery of South Australia, Adelaide;
Gift of the South Australian Mining Association 1914

(AGSA 0.650)

64   *The Opening of Lode in Stocks's Air-Hole from top of N.W. Entrance, April 12th 1847*   1847

watercolour on paper 21.0 x 33.4 cm (image), 27.5 x 40.0 cm
Not signed. Inscribed decorative label affixed to sheet centrally below image, brush and watercolour *THE OPENING OF LODE in STOCKS'S AIR-HOLE/ from top of N.W. ENTRANCE APRIL 12th 1847.*

A version of one of the seven watercolours commissioned by the South Australian Mining Association.[11] A wood-engraving of this painting wrongly titled

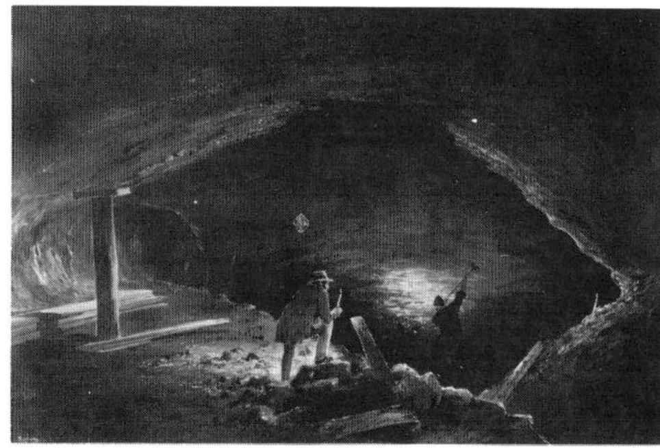

Interior of the Mine appeared in the *Illustrated London News*, 2 December 1848, p.340, and in the *Mining Journal*, London, 30 December 1848, p.611.

Six Burra subjects were included in the *Exhibition of Pictures*, Adelaide 1848, this one probably as no. 7, *Stocks's Lode, Burra Burra.*

Rex Nan Kivell Collection;
National Library of Australia, Canberra

(NLA NK. 1411/A)

65   *Leading from Stocks's to Paxton's Lode, Burra Burra Mine, April 12 1847*   1847

watercolour on paper 20.2 x 32.2 cm (image), 26.8 x 39.5 cm
Not signed. Inscribed decorative label affixed to sheet centrally below image,

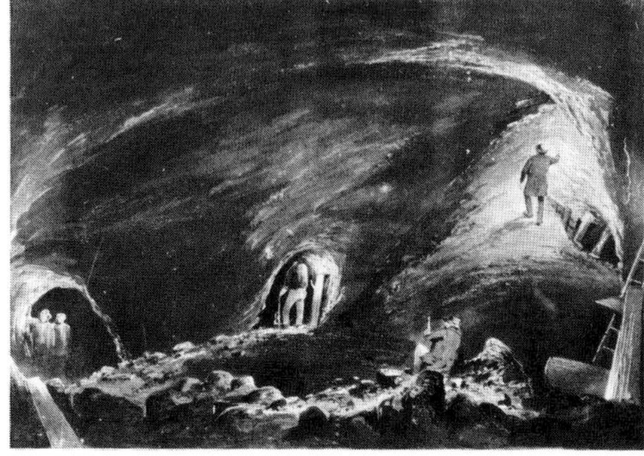

brush and watercolour *LEADING from STOCKS to PAXTON'S LODE/ B.B. MINE APR^L 12th 1847.*

A version of one of the seven watercolours commissioned by the South Australian Mining Association.[11]

Six Burra subjects were included in the *Exhibition of Pictures*, Adelaide 1848, this one probably as no. 10, *Stocks's Air-hole, Burra Burra.*

Rex Nan Kivell Collection;
National Library of Australia, Canberra

(NLA NK.1411/D)

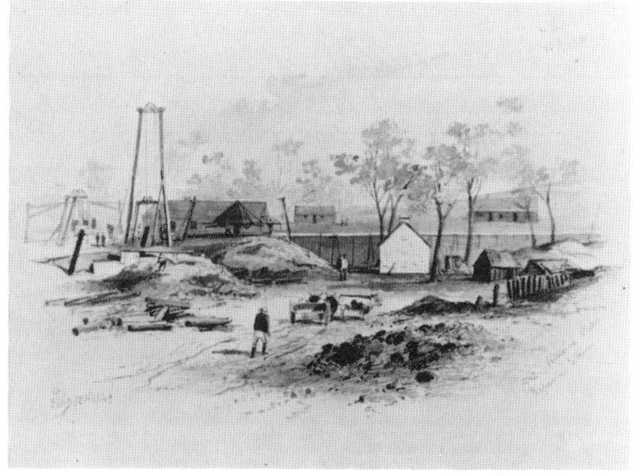

66   *(Kapunda Copper Mine No. 2 Sectional Sketch)*   1849

pencil and grey watercolour wash on paper 20.2 x 26.5 cm
Not signed. Dated l.l. corner, pencil *Feby 12th 1849.* Inscribed l.r. corner, pencil *No 2 Sectional Sketch/ Kapunda C Mine.*

One of a series of six sectional sketches depicting the surface workings, engine house, cottages and offices as they appeared in 1849. The sketches were acquired from the Royal Commonwealth Society, London, which had received them as a gift from Mr Peter D. Prankerd, a member from 1881 to 1902.

Art Gallery of South Australia, Adelaide;
A.R. Ragless Bequest Fund 1971   (AGSA 7110D9)

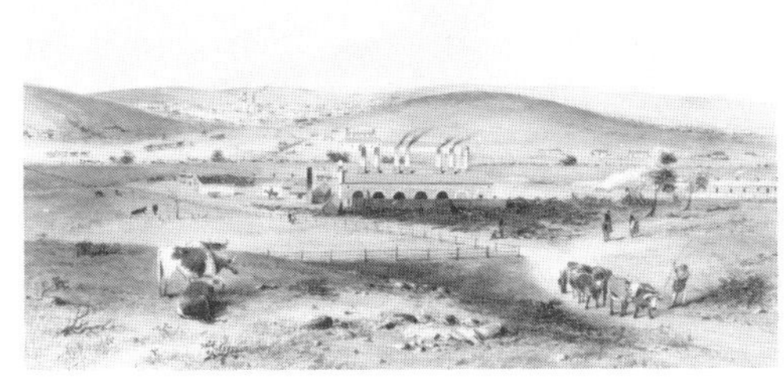

67 *(Patent Copper Company's Smelting Works and the Burra Burra Mine, 1850)*

1850

watercolour on paper, mounted on linen
27.2 x 49.6 cm (image), 29.5 x 52.0 cm
Signed l.l. corner, brush and brown
watercolour *S.T.G.* Not dated.

In 1850 Gill produced three views, one of
Kooringa and two of the surface
operations at Burra Burra as a commission
from the South Australian Mining
Association to record the dramatic
developments since 1847. In this work the
Patent Copper Company's smelter, which
boasted nineteen furnaces, occupies the
foreground, whilst the pumphouse
dominates the mine workings in the
distance. This version was previously titled
Burra Burra Mines 1850. A larger version,
*Burra Burra Mine, So. Australia from the rear
of P.C.C. Smelting works, near Kooringa, Feby
26th 1850* (AGSA.1350), with compositional
variations was painted for J.B. Graham.[16]

Art Gallery of South Australia, Adelaide;
Gift of the South Australian Mining Association 1914
(AGSA 0.653)

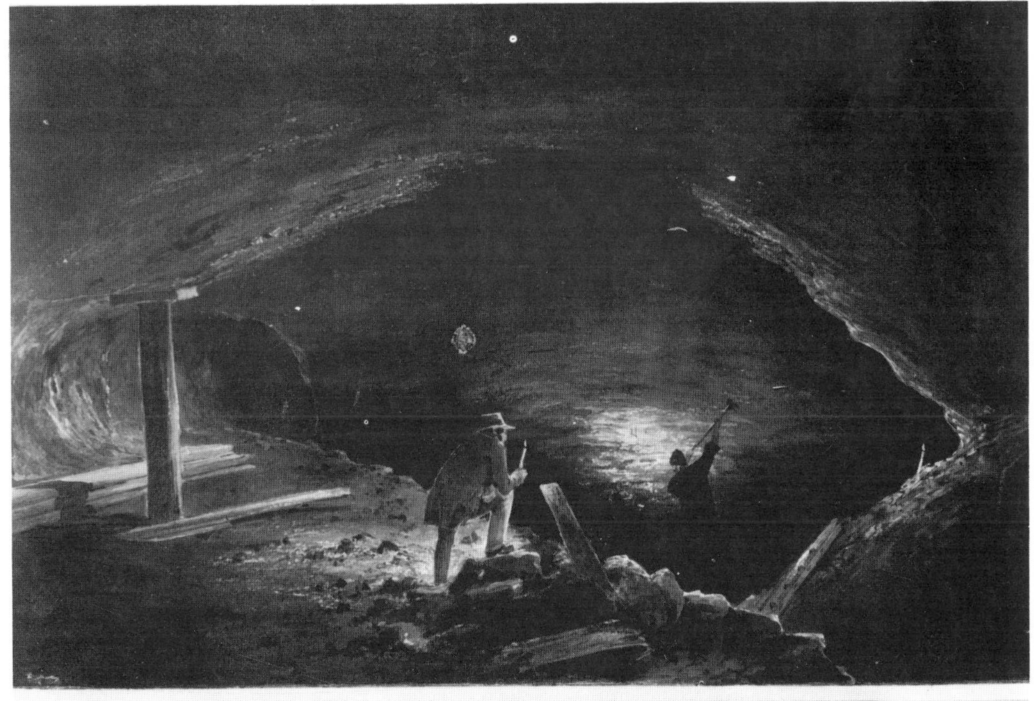

64 *The Opening of Lode in Stocks's Air-Hole from top of N.W. Entrance, April 12th 1847*, watercolour on paper, 27.5 x 40.0 cm, National Library of Australia.

Sport and Recreation

Once the planning of the city of Adelaide was completed, the colonists lost no time in organising sporting pastimes to add pleasure to their lives and to recreate the established pattern of English social life in Australia.

Within a year of settlement the first 'Adelaide Races' were held in January 1838 on the flat plains to the west of the city. While it was reported that 'the paddock at Thebarton was far removed from the animation and excitement of Epsom Downs . . . these colonial sportsmen did their best',[1] the fact as noted by the *South Australian Gazette and Colonial Register*, that 800 out of a population of 2,500 attended seems to indicate the popularity of the sport. The correspondent also noted that the event was 'a great sensation' and described the excellent booths for refreshment and dancing which had been set up. The stewards for the four races were Colonel Light and James Hurtle Fisher.

James Crawford writing his impressions of Adelaide in 1839[2] noted how popular hunting and horse racing had become '. . . and the loud tally-ho is heard on the plains of Adelaide'. The tally-ho must have been prominent enough for James Allen to include hunting and horseracing subjects in his commission to S.T. Gill for paintings to be used for his lecture tour of England 1846-47 (see Appendix A). Along with the Adelaide street scenes and Port Adelaide and other subjects, Gill depicted *Hunt Meet at Dry Creek near Adelaide* (cat. 72) and *A Race Meeting at Adelaide* (cat. 73), both vigorous accounts of the sporting life of Adelaide in 1845 and of the evident pleasure of the spectators.

Henry Lawson described Australia as 'a land where sport is sacred', but in the experimental colony of South Australia in the 1840s with its strongly Christian emphasis, horseracing and other sporting activities which involved the transaction of money and partaking of alcohol were sometimes frowned on and the young in particular were encouraged to pursue team games as 'a manly and moral pastime'.

Anthony Trollope, discoursing on the influence of an imperial nation in the nineteenth century, claimed that Britain's impact on developing colonies would be its 'contagious passion for our national pastimes such as fox hunting, cricket and horseracing.'[3] In South Australia other British characteristics came to the fore in the chosen pastimes of the early colonists. Horticulture and agriculture, while an urgent means of survival, could also lead to friendly rivalry and competition and the early development of the Agricultural and Horticultural Society of South Australia's annual exhibitions is evidence of the importance of the idea of fostering the display of the best of the colony's produce, in the style of the Village or County Show in England.

The fourth such annual exhibition or show took place in Adelaide in 1845 and was recorded by Gill on the spot in a swift grey wash drawing *Agricultural and Horticultural Exhibition, Parklands 1845* (cat. 68) and then developed fully as a watercolour *Agricultural and Horticultural Show, Adelaide 1845* (cat. 69). Both works were commissioned by James Allen (see Appendix A).

Two other watercolours were developed on this theme (cat. 69 and 71) and they show Gill at his best in evoking a sense of crowded excitement and grand occasion. The correspondent of the *South Australian Register*[4] was equally euphoric in describing the previous day's events, 'Never more sweetly than yesterday did Aurora smile . . . parting her golden ringlets . . . and at her back arose a bright, but not burning sun from a cloudless sky. . . Smiles were on every face — care was thrown aside — and the holiday, as our holidays in Adelaide always are, was a holiday indeed.' He went on to describe the quantity and high quality of the produce shown and to develop his theme of prosperity and burgeoning confidence in the growing colony. Gill painted the event again in 1846 (cat. 74) and showed a bigger crowd and more marquees, tents and booths dispersed under the shade of dense tall trees. While the general scene looked tranquil enough, inside the marquees a more dramatic tale was told.

The South Australian Register in reporting the event[5] hinted at mumblings of discontent from the settlers, some of whom had not exhibited because of rumours that the judges were not as impartial as could be expected. Nevertheless Mr Cobbledick of Mount Lofty was highly commended for his fine collection of vegetables even if Mr Ind was taken to task for a towering floral display described as 'an unmitigated monument of dahlias'. He later indignantly explained it was 'a portrait of a kangaroo!'

Having dealt successfully with complex scenes such as the annual events just described, Gill later moved on to more specific subjects. He had advertised in 1840 his ability to draw 'correct resemblances of horses, dogs &c.' and in the lithograph *Merry Monarch, The Property of W. Vansittart Esqr* (cat. 78) Gill shows a mastery of the new technique of lithography as well as a fine understanding of the sought-after qualities in a thoroughbred, here seen in his stable. In the sporting portraits of Cydnus and Fidget (cat. 76 and 77) Gill shows his flair for capturing the action and excitement of the moment, whereas Fus-buz, a favourite old horse stands quietly, saddled and patient with the hounds at his feet (cat. 75). All four horse portraits show Gill as an artist who loved horses and could paint them with a sense of style to match any fashionable sporting print of the day.

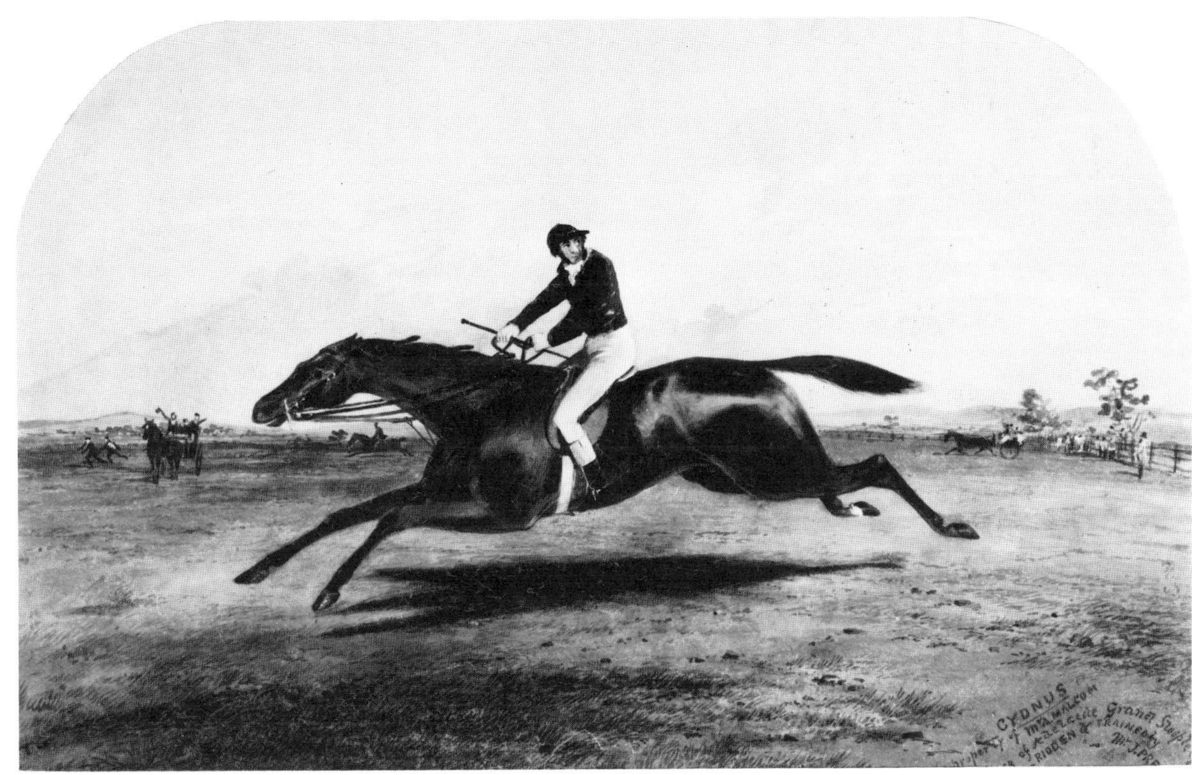

76 *Cydnus, the property of Mr A. Malcom, winner of Adelaide Grand Steeplechase 1851, ridden and trained by Mr J. Prest,* watercolour on paper, 29.2 x 46.4 cm, National Library of Australia.

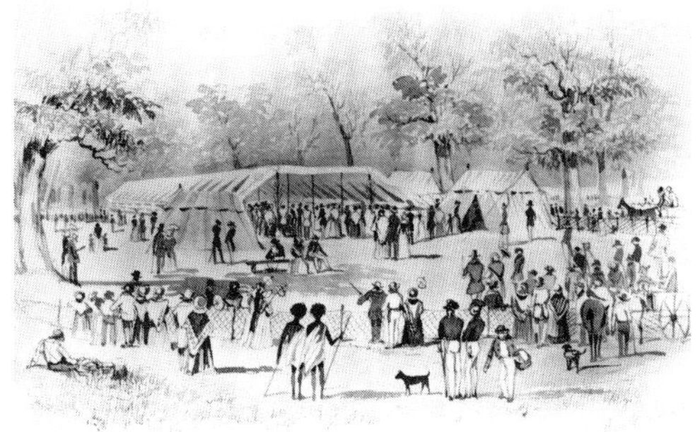

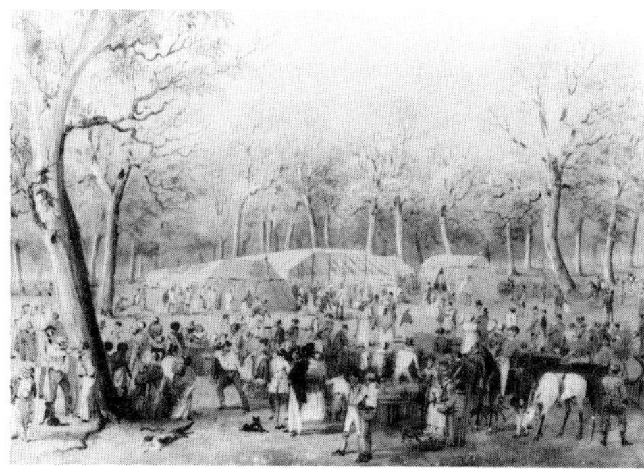

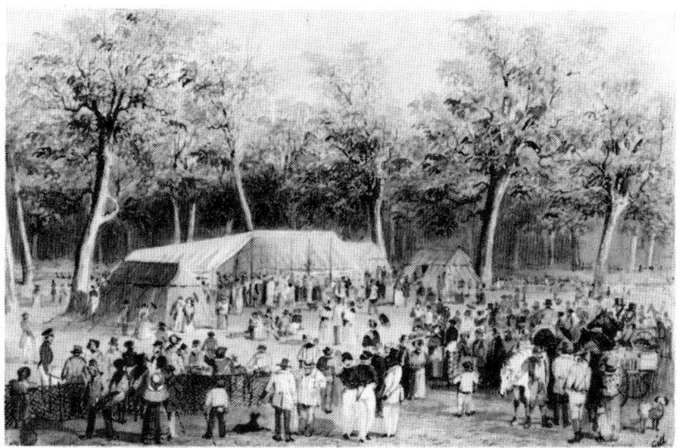

68 *Agricultural and Horticultural Exhibition*   1845
pen and ink, grey watercolour wash on paper 11.5 x 17.4 cm
Signed l.l. corner, pen and grey watercolour *S.T.G.* Inscribed l.r. corner, pencil *A & H Exhibition Park Lands*, on reverse, pencil *Mr. Allen.*

This seems to be the original on-the-spot grey wash drawing from which the three larger versions were developed (cat. 69, 70, and 71). The quick brush strokes have captured the activity of the scene while firmly establishing positions of marquees and tents and fencing. The two onlooking Aborigines in the foreground have gone from the three versions just mentioned, but the soldiers remain in (cat. 70).

National Library of Australia, Canberra

(NLAR. 108)

69 *Agricultural and Horticultural Show, Adelaide 1845*   1845
watercolour on paper 27.1 x 40.0 cm (original linen backing removed during conservation)
Signed l.l. corner, brush and grey watercolour *S T G.* Not dated. Inscribed, reverse, on removed linen backing, pencil *Agricultural & Horticultural Show/ Adelaide*

1845, also imprinted in black in three places with oval stamp *South Australian Company* each inscribed in centre, pencil *No 14.*

Another large version of the grey wash drawing (cat. 68) with the same placing of marquees and tents but another arrangement of the foreground crowd. Only one red-coated soldier remains, now on horseback, and a very large tree is placed at the left.
   Of interest is the fact that when the linen backing was removed, a pencil drawing was revealed on the reverse which appears to be very similar to *Port Adelaide 1847* (cat. 53).

Art Gallery of South Australia, Adelaide; Gift of the South Australian Company 1890

(AGSA 0.641)

70 *(Agricultural & Horticultural Show, Adelaide 1845)*   *c.*1845
watercolour on paper 20.0 x 30.8 cm
Signed l.l. corner, brush and brown ink *S T G.* Not dated. Inscribed l.r. corner, pen and brown ink *Gill.* (possibly not by artist)

This version has a very complex crowd scene in the foreground blending away to suggested figures shaded by dense trees. The large open marquee and other side

tents are placed in much the same arrangement as those in *Agricultural and Horticultural Exhibition 1845* (cat. 68) which was presumably a quick wash field sketch executed on the spot, and the two red-coated soldiers have been retained.

M.J.M. Carter Collection, Art Gallery of South Australia, Adelaide

71 *(The Agricultural and Horticultural Exhibition, Adelaide)*   1845
watercolour on paper 19.7 x 30.2 cm (sight)
Signed and dated, l.r. corner, *S T G /45/ Adelaide*
The following title was taken from an old mount before reframing:
'The South Australian and Agricultural Exhibition, 1845 held on the old Exhibition Ground, Frome Road, Adelaide'

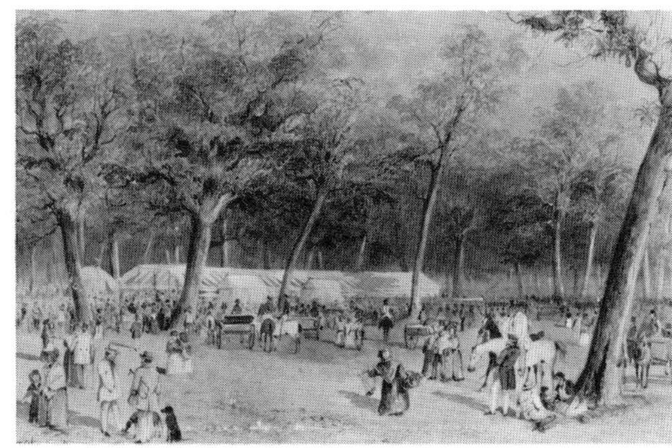

There are three watercolour paintings of the event held on 14 February, 1845 and this version approaches the pitched tents and marquees from a different angle and from a greater distance than the other two, giving the impression of walking towards the exhibition. Held in the Parklands opposite North Terrace, *The South Australian Register* of 3 February 1845 gave instructions to enter by a gate at the corner of Frome Bridge Road. The same newspaper on 15 February carried a detailed report of the event and a list of prizewinners.

Miller Anderson Limited, Adelaide

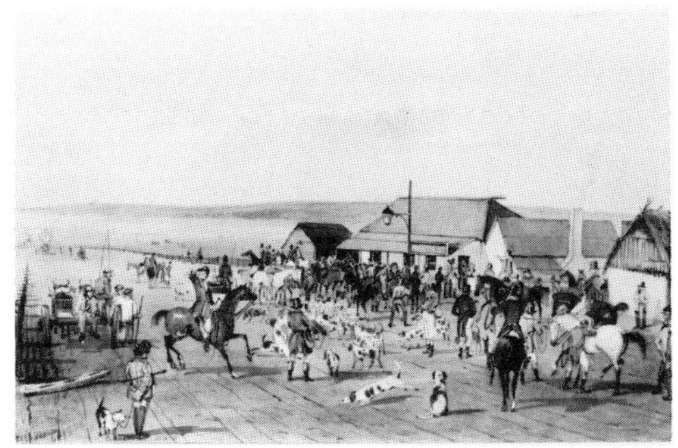

72 (*Hunt Meet at Dry Creek near Adelaide*) 1845

watercolour on paper 22.0 x 35.5 cm (sight)
Signed and dated l.l. corner, brush and brown watercolour *S.T.G. Adelaide/ 45.*

One of the paintings commissioned by James Allen (see Appendix A).

University of Adelaide;
Bequest of Sir George Murray 1942

73 (*A Race Meeting at Adelaide*) 1845

watercolour on paper 19.5 x 30.0 cm (sight)
Signed and dated l.l. corner, brush and brown watercolour *S.T.G. Adelaide/ 45.*

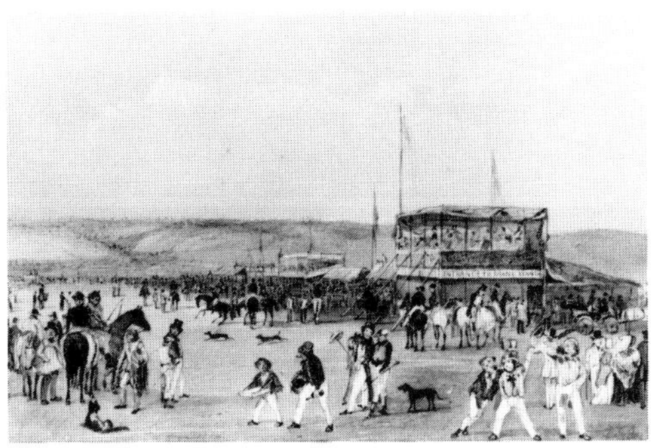

This work and its companion piece (*Hunt Meet at Dry Creek near Adelaide*) show Gill's ability to make the most of a social event as a subject for composition. Distant hills form a backdrop to the busy scene with grandstand, booths, crowd and foreground drunks.
One of the paintings commissioned by James Allen (see Appendix A)

University of Adelaide;
Bequest of Sir George Murray 1942

74 (*Agricultural and Horticultural Society of South Australia, Autumn Show 1846*) 1846

watercolour on paper 26.0 x 39.8 cm, mounted on cardboard
Signed and dated l.l. corner, brush and

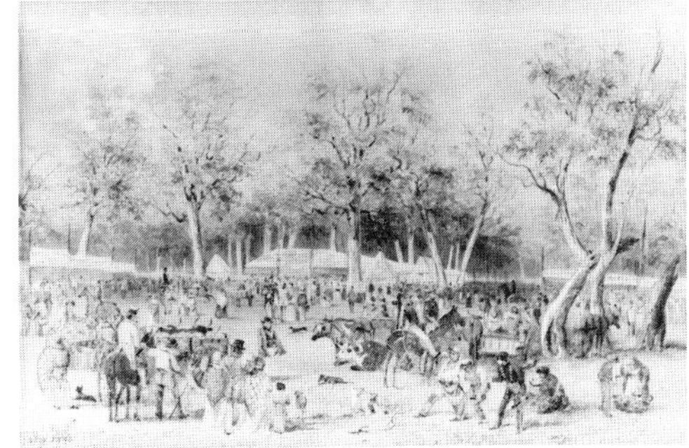

watercolour . . . *TG/ . . . 46* (Original signature and date cropped when sheet trimmed and mounted on cardboard and the initials and date *S.T.G. 1846* added above by another hand.)

The annual event one year later than the other four paintings on this subject. Here the marquees, tents and hoardings have been placed in the background, leaving the foreground free to accommodate a larger and more varied crowd, and more animals.

Art Gallery of South Australia, Adelaide;
Gift of Dr E. Angas Johnson 1917

(AGSA 0.38)

75 *Fus-Buz, A Favourite Old Hunter: The property of Mr J. Chambers, Adelaide 1849.* 1849

watercolour on paper 32.5 x 43.5 cm.
Signed and dated, l.l. corner *Sam¹ Thoˢ Gill./1849*

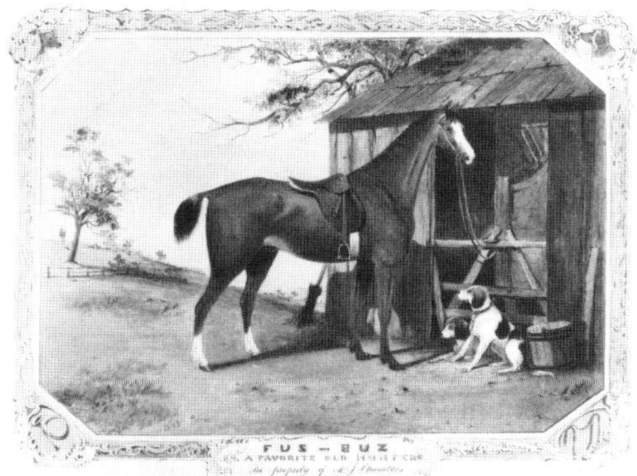

The image surrounded by a decorative border, incorporating hunting motifs in vignettes at each of the four corners and the title in a panel centrally below the image, brush and watercolour *FUS - BUZ/ A FAVOURITE OLD HUNTER/ The property of Mr. J. Chambers/ ADELAIDE 1849*

This charming portrait of a horse shows

Gill's skill in capturing the sporting life.
Here a patient old hunter waits for the
day's riding to begin. Symbols of the
hunting life are the subjects for the four
corner vignettes, and the decorative border
is reminiscent of a similar design
surrounding *Prospect House, the Seat of J.B.
Graham, Esqr., near Adelaide South Australia*
(cat. 106)

On loan from Deutscher Fine Art, Melbourne.

76 *Cydnus, the property of
Mr A. Malcom, winner of
Adelaide Grand Steeplechase 1851, ridden and
trained by Mr J. Prest*   1851
watercolour on paper 29.2 x 46.4 cm
Signed l.l. corner, brush and brown

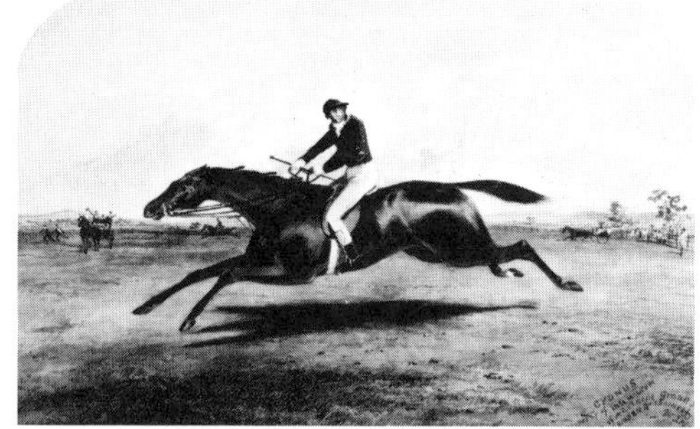

watercolour *S T G*. Inscribed l.r. corner,
brush and brown watercolour *CYDNUS/
The property of Mr A. MALCOLM/ - INNER of
Adelaide Grand Steeplec----/ --51 — RIDDEN &
TRAINED by / Mr. J. PREST*

When the first Adelaide Steeplechase was
held in 1846 'the whole town migrated to
Glen Osmond' to watch the event, run
over four miles of rough country. Gill has
captured the speed and excitement of the
1851 race which was won by Cydnus,
whose trainer-jockey looks anxiously over
one shoulder to see if he is being
followed.

National Library of Australia, Canberra

(NLA R.4757)

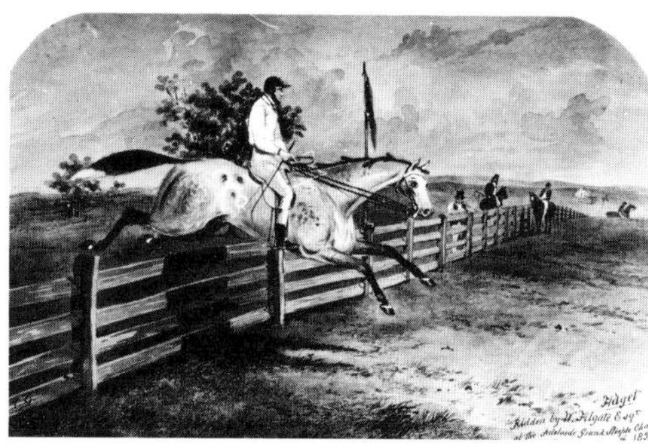

77 *Fidget, ridden by W. Filgate Esqr. at
the Adelaide Grand Steeplechase of 1851*
                                          1851

watercolour on paper 29.0 x 46.0 cm
Signed l.l. corner, brush and watercolour
S.T.G. Inscribed l.r. corner, brush and
watercolour *Fidget/ Ridden by W. Filgate
Esqr/ at the Adelaide Steeple Chase/ of
1851*

All the excitement of the big race has
been retained by Gill while at the same
time producing a work that fitted the
concept of the stylish sporting print of the
day. Though not the winner of the race
the dapple grey Fidget shows his paces
over formidable fences.

National Library of Australia, Canberra

(NLA R.6372)

78 *Merry Monarch, The Property of W.
Vansittart Esqr.*   1851
Lithograph, two stones 29.2 x 44.5 cm (image),
33.7 x 47.0 cm
Signed and dated l.l. corner on the stone
(vertically on cobblestone, the S reversed)
S.T.G./ 1851

William Vansittart was once described as
'a thorough sportsman . . . a perfect Irish
gentleman'. A wealthy pastoralist from the
south-east of South Australia, he imported

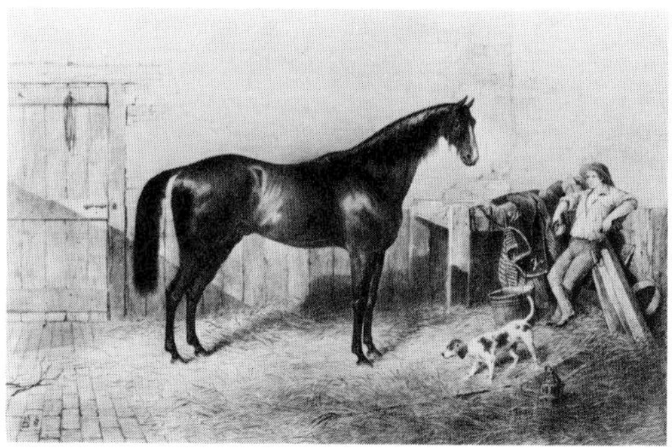

several thoroughbreds of whom Merry
Monarch was one. Gill was commissioned
to paint them, and he made a lithograph
of this particular horse. The study of the
indolent stablehand leaning against the
manger surrounded by all the
paraphernalia of the stable makes this
work doubly interesting.

Art Gallery of South Australia, Adelaide;
Transferred from the South Australian Archives,
Ware Estate 1948

(AGSA 4811G47)

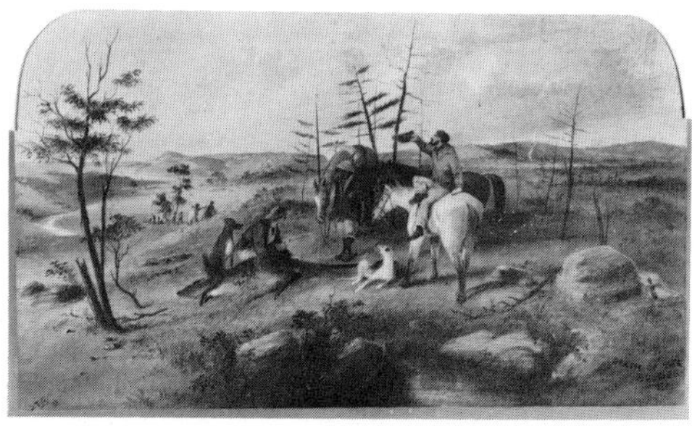

79 *Death of the Boomer 1853*   1853
watercolour on paper, mounted on paper,
mounted on linen 37.5 x 63.7 cm (image)
Signed l.l. corner, brush and brown
watercolour *S.T.G./ /53*. Inscribed l.r.
corner, brush and brown watercolour
DEATH OF THE/ BOOMER/ 1853. Inscribed
on reverse, pen and ink *Saml Thos Gill/*

1850 and *The Death of the Kangaroo/------ North of Mt Horrocks/ South Australia*

This large composition is interesting from several points of view, not least its title inscribed on the reverse of the work. As Gill had left Adelaide by 1853, this work must have been painted in Melbourne from a sketch made during a visit to Mount Horrocks in the Clare district north of Adelaide. Kangaroo hunting was a favourite sport often depicted by Gill. A boomer is an old man kangaroo.

La Trobe Collection,
State Library of Victoria, Melbourne;
Gift of Miss E. Blundell 1930

(SLV LT H 956, LT 61)

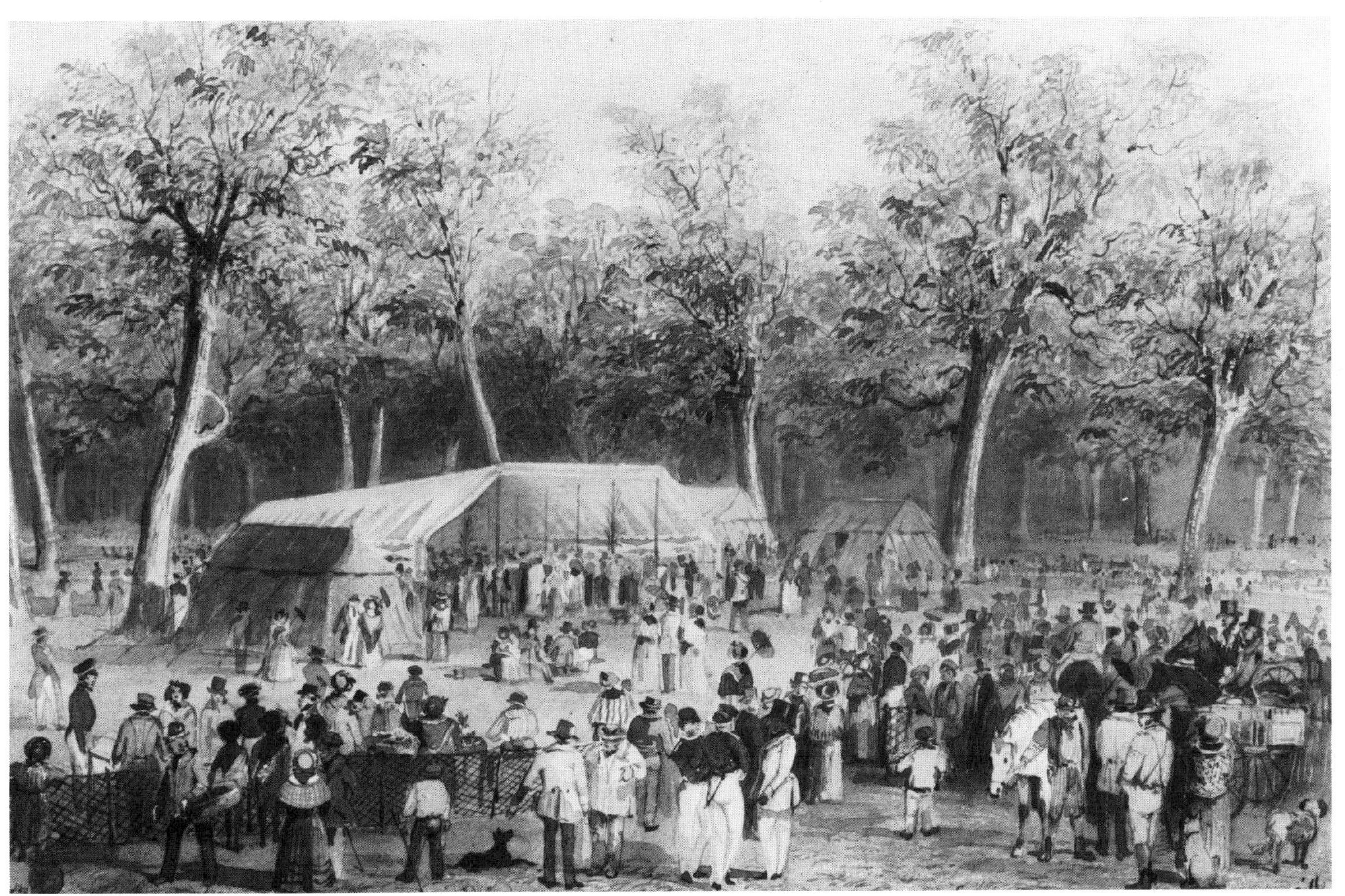

70 *Agricultural and Horticultural Show, Adelaide 1845*, watercolour on paper, 20.0 x 30.8 cm, Art Gallery of South Australia.

Sturt's Expedition into Central Australia

When Captain Charles Sturt (1795–1865) departed on his expedition into Central Australia in 1844, he was forty-nine years of age and had already had a distinguished, if somewhat chequered career as a soldier, explorer and public servant. The official purpose of the expedition was to establish the existence of a supposed mountain range trending NE to SW near latitude 28°S and to report on the rise of any rivers, but Sturt, who had believed in its existence for many years, hoped to find an inland sea.

Saturday 10 August 1844 was declared a public holiday in Adelaide in honour of Sturt's departure. A public Breakfast was held at 11 am at Stocks's Stores in Grenfell Street, attended by leading citizens and His Excellency the Governor, Captain Grey, who hailed Sturt as the 'Father of Australian Exploration'.[1] Gill's two paintings (cat. 80 and 81) capture all the excitement and atmosphere of the occasion as the expedition moved off at about 2 pm accompanied by 'ladies and gentlemen on horseback and in carriages'[2] down King William Street and out along the Great North Road as far as Dry Creek. At this point the main party proceeded under the second-in-command, James Poole, whilst Sturt returned to Adelaide to finalise some details.

The rendezvous was Eyre's station on the Murray at Moorundie where the party of sixteen men camped under the remarkable natural avenue of trees[3] and assembled their equipment for the final departure on 18 August. Moving up the Murray and the Darling the party camped near Lake Cawndilla for several months scouting into and beyond the Stanley Range. Sturt made pen and wash sketches in his journal which were later developed by Gill, for example *View from Stanley Range* (cat. 82), and subsequently engraved to illustrate Sturt's *Narrative of an Expedition into Central Australia,* London: Boone, 1849.

A camp was then established further north at Depot Glen on permanent water at Preservation Creek. The extreme summer heat soon dried up any water within reach and the party was trapped from 27 January 1845 until mid July when heavy rains fell. During this period James Poole died from scurvy.

The rain enabled the party to move a further sixty-one miles north where a depot, Fort Grey, was established. From here a number of excursions were made, seventy-one miles west to Lake Torrens (cat. 84), 450 miles north-west towards Simpson Desert and finally to Cooper's Creek. By November, water was again drying up and having encountered nothing but inhospitable country, sandhills and stony desert, Sturt was forced to abandon the idea of an inland sea and he and his party returned exhausted to Adelaide in January 1846 after an absence of seventeen months.

Following his return, Sturt was appointed Colonial Treasurer and in April 1847 was granted leave of absence to visit England where he remained until 1849, completing his *Narrative of an Expedition into Central Australia* which was published in that year. A number of the illustrations were engraved from watercolours developed by S.T. Gill from sketches by Sturt or members of his party.[4] Gill is acknowledged as the delineator of three of these watercolours, gifts to Australia from Her Majesty Queen Elizabeth II, (cat. 82, 83, 84), but there are others for which he receives no credit.[5]

In 1849 Captain Sturt presented a group of drawings and specimens of ore to Queen Victoria[6] and whereas a list has not been found, it is reasonable to assume that these three works and ten others presented by Queen Elizabeth II from the Royal Library, Windsor to the Commonwealth of Australia in 1956[7] and now in the National Library of Australia were part of Sturt's original gift.

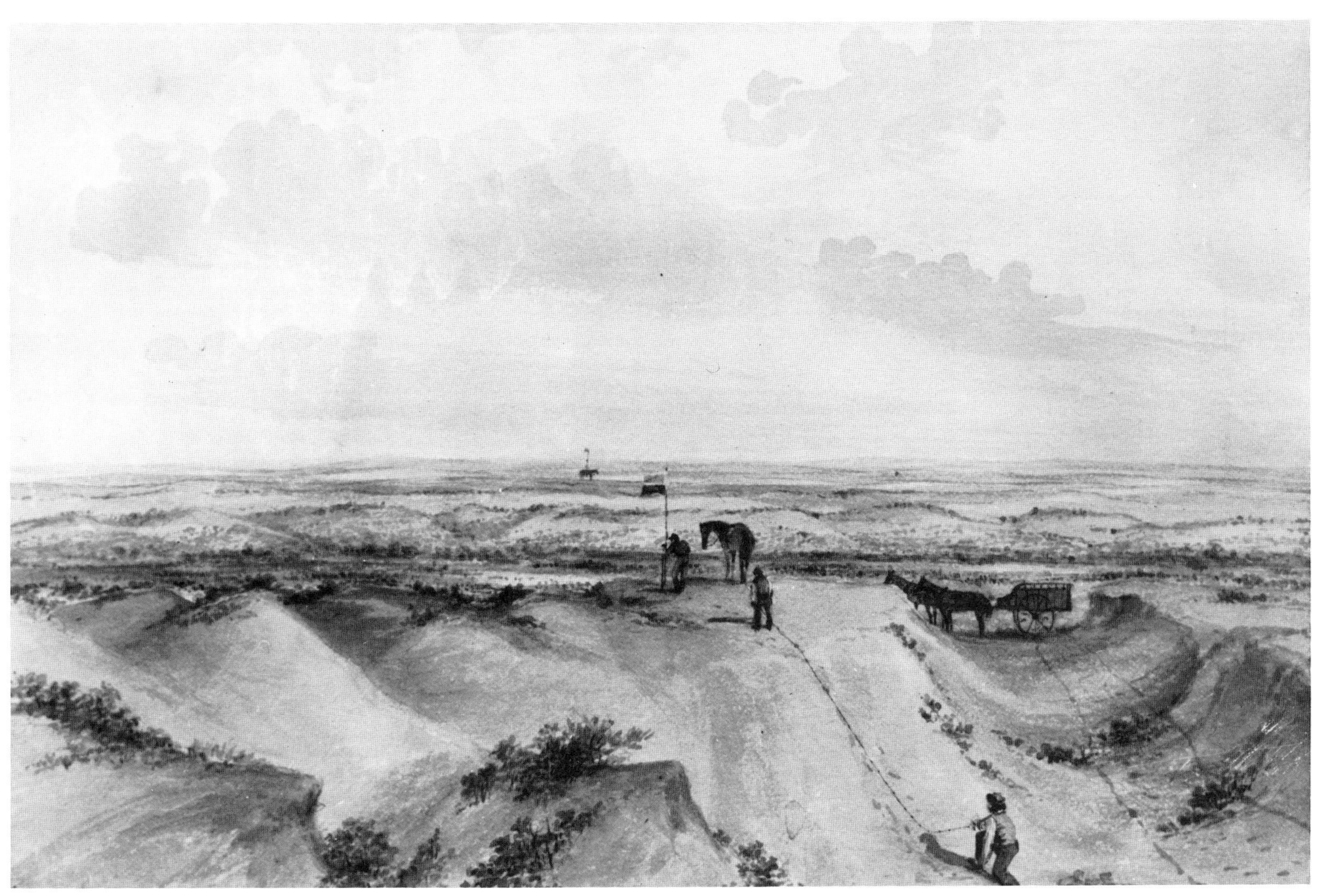

84 *Chaining over the Sand Hills to Lake Torrens*, watercolour on paper, 15.2 x 22.9 cm, National Library of Australia.

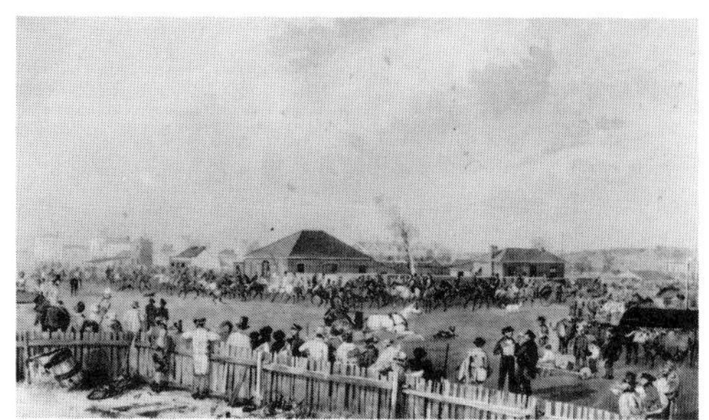

80   *Sturt's Overland Expedition leaving Adelaide, 10th August, 1844*   *c.*1844-45
watercolour on paper 41.0 x 72.2 cm
Signed l.l. corner, pen and brown ink
S T G/ ADELAIDE. Not dated.

A public holiday was declared in Adelaide to honour Captain Sturt's departure. Following the public Breakfast, the procession of explorers and citizens is seen turning from Grenfell Street, north into King William Street, the bullock team with the boat waiting at the right to follow the procession. This *tour de force* captures the atmosphere and spectacle of the occasion which 'elicited from the Colonists of all ranks, and of all shades of opinion, such a general burst of united and enthusiastic public feeling'.[8]

The Art Gallery of South Australia owns another watercolour, a smaller version of this subject with some foreground variations, signed and dated *S T G Adelaide /44* (AGSA 0.1522) and the National Library of Australia owns a brown wash drawing (NLA R.113) from which both watercolours were probably developed.

Art Gallery of South Australia, Adelaide;
South Australian Government Grant 1939

(AGSA 0.1128)

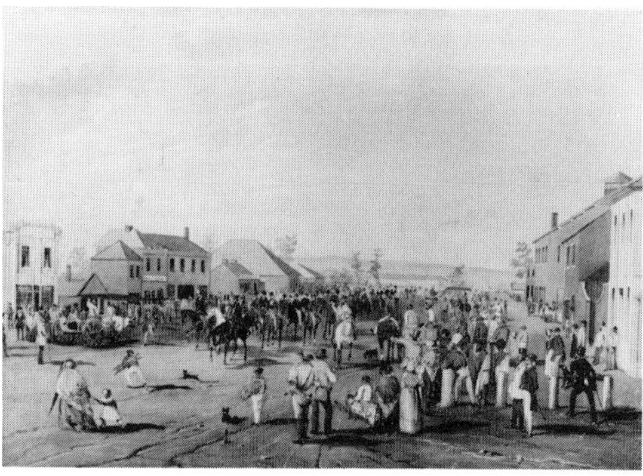

81   *Sturt's Overland Expedition leaving Adelaide, August 10th, 1844*   *c.*1844-45
watercolour on paper 27.2 x 40.0 cm (original linen backing removed during conservation).
Not signed. Not dated. Inscribed, reverse, on removed linen backing, pencil *Rundle St looking out/ from the East Terrace to the Corner/ of King William St* (possibly not by the artist), also imprinted in black in three places with oval stamp *South Australian Company* each inscribed in centre, pencil *No 10*.

The head of the procession, no doubt led by Governor Grey and Captain Sturt, seen from the north-west corner of Hindley Street, is moving north along King William Street. This view, which appears to have been drawn at exactly the same moment as the previous picture (cat. 80) but from a different point was probably commissioned by James Allen to illustrate his lectures in England in 1846[9] and was subsequently lithographed by J.W. Giles for George French Angas's *South Australia Illustrated*, London: McLean, 1846-47, plate LIV, *The Departure of Captain Sturt August 1844*. The title inscribed on the linen backing is incorrect.

Art Gallery of South Australia, Adelaide;
Gift of the South Australian Company 1890

(AGSA 0.644)

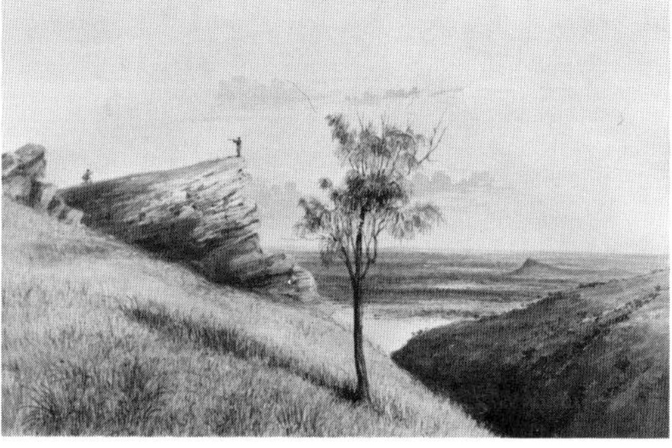

82   *View from Stanley Range*   *c.*1846-47
watercolour on paper 15.2 x 22.7 cm.
Not signed. Not dated. Inscribed on reverse, pencil *No 4 View from Stanley Range* (possibly not by the artist).

Developed by Gill from an original sketch by Captain Sturt and made into a steel-engraving to illustrate Sturt's *Narrative of an Expedition into Central Australia*, 1849, vol. 2, as frontispiece, with the title as catalogued here.

The original sketch may have been taken when the party was camped at 'Parnari' water-hole when, between 1 and 5 November 1844, the men were 'employed in taking bearings from the loftiest points of the [Stanley's Barrier] range'.[10]

National Library of Australia, Canberra;
Gift of Her Majesty Queen Elizabeth II 1956

(NLA R.346)

83   *A Native Village in the Northern Interior*   *c.*1846-47
watercolour on paper 15.1 x 22.0 cm
Not signed. Not dated. Inscribed on reverse, pencil *No 3 A Native Village in the Northern Interior of S. Australia* (possibly not by the artist).

Developed by Gill from an original sketch by Captain Sturt and made into a steel-

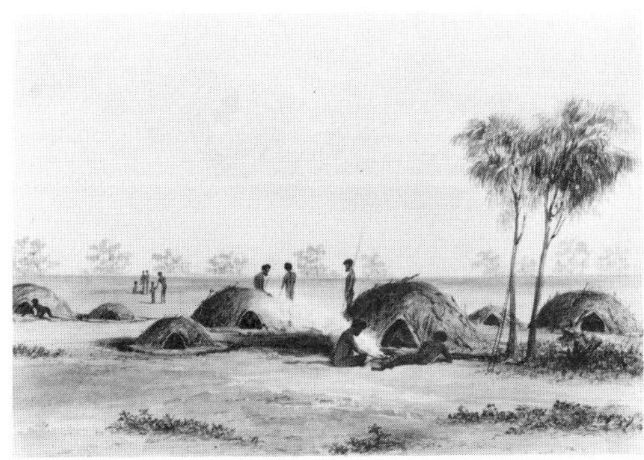

engraving to illustrate Sturt's *Narrative of an Expedition into Central Australia*, 1849, vol. 1, facing p.254 with the title *Native Village in the Northern Interior*. The National Library of Australia titles this work *A Native Village in the Northern Interior of South Australia*. The scene in fact is probably situated in New South Wales.

Sturt describes the construction of these huts, several groups of which were found deserted about 19 or 20 January whilst *en route* to Depot Glen.[11] Sturt or Gill apparently added the Aborigines to create greater interest.

National Library of Australia, Canberra;
Gift of Her Majesty Queen Elizbaeth II 1956
(NLA R.345)

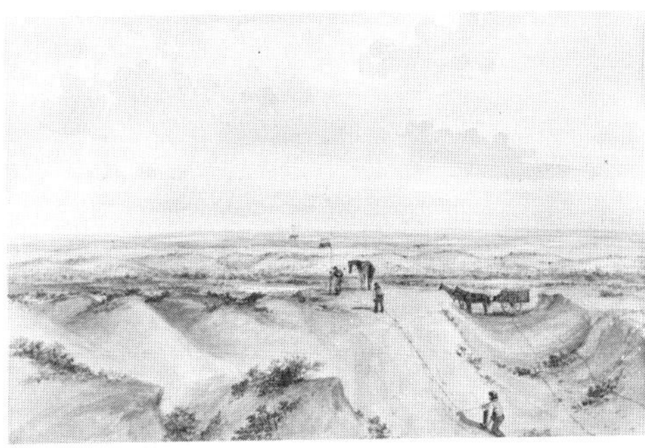

84   *Chaining over the Sand Hills to Lake Torrens*   *c.*1846-47

watercolour on paper 15.2 x 22.9 cm
Not signed. Not dated. Inscribed on reverse, pencil *No. 2 The Sandy Ridges of Central Australia* (possibly not by the artist).

Developed by Gill from an original sketch by Captain Sturt and made into a steel-engraving to illustrate Sturt's *Narrative of an Expedition into Central Australia*, 1849, vol. 1, as frontispiece, with the title *Chaining over the Sand Hills to Lake Torrens*. The National Library of Australia titles this work *The Sandy Ridges of Central Australia*.

After the rains in July 1845, the party moved 61 miles NW, chaining as they went, and established a new depot at Fort Grey, 28-30 July, from where J. McDouall Stuart, Draftsman, and J.H. Browne, Surgeon, chained a further 70¾ miles 75°W of S direct on Mount Hopeless over sandhills. Reaching Lake Torrens on 4 August, Sturt and Stuart examined the shores to the north and to the south and determined it would be 'impracticable to proceed further'.[12]

National Library of Australia, Canberra;
Gift of Her Majesty Queen Elizabeth II 1956
(NLA R.343)

The Horrocks Expedition 1846

John Ainsworth Horrocks (1818-1846) who arrived in South Australia in 1839 was the first settler in the Clare district. He established Hope Farm at Penwortham, where nearby Mount Horrocks bears his name. An energetic figure, he explored the country further north and in 1841 named Gulnare Plain after his favourite hunting dog. In 1846 he mounted a more ambitious, privately-financed expedition to search for pastoral country to the north-west of Mount Arden.

Gill, who was a friend of Horrocks, joined the expedition 'as an amateur [explorer] for the purpose of filling his note book'.[1] On 10 July 1846, the evening prior to his departure from Adelaide 'our much respected and talented fellow colonist, Mr Gill gave a parting supper to a few of his friends' and was enthusiastically toasted. He responded to the effect that he was entering upon a journey entirely novel to him, unremunerated, and hoped 'to give a full, true and accurate report of his adventures with . . . faithful scenic representations'.[2]

In the event, he not only produced a dramatic series of pictures of the dangers and hardships experienced in a hostile land, but he was the first artist to capture the atmosphere and sheer grandeur of the craggy rock-faces, rugged hills and deep gorges of the Flinders Range. In addition to this remarkable pictorial record, Gill kept a diary of the expedition, published in the *South Australian Gazette*, 10 October 1846[3], which together with Horrocks's journal[4] has made it possible to plot the route taken and to locate the sites of many of his watercolours.[5] The pictures in the exhibition have been catalogued in chronological order of the progress of the expedition, which left Penwortham on Monday 27 July 1846.[6]

The party comprised six men, J.A. Horrocks, J.H. Theakston (second-in-charge)[7], Bernard Kilroy, Garlick the cook, S.T. Gill and an Aborigine, Jimmy Moorhouse. It was equipped with horses, drays and a camel, Harry, the first to be imported into Australia and used on an expedition. The *South Australian Register* noted that the camel 'will doubtless prove a valuable appendage'[8], but in fact it proved to be troublesome and was the innocent cause of the accident which brought the expedition to an abrupt end and resulted in the death of Horrocks.

The expedition travelled slowly, past Clare to the Mount Remarkable area, discovered and went through Horrocks Pass, then along the western side of Flinders Range. On 21 August it reached Eyre's old camp at Depot Creek[9] where a base was established. The party had taken twenty-six days to cover some 125 miles. There had been many delays to repair equipment and overcome other difficulties, during which time Gill was 'engaged in rectifying some sketches' or used the opportunity to go 'out on the hills sketching'.[10]

On 22 and 23 August, Horrocks and Gill made an exploratory journey on horseback, west-north-west from Depot Creek, to search for water in order to establish a new base for the main party. They found little water and had several unpleasant confrontations with the Aborigines which Gill has graphically represented. Horrocks decided to make another thrust into the inhospitable country and, because of the uncertainty of finding water, he decided the party should go on foot. On 28 August, he set out with Gill and Kilroy and the camel laden with three weeks supply of food and water. On 1 September the three men reached what is now known as Lake Dutton (which Horrocks originally named Lake Gill) where, during the afternoon, Horrocks was accidentally shot. The camel was kneeling whilst Horrocks was standing alongside withdrawing a charge from his shotgun. The animal lurched and caught its pack in the cock of the gun, discharging the barrel. The contents took away the middle finger of Horrocks's right hand, entered his left cheek and knocked out a row of teeth. Gill nursed Horrocks whilst Kilroy walked some seventy-five miles, mostly at night, back to Depot Creek for assistance.

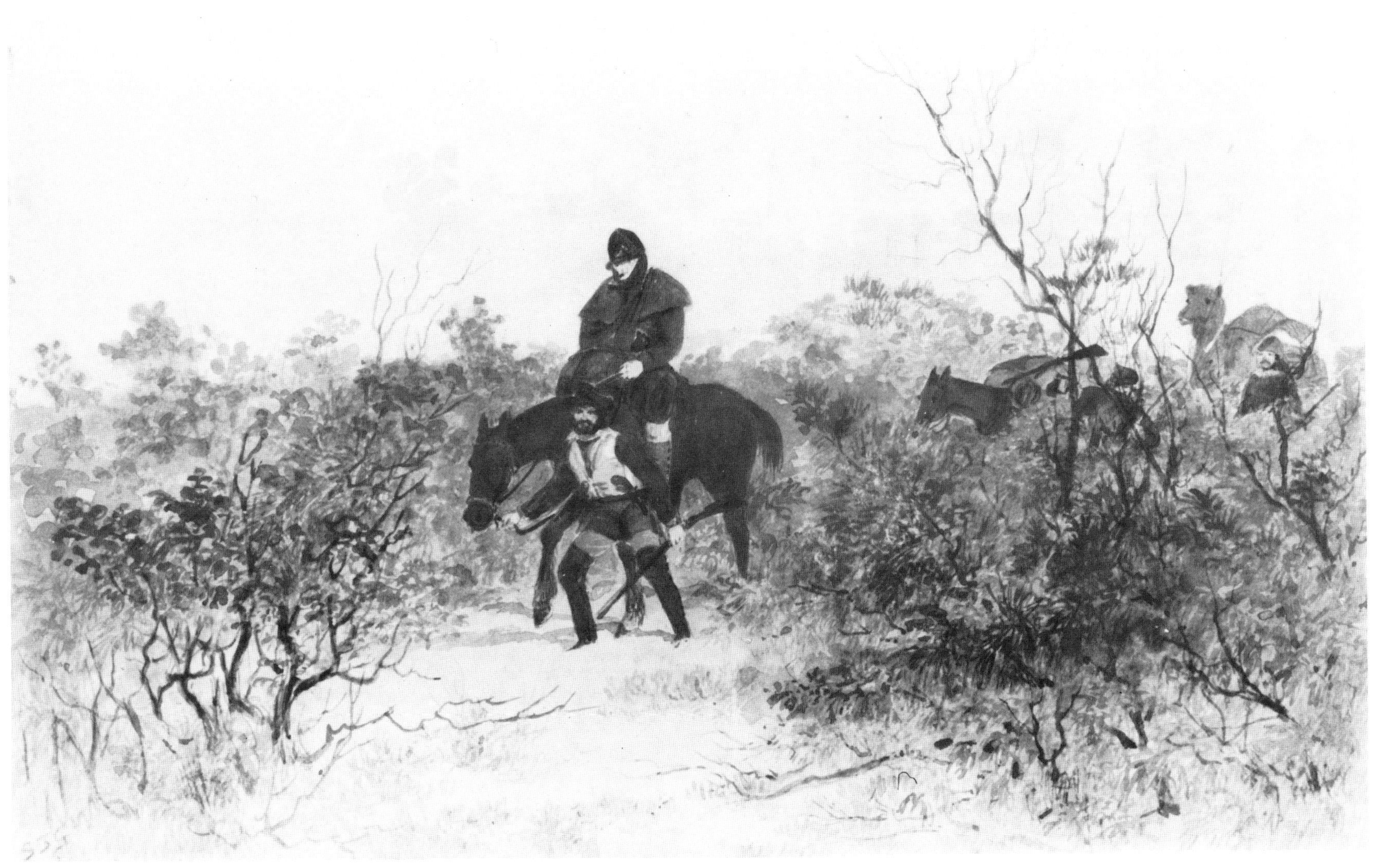

99 *Return of invalid*, watercolour on paper, 18.4 x 30.3 cm, Art Gallery of South Australia.

After three days, he returned with Theakston and two horses whereupon the party immediately set off with Horrocks to Depot Creek which they reached on 6 September. There they awaited a doctor, but as one did not arrive, on 10 September the party travelled south. At Saltia Creek, Kilroy left without delay for Penwortham with Horrocks, whilst Gill, Theakston and Jimmy followed behind, possibly by a different route along the west side of the Range to Crystal Brook.

Gill and Theakston reached Penwortham on 19 September to find Horrocks critically ill. He died on 23 September and was buried next day in ground which he had set aside for the establishment of St Mark's Church, Penwortham.

Returning to Adelaide, Gill set to work to develop his sketches. Within the space of three months he had produced a series of thirty-three watercolours 'depicting the most remarkable scenes met with by the expedition'. Five of these, (three of them works in the present exhibition (cat. 92, 98, 99), were reviewed by the press on 5 January 1847.[11] The same article announced that this 'interesting series is to be raffled', an event that took place next day among 'thirty members at one guinea each'.[12]

Two weeks later the press announced that a Committee had been formed to make arrangements for an 'exhibition of paintings and drawings by our South Australian artists' and that 'Mr Gill, the artist will receive [them] at his rooms in Leigh Street'.[13] The *Exhibition of Pictures, the Works of Colonial Artists* was held in the Council Room, North Terrace from 10 to 17 February 1847. Captain Charles Sturt, then Colonial Secretary, was Chairman of the Committee, which set an admission fee of one shilling and published a catalogue at sixpence. The surplus proceeds were held as a 'fund towards the formation of a Society for the promotion of art in the Colony'.[14]

Gill displayed sixty-two works in the exhibition, including thirty-three watercolours relating to the Horrocks expedition, presumably the ones which had been raffled. They were catalogued in what appears to be a chronological sequence from no. 90, *Horrocks Camp, Penwortham Flat*, to no. 122, *Funeral of Mr Horrocks*.[15] Based on style, signature, subject and inscriptions it has been possible to identify a number of these original thirty-three watercolours (cat. 91, 92, 96, 97, 98, 99) Two of these works (cat. 91, 97) are part of a group of eight Horrocks watercolours held by the National Library of Australia. Presented by Her Majesty Queen Elizabeth II from the Royal Library, Windsor, it is possible that they were originally won in the raffle by Captain Sturt and formed part of a gift of drawings he made to Queen Victoria in 1849.[16]

It seems likely that Gill made subsequent visits to the lower Flinders Range when undertaking commissions for northern pastoralists although there is no reliable evidence upon which to base this assumption.[17] Certainly he continued to produce watercolours of the Horrocks expedition and the Flinders Range until as late as 1865-70.[18]

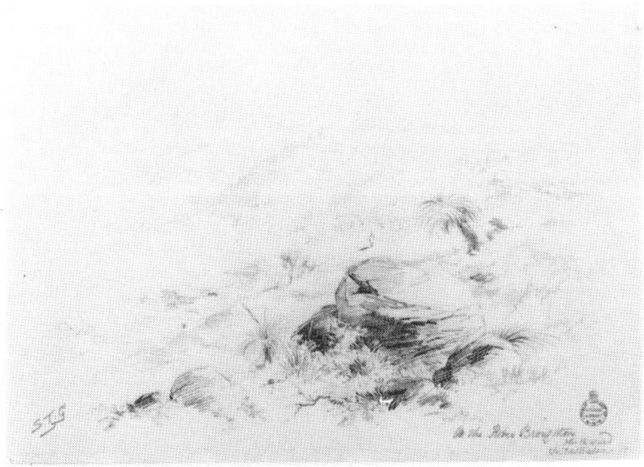

85 *On the River Broughton, Northward,
South Australia*   *c.*1846

pencil on buff paper 25.9 x 36.8 cm
Signed l.l. corner, pencil *S.T.G.* Not
dated. Inscribed l.r. corner, pencil *On the
River Broughton/ Northward/ So Australia. 18--.*
(Last two figures of date omitted.)

Gill included a picture entitled *Camp on
the Broughton River* as no. 92 in the
Horrocks group shown in the *Exhibition of
Pictures*, Adelaide 1847. This drawing with
artist's notes is probably one of a series of
sketches taken when Horrocks's party
camped overnight on 29 July 'on the
second crossing of the Broughton'.[19] The
view has been identified as toward the
south west tip (Mount Misery) of
Campbell Range from the township of
Yacka.[20] The signature, which is later in
style, *c.*1864-80, and part of the inscription,
may have been added some years later.
See Appendix B.

Mitchell Library,
State Library of New South Wales, Sydney.
                         (ML PX* D383 f2)

86 *(Spencer Gulf from the Top of
Flinders Range)*   1846-47

watercolour on paper, mounted on
cardboard 26.8 x 39.7 cm

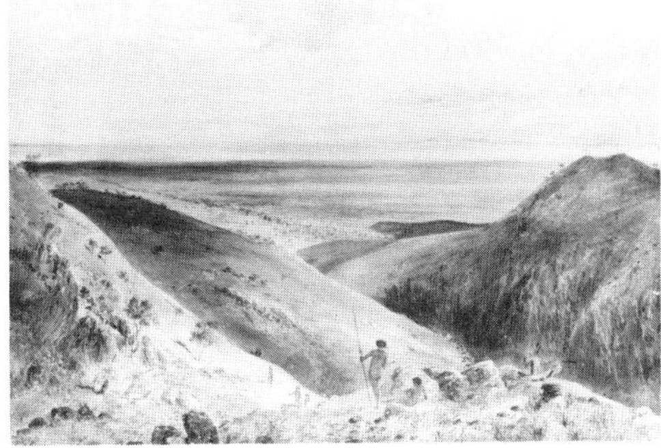

Signed l.l. corner, brush and brown
watercolour *S T G.* Not dated. Inscribed,
reverse, pencil *Spencers Gulf from the Top of
Flinders Range* (possibly not by artist).

The expedition reached White's Station on
Rocky River, just north of Wirrabara, on
3 August and camped for four nights. Gill
probably spent two days painting since
quite a number of watercolours of this
area have been identified.[21] Horrocks
recorded in his journal for 4 August 'Mr
White rode to a gum-tree in Flinders
Range with Mr Gill to take a sketch of
the north of the gulf and the hills on the
opposite road'[22] and this may well be one
of the sketches taken at that time. The
view, until recently catalogued by the Art
Gallery of South Australia as *Spencers Gulf*,
overlooks the lower section of the gorge
of Waterfall Creek, east of Baroota
Reservoir and downstream from the next
three paintings (cat. 87, 88, 89).

Art Gallery of South Australia, Adelaide;
Gift of Mrs E.S. Levinson 1954   (AGSA 0.1543)

87 *(Great Fall, Stony Creek)*   1846-47

watercolour on paper 25.2 x 37.8 cm
Signed l.l. corner, pen and brown
watercolour *S.T.G.*. Not dated.

One of the views taken in the west ranges
whilst Horrocks's party was camped at

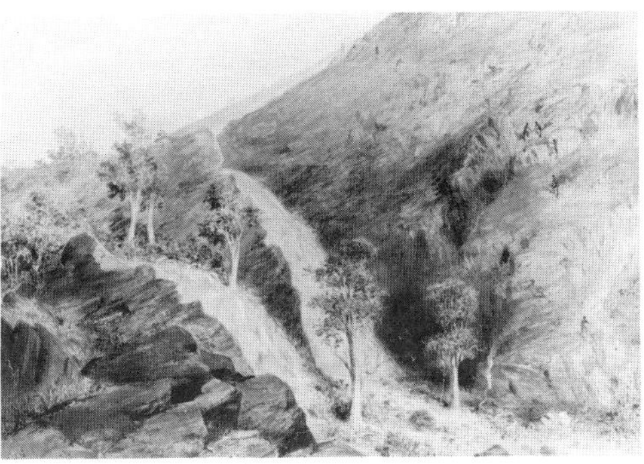

White's Station from 3 to 6 August 1846.
This waterfall, which branches into two
falls after heavy rains, was known in Gill's
day as the 'Great Fall' on Stony Creek.[23]
The title of the painting has therefore
been changed from *Landscape with Waterfall*.
The fall is on Waterfall Creek which runs
into Baroota Reservoir.[24] On today's maps
there is a Stony Creek which runs into
Waterfall Creek higher upstream, but
previously the entire watercourse must
have been known as Stony Creek.

Art Gallery of South Australia, Adelaide;
Gift of Mrs E.S. Levinson 1954   (AGSA 0.1544)

88 *(Stony Creek from the Top of the
Waterfall)*   1846-47

watercolour on paper 27.5 x 40.2 cm
(cardboard backing removed during
conservation)

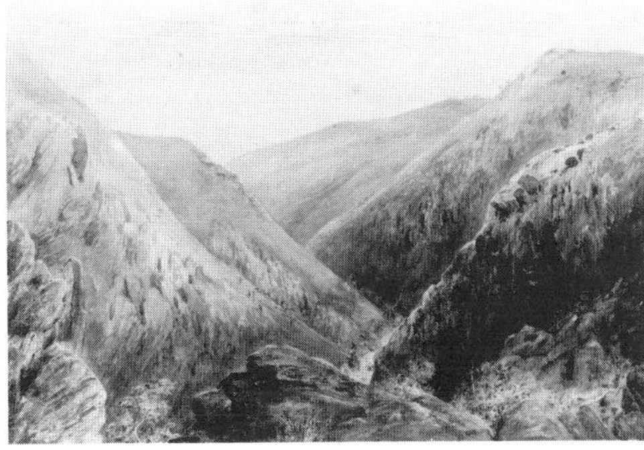

Signed l.l. corner, brush and brown watercolour *S T G*. Not dated. Inscribed on cardboard backing, pencil *Stony Creek From the Top of the Waterfall* (possibly not by the artist).

Sketched whilst the party was camped at White's Station from 3 to 6 August 1846, this watercolour, for many years incorrectly catalogued as *Pichi Richi Pass* is a view from the top of the higher of the two falls in the previous picture (cat. 87) looking down into the gorge of Waterfall Creek.[25]

Art Gallery of South Australia, Adelaide;
Gift of Mrs E.S. Levinson 1954   (AGSA 0.1542)

89 *(Stony Creek, Mount Remarkable Survey, from above the fall)*   1846-47
watercolour on paper 26.3 x 39.2 cm (cardboard backing removed during conservation)
Signed l.l. corner, pen and brown watercolour *S T G*. Not dated.

Derived from a sketch made whilst the party was camped at White's Station from 3 to 6 August 1846, this watercolour relates to the two previous pictures and is taken from a more distant point, looking between the two rocky crags of the higher, usually dry fall into the gorge of Waterfall Creek.[26] Previously titled

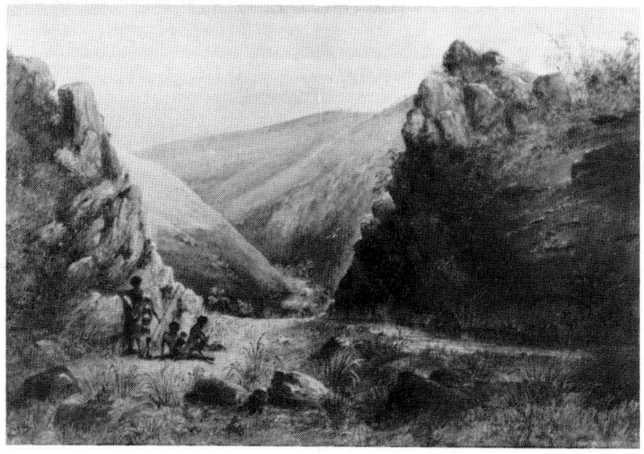

Aborigines in a Gorge, the new title has been taken from the photograph of another version once in the possession of the Horrocks family in England.[27]

Art Gallery of South Australia, Adelaide;
Bequest of Christine Margaret MacGregor 1975
(AGSA 758HP14)

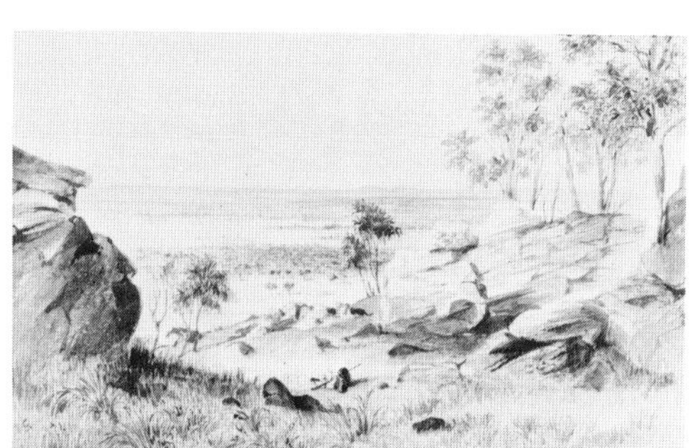

90 *(Looking north-east from Flinders Range)*   1846
watercolour on paper 18.8 x 31.5 cm
Signed l.l. corner, brush and watercolour *S T G*. Inscribed, reverse, pencil *Looking N E Augst 10/??/ From F Range*.

On 9 August the party camped 'on the edge of the scrub by stony point' and on the following day Horrocks with Mr C. Campbell of Mount Remarkable Station went to search for a pass through the ranges,[28] discovering Horrocks Pass. During their absence Gill 'took two sketches from Stoney [*sic*] Point behind the camp'.[29] This watercolour may be one of them. The site has been located in the rocky outcrops of Mount Maria, near Wilmington, looking east-north-east.[30] Another sketch may have been shown in the *Exhibition of Pictures*, Adelaide 1847, as no. 98 with the title *Sketch from Stony Point, looking E.S.E.*

This picture which the National Library of

Australia catalogues as *Looking north from Flinders Range* was titled *Distant View from Mt. Arden* when presented by Her Majesty Queen Elizabeth II in 1956.

National Library of Australia, Canberra;
Gift of Her Majesty Queen Elizabeth II 1956
(NLA R.348)

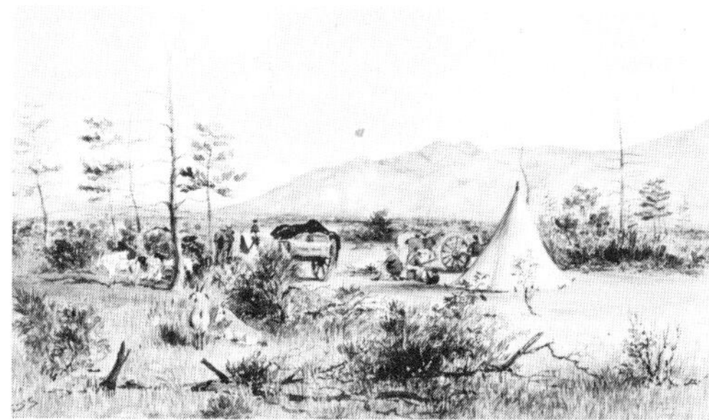

91 *Mount Brown from Camp looking north-north-east, August 20th*   1846
watercolour on paper 18.0 x 31.2 cm
Signed l.l. corner, brush and watercolour *S T G*. Inscribed, reverse, pencil *Mt. Brown from Camp looking N.N.E. Augst. 20th*.

The party finally made its way out of the Horrocks pass on 19 August[31] and camped on the plains near Spear Creek[32] on the western side of the Range. Gill would have sketched the scene that evening or the next morning and this may be the picture shown in the *Exhibition of Pictures*, Adelaide 1847 as no. 102 with the title *Mt. Brown, from camp W. side of Flinders Range.*

This picture which the National Library of Australia titles *Mt. Brown looking N.N.E. Augst. 20th* was titled *Mount Brown at the Head of St. Vincent's Gulf, South Australia* when presented by Her Majesty Queen Elizabeth II in 1956.

National Library of Australia, Canberra;
Gift of Her Majesty Queen Elizabeth II 1956
(NLA R.354)

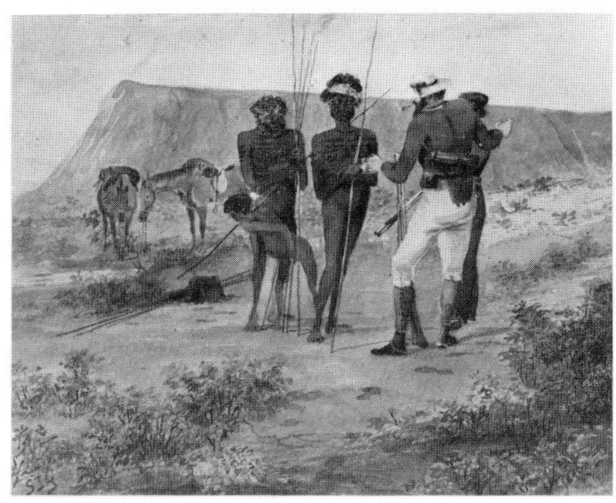

92   *Interview with Blacks near Table-land*
1846

watercolour on paper 23.3 x 27.6 cm
Signed l.l. corner, brush and brown
watercolour *S T G.* Not dated.

Having established a base camp at Depot
Creek, Horrocks and Gill set out on 22
August and rode some 25 miles west-
north-west to Uro Bluff returning the
next morning. Their experiences are well
documented both in Gill's diary[33] and in
Horrocks's journal.[34]

This scene depicts Gill, and Horrocks
with pistols and telescope at his back,
asking Aborigines for directions to water.
According to Gill the Aborigines 'appeared
ill-pleased with us, the old man more
particularly; the young one had bound
round his head a piece of red night cap
. . . and knew a knife by name'. In the
background is Uro Bluff.

This painting must be *Interview with
Blacks near Table-land,* which was included
by Gill as no. 108 in the *Exhibition of
Pictures,* Adelaide 1847 and was previewed
by the press as a 'graphic representation'
of an 'interview with a sable pair, whose
expression of countenance is absolutely
satanic'.[35] The work was formerly
catalogued by the State Library of

Victoria as *Drawing of a meeting of two white
men and a group of natives.*

La Trobe Collection,
State Library of Victoria, Melbourne
(SLV LT H.8213 LT.63)

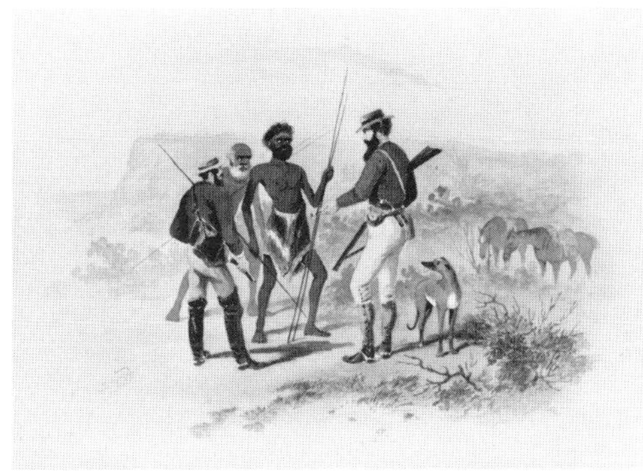

93   *Interview with Blacks before Attack,
Horrocks Expedition, South Australia*
*c.*1865-70

watercolour on buff paper 27.3 x 38.1 cm
Signed l.l. corner, pencil *S.T.G.* Not
dated. Inscribed l.r. corner, pencil *Interview
with Blacks/ before Attack/ H's Exn/ S°. A.*

Another version of the previous subject
and one of a group of six watercolours
relating to the expedition acquired from
Arthur Horrocks, a great-nephew of J.A.
Horrocks. The style and signature of these
works indicate that they were painted in
Melbourne *c.*1865-70, but there is no
extant family record of a commission.
Several of the group are inscribed with
the incorrect date 1844 instead of 1846.
This one is not dated.

Art Gallery of South Australia, Adelaide;
Morgan Thomas Bequest Fund 1944   (AGSA 0.1251)

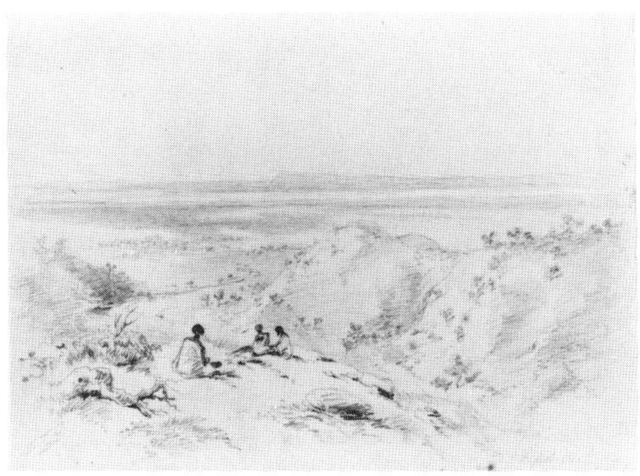

94   *Depot Creek, South Australia, looking
west*
1846

pencil on paper 20.6 x 29.0 cm
Signed l.l. corner, pencil *S.T.G* Not dated.
Inscribed l.r. corner, pencil *Depot Creek S°.
A/ looking West.*

Gill was camped at Depot Creek for two
periods, from 21 to 27 August when he
recorded in his diary that he was 'engaged
with my sketches' and again from 7 to 9
September when he 'went to the top of
the range sketching'.[36] This field sketch,
showing Uro Bluff in the distance, may
have been used in the development of a
number of finished watercolours
immediately after the expedition, and later
in Melbourne in the 1860s, for example,
Horrocks's Party in the North (cat. 95). The
signature appears to be a later addition,
*c.*1864-80. See Appendix B.

Art Gallery of South Australia, Adelaide;
South Australian Government Grant 1969
(AGSA 697HP7)

95   *(Horrocks's Party in the North)*
*c.*1865-70

watercolour on paper 40.5 x 73.2 cm
(sight)
Signed l.l. corner, brush and brown
watercolour *S.T.G.* Not dated.

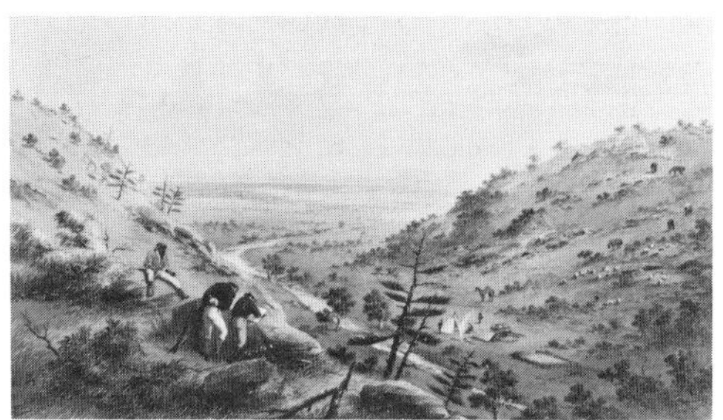

A picturesque view of the first camp at Depot Creek 21-23 August 1846 looking across the salt lakes towards Uro Bluff with Gill sketching, Horrocks looking on and Jimmy Moorhouse nearby. Gill appears to have used some artistic licence while executing this painting in Melbourne (*c*.1865-70) from sketches such as *Depot Creek, South Australia, looking west* (cat. 94). It is doubtful whether there was water in the lower part of the creek at the time as Gill records in his diary on 24 August that the party was engaged in moving the camp higher up the creek 'so that time be not so long occupied in fetching water'.[37]

Art Gallery of South Australia, Adelaide;
Morgan Thomas Bequest Fund 1946   (AGSA 0.1322)

96   *Travelling through the brush and sandridges, August 30*   1846
watercolour on paper 18.6 x 30.3 cm
Signed l.l. corner, brush and brown watercolour *S T G*. Not dated. Inscribed, reverse, pencil *Travelling through the brush and Sandridges/ August 30.*

On 28 August Horrocks set off from Depot Creek to the north-west on foot with Gill, Bernard Kilroy and the camel laden with equipment, ten gallons of water and provisions for three weeks.[38] On 30 August, Gill recorded in his diary that they had crossed 'many red sandy and thickly scrub'd ridges'[39] and in this

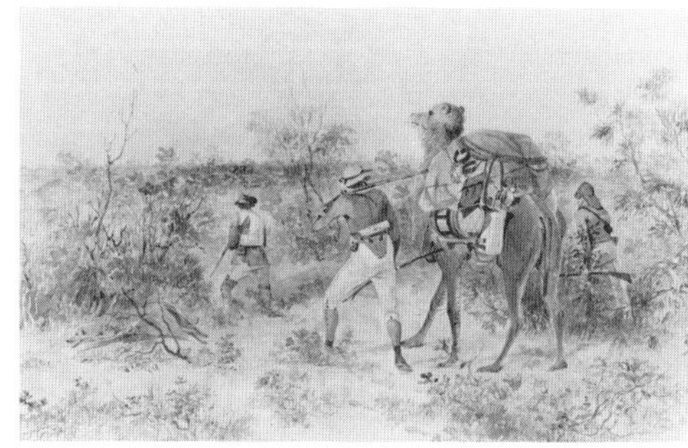

watercolour he depicts himself in the lead, followed by Horrocks with Kilroy on the other side of the laden camel. Both Horrocks and Gill are dressed as in cat. 92. Stylistically this painting was probably one of those included in the *Exhibition of Pictures*, Adelaide 1847, possibly no. 112, *Party travelling en route to N.W. country.* The Art Gallery of South Australia formerly titled this work *The Horrocks Expedition 1846.*

Art Gallery of South Australia, Adelaide;
Gift of Mrs Howard Davenport 1939   (AGSA 0.1126)

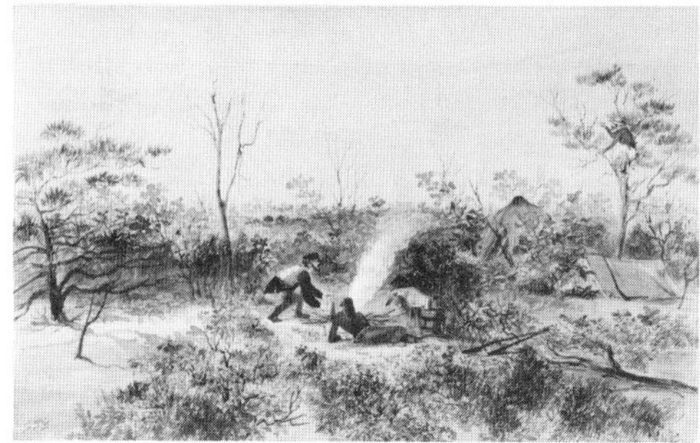

97   *Camp in desert Sept[r]. 1st.*   1846
watercolour on paper 19.0 x 30.6 cm
Signed l.l. corner, brush and watercolour *S T G*. Not dated. Inscribed, reverse, pencil *Camp in desert Sept[r] 1st.*

The date inscribed on this picture 'Sept[r]

1st', the day of the accident, is incorrect. After a sixteen-mile tramp over thickly scrubbed ridges Gill states in his diary for 30 August 'having to camp in scrub [and] set watch through the night'. The next day the party travelled mostly through similar country, the 'scrub appeared to increase in size'.[40] Gill depicts himself and Kilroy at the campfire with Horrocks in a tree, either getting his bearings, or keeping watch. The scene must represent the camp on the evening of 30 or 31 August. The picture was one of the originals shown in the *Exhibition of Pictures*, Adelaide 1847 as no. 113, *Camp in the scrub, evening.* When presented by Her Majesty Queen Elizabeth II the picture was titled *Camp in the Desert.*

National Library of Australia, Canberra;
Gift of Her Majesty Queen Elizabeth II 1956

(NLA R.350)

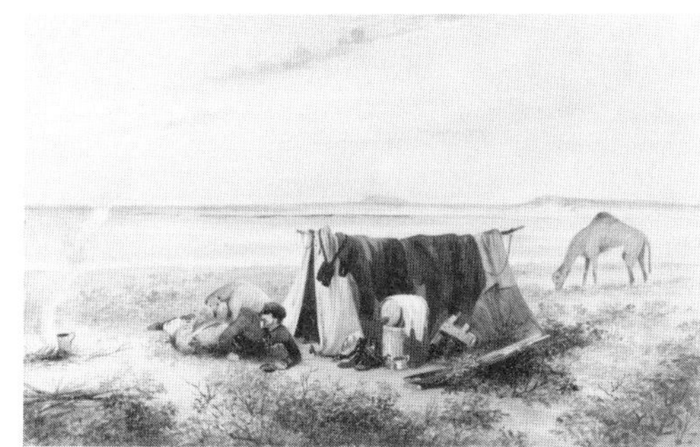

98   *Invalid's tent, salt lake 75 miles north-west of Mount Arden*   1846
watercolour on paper 21.4 x 34.2 cm
Signed l.l. corner, brush and brown watercolour *S T G*. Not dated. Inscribed, reverse, pencil, *Sept[r] 1st 1846/ Invalids Tent Salt Lake 75 miles N.W. of/ Mt. Arden South Australia. F.R./ The furthest point attained in Horrocks'/N.W. Expedition — at the scene of his fatal/ accident.*

Following the accident in the afternoon of 1 September 1846, Gill and Kilroy dressed Horrocks's wounds and pitched the tent to shelter him. Kilroy left that evening for Depot Creek returning three days later, 4 September, with Theakston and two horses. Gill portrays himself waiting by the salt lake, which Horrocks named Lake Gill (now Lake Dutton). Water was short and Gill was 'much fatigued from anxiety and want of rest'.[41] Shown in the *Exhibition of Pictures*, Adelaide 1847, probably as no. 117, *Invalid's tent, furthest point attained*, the painting was also previewed in the press.[42] The inscription on this watercolour was revealed during conservation. It had been mounted on card, possibly by Celia Horrocks, John's sister, who had written on the card mount a version of the inscription and a lengthy account of the expedition. The picture was acquired from Arthur Horrocks, a great-nephew of Celia and John Horrocks, in 1944 and titled *Horrocks wounded — S.T. Gill awaiting help outside Horrocks's tent, 1 September 1846.*

Art Gallery of South Australia, Adelaide;
Morgan Thomas Bequest Fund 1944   (AGSA 0.1253)

99   *Return of invalid*   1846
watercolour on paper 18.4 x 30.3 cm
Signed l.l. corner, brush and brown watercolour *S T G*. Not dated. Inscribed, reverse, pencil *Return of invalid/ Sept. 5th.*

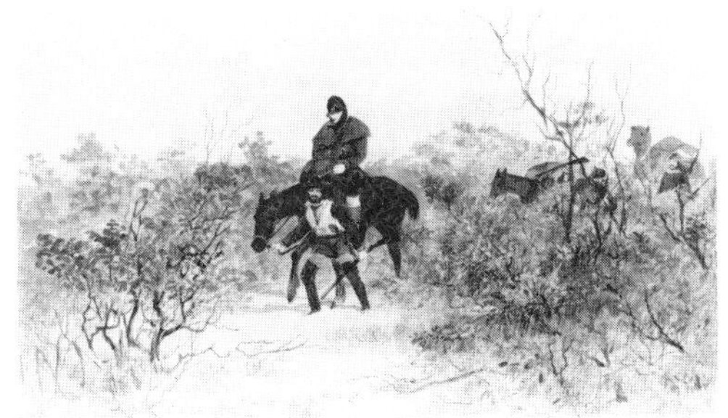

Gill leads Horrocks on horseback, followed by Theakston with the packhorse and Kilroy with the camel. The party covered the seventy miles back to Depot Creek in a little more than two days, arriving late on 6 September. On the 5th 'Mr Horrocks was very exhausted' and the men and horses 'were all nearly knocked up for want of water and rest'.[43] Shown in the *Exhibition of Pictures*, Adelaide 1847, as no. 118 *Invalid's return to Depot*, it was also previewed in the press.[44] Formerly titled *The Return of Horrocks 1846.*

Art Gallery of South Australia, Adelaide;
Gift of Mrs Howard Davenport 1939   (AGSA 0.1127)

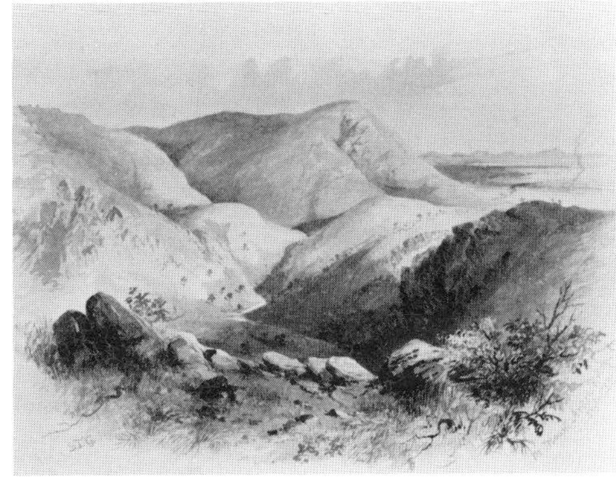

100   *Near Mount Arden, Flinders Range, South Australia*   1846
grey wash drawing on paper 16.8 x 21.6 cm
Signed l.l. corner, brush and grey watercolour *S.T.G.* Not dated. Inscribed, l.r. corner, diagonally, brush and grey watercolour *Nr Mount Arden. F.R./ So Australia*; reverse, pencil *looking E.S.E. from F. Range near Mt Arden/ Sept 7th 1846.*

The party remained at Depot Creek from 7 to 9 September. On the latter day, Gill

recorded in his diary that he 'went to the top of the range sketching'.[45] This is a typical field sketch taken after a long climb to a vantage point in the vicinity of Depot Creek which is approximately 8 km south of Mount Arden.

Art Gallery of South Australia, Adelaide;
South Australian Government Grant 1981

(AGSA 8113HP94)

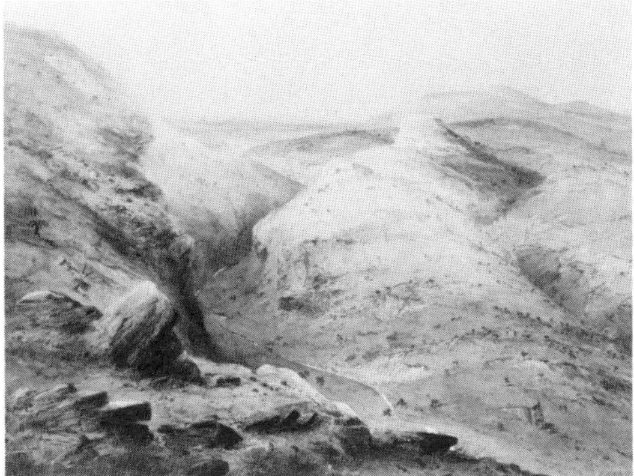

101   *Flinders Range, north of Mount Brown,*   *c*.1846-50
watercolour on paper 32.8 x 44.8 cm (sight)
Signed l.l. corner, brush and grey watercolour *S T G*. Not dated. Inscribed l.r. corner, brush and grey watercolour *F. RANGE/ N M^T BROWN.*

This is one of the many fine watercolours developed by Gill in the period *c*.1846-50 from sketches made during the expedition or possibly during a subsequent visit. The site has not yet been identified, but recent investigations suggest that it might be the gorge of Spear Creek, near Mount Brown[46].

Art Gallery of South Australia, Adelaide;
South Australian Government Grant 1981

(AGSA 811HP88)

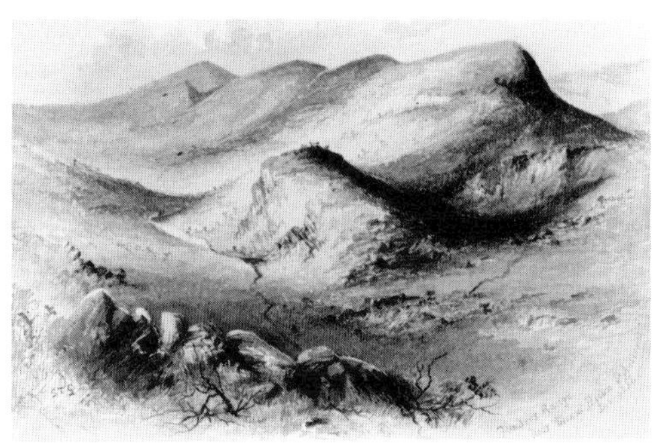

102 *Flinders Range, near Mount Brown, South Australia, looking east-south-east*
c.1846-1848

grey wash on paper 15.5 x 24.3 cm
Signed l.l. corner, brush and grey wash
S T G. Not dated. Inscribed, l.r. corner, diagonally, brush and grey wash *Flinders Range/ Near Mount Brown So Australia/ Looking E S E'*; reverse, pencil *Looking E.S.E. 2 miles South of/ Mt. Brown —/ Flinders R* [cropped?]*/ Sept*^r *16th 184* [cropped].

This view has been located at Woolundunga, just south of Mount Brown. The location given in the inscription is correct, but the date is wrong, as by 16 September Gill had reached Hope's Station, well south of Crystal Brook. The sketch may have been made during the expedition or possibly during a subsequent visit.[47]

Art Gallery of South Australia, Adelaide;
South Australian Government Grant 1981
(AGSA 8113HP95)

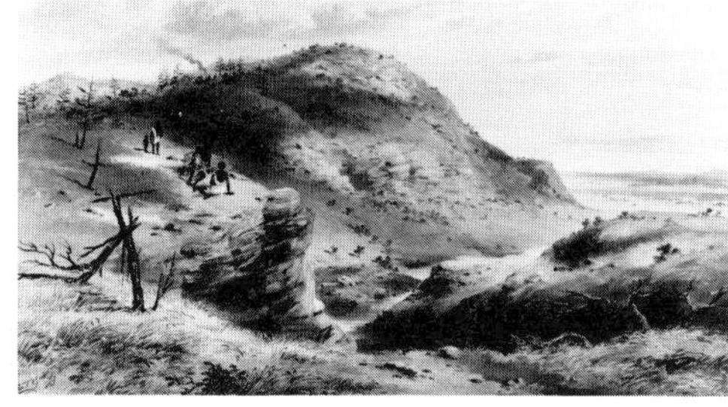

103 *(The Flinders Range)* *c.1865-70*
watercolour on paper 36.5 x 68.0 cm
(sight)
Signed l.l. corner, brush and brown watercolour *S.T.G* Not dated.

This view has been located on the western side of the Flinders Range above Woolundunga in the vicinity of Mount Brown. The signature and style of this large watercolour indicate that it was painted in Melbourne *c.*1865-70 from sketches made during the Horrocks Expedition or on a subsequent visit.[48]

M.J.M. Carter Collection,
Art Gallery of South Australia, Adelaide.

Houses

Gill would have foreseen a market for paintings of new houses built by the colonists when he included a section in his advertisement of 1840: 'Residences sketched and transferred to paper suited for home conveyance'. Watercolour painting was frequently used for a simple visual record, serving a need the camera was later to meet, and Gill appears to have fulfilled several requests for this kind of work.

Gill frequently rode out to country homesteads and some of his loveliest watercolours were the result of these expeditions. In these works the landscape was often as much a feature as the makeshift dwelling, as is apparent in *Rankine's Station, Mount Crawford, Barossa Range, South Australia* and *Approach to Mount Crawford* (cat. 19 and cat. 20). *The Gawler River* and *Rhodes's Cattle Station on the Gawler, Section 471, November 1844* (cat. 22 and 23) are two views of the same holding with its small out-station building. In *Floraville, property of Wm. Younghusband, Esq., near Gawler* (cat. 28) Gill has carefully represented a small farmhouse surrounded by a walled garden and neat path while in the paddocks in front, the harvest home completes the contented, sunlit scene. By the middle of the nineteenth century, grander houses were being built in South Australia and paintings of a larger size were being commissioned by the owners, who often requested several views of the same house. Gill's records of colonists' property mirror the progress of the colony. His depictions of South Australian houses were forerunners of works by a later South Australian artist, James Shaw, who arrived in Adelaide in 1850 and died in 1881, and produced numerous oil paintings of residences in Adelaide.

Vale Farm was built near the River Torrens in what is now the Adelaide suburb of Vale Park. It appears to have been a Manning House, a type of dwelling prefabricated in Britain, as were many houses of this period. It was assembled in 1841 and by 1845 it had been bought by Jonas Moses Phillipson. He appears to have commissioned two paintings from Gill, one of the house itself and one of the view from the verandah with the developing garden and hills beyond (cat 104 and 105). The rather formal record of the house, which looks strangely like a 1930s bungalow, must have pleased the owners who are shown strolling contentedly along the garden path in front of their new colonial home.

Prospect House was far more pretentious, built of local white limestone, topped with a crenellated parapet which gave it the appearance of a castle. J.B. Graham, one of the main shareholders in the Burra Burra Mines and a Director of the South Australian Mining Association, bought the house for £500 from the original owner, John Richmond, in 1846. A bachelor, Graham made improvements and extensions to the house with the help of an architect, until it was quite palatial and lavishly fitted inside with a 'rosewood pipe organ with swell' completing the picture of luxury. Wide driveways ran through the grounds which were surrounded by a high stone wall.

The gardens were set out formally with exotic trees and geometric flower beds edged with blue copper waste, presumably from the Burra Burra Mines. Vegetable gardens, stables, coachhouse and coachman's cottage completed the appointments at Prospect House. When Graham left for England, the house was occupied by his mother who had recently remarried. She and her husband, John Adams, held a fete there in 1849 as part of their lavish style of entertainment and which Gill recorded (cat. 111). It is assumed that the house portraits by Gill were commissioned by Mrs Adams on behalf of her son J.B. Graham.

Working on large sheets, Gill has produced formal records of Prospect House and its gardens. The two views of the house from ground level (cat. 106 and 107) have made the most of a difficult subject but the views from the roof of the house seem strangely awkward although they do convey the desolation of the plain between Prospect and the metropolis of Adelaide.

There is no known record by Gill of the interior of the house to compare with the series of eight paintings, executed in Sydney in 1857, of Monsieur Noufflard's house where external and internal views are faithfully and delightfully represented.

These watercolour paintings of houses are among the last executed in South Australia by Gill and show him working on a larger scale (possibly due to availability of larger sizes of paper). They also reflect the sudden peak of South Australian prosperity brought about by the copper boom with the colonists translating their new found wealth into gentlemen's residences of a scale which matched their aspirations.

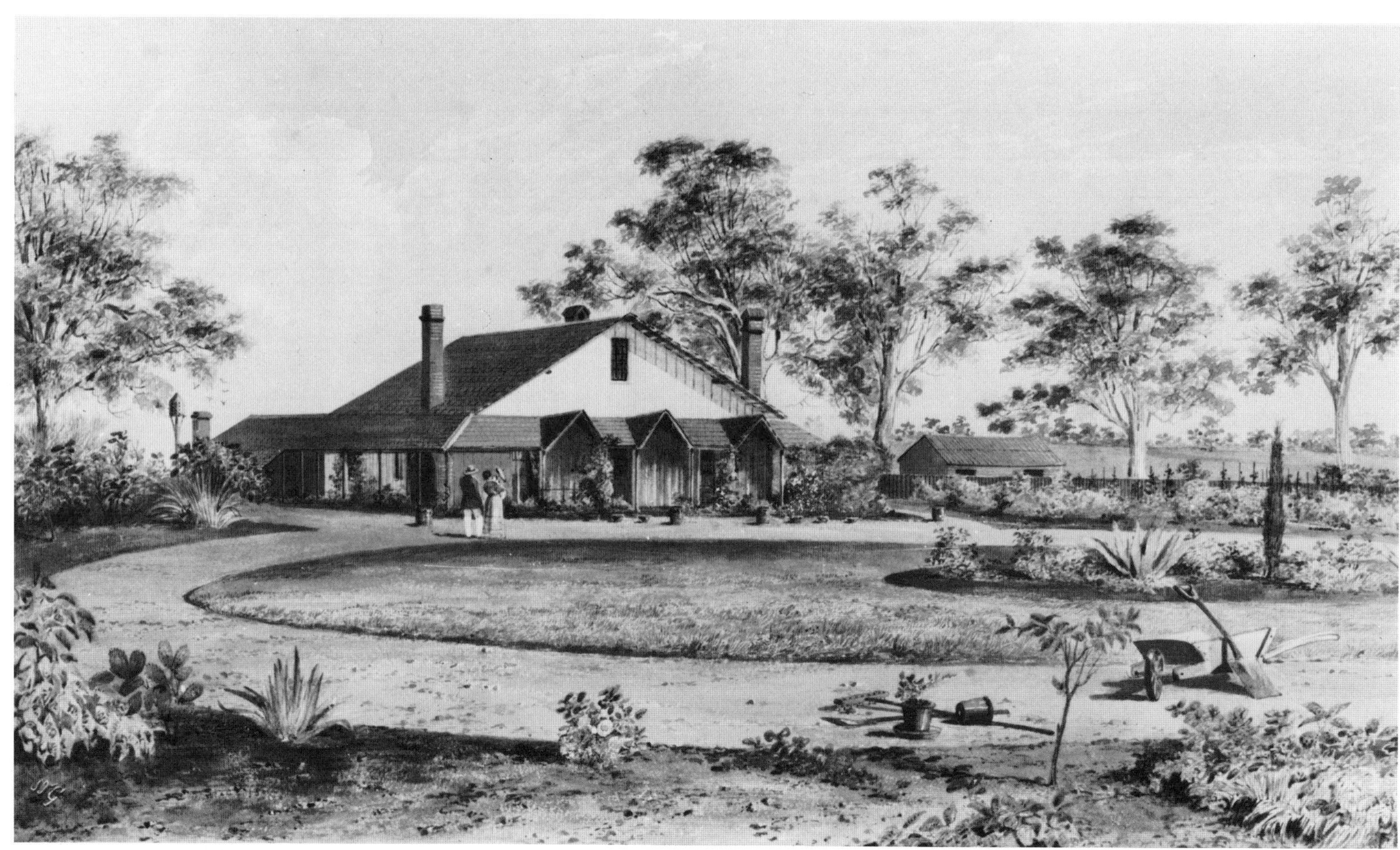

104 *Vale Farm*, watercolour on paper, 33.3 x 57.5 cm (image), Art Gallery of South Australia.

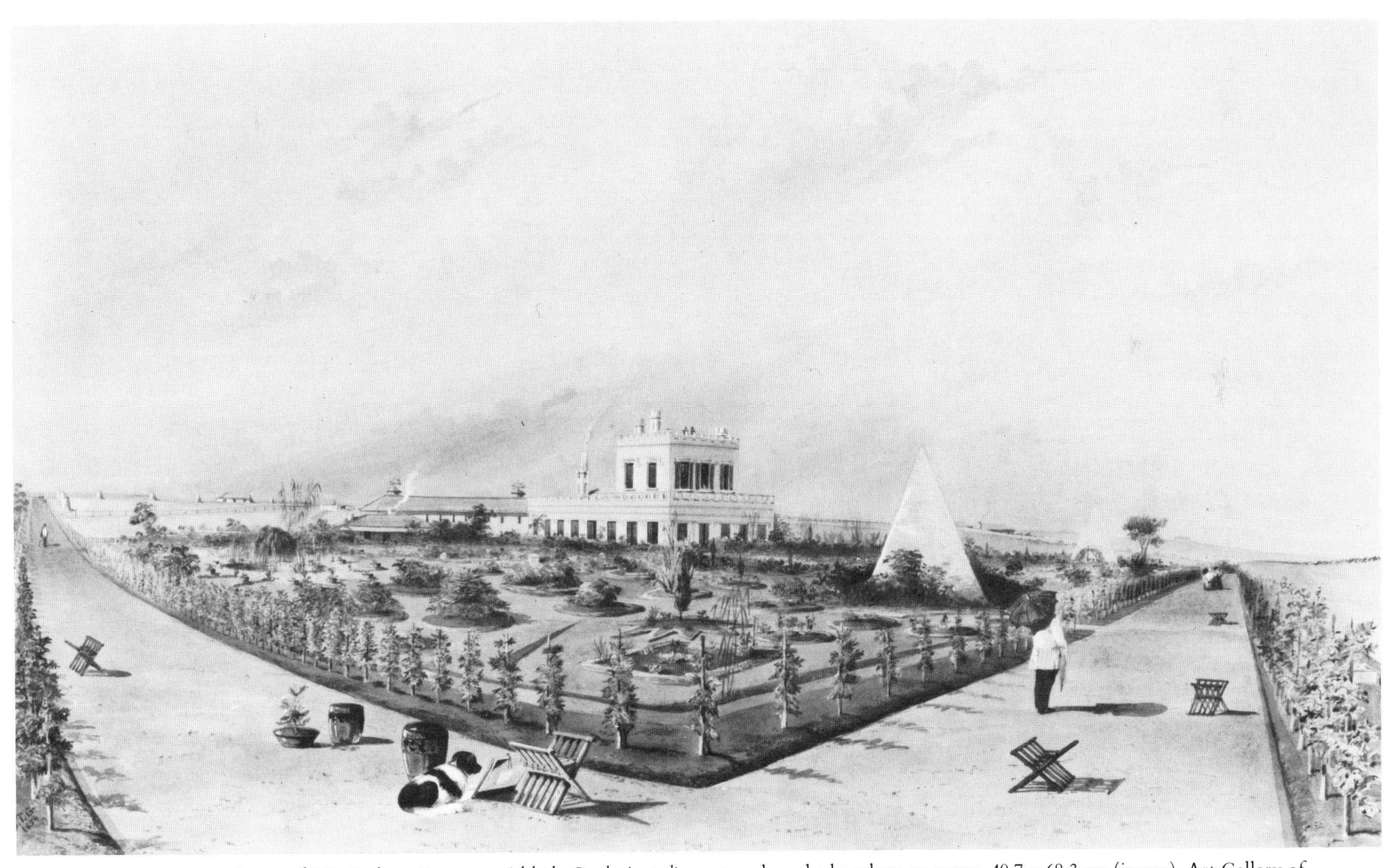

106 *Prospect House, the seat of J.B. Graham, Esqr., near Adelaide, South Australia,* watercolour, body colour on paper, 40.7 x 68.3 cm (image), Art Gallery of South Australia.

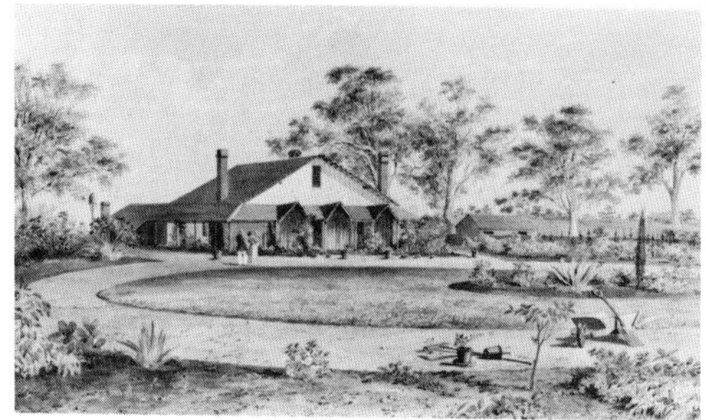 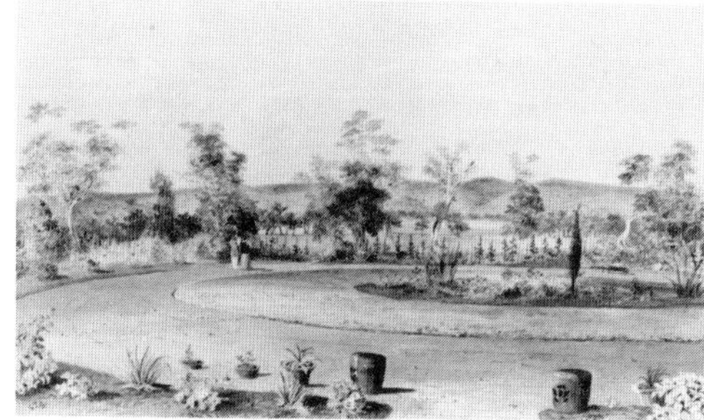 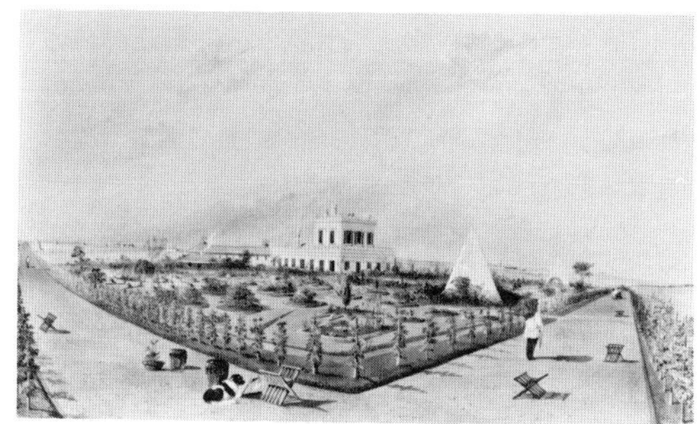

104   Vale Farm   c.1850

watercolour on paper, mounted on linen
33.3 x 57.5 cm (image), 38.5 x 64.4 cm
Signed l.l. corner, brush, and brown
watercolour and scratched line *S T G*. Not
dated. Inscribed, bot. c., pencil *Vale Farm*
(possibly not by artist), reverse, pencil *M
Philipson Esqr/ No 1*.

It is difficult to realise that this bungalow-
style house was built in the mid-nineteenth
century rather than the mid-twentieth.

Vale Farm is said to have been a Manning
House and was constructed near the River
Torrens in what is now the suburb of Vale
Park.

A Manning House was a prefabricated
design made in England and shipped out to
Australia for erection at a chosen site, with
the possible addition of brickwork for
chimneys.

Gill has captured a feeling of sunny
ambience, the owner and his wife taking the
air in front of their unpretentious dwelling
and simple, but serviceable, circular drive
and garden.

As in earlier works such as *The Seasons* and
The Months, Gill has made excellent use of a
foreground arrangement of gardening tools
and wheelbarrow.

Art Gallery of South Australia, Adelaide;
Gift of Mrs C. Phillipson 1935   (AGSA 0.854)

105   (From the Verandah of Vale Farm)

                                   c.1850

watercolour on paper 32.8 x 56.8 cm
(image), 38.6 x 64.3 cm (original linen
backing removed during conservation)
Signed l.l. corner, brush and brown
watercolour *S.T.G.* Not dated. Inscribed l.l.
corner, pencil *from The Verandah* (possibly not
by the artist), reverse on removed linen
backing, pencil *M Philipson* [*sic*] *Esq/ No 2*.

A quiet domestic scene bathed in golden
sunlight, with hills glimpsed through the
trees. Gill has captured a sense of tranquillity
and peacefulness in the garden which is
obviously still being planted and developed,
the owners strolling quietly in the sun. The
oriental blue pots are exactly the same as
those seen in the paintings of Prospect House
(cat. 106).

Art Gallery of South Australia, Adelaide;
Gift of Mrs C Phillipson 1935   (AGSA 0.855)

**106   Prospect House, the Seat of
J.B. Graham, Esqr., near Adelaide, South
Australia**   1850

watercolour, body colour on paper,
mounted on linen 40.7 x 68.3 cm (image),
51.0 x 77.0 cm
Signed and dated l.l. corner, brush and
brown watercolour *S.T.G/ 1850*. Inscribed
decorative label affixed to sheet centrally
below image, pen and brown ink, brush

and brown watercolour *PROSPECT
HOUSE/ The Seat of J.B. Graham, Esqr/
NEAR ADELAIDE S. AUSTRALIA.*

This formal portrait of an Australian
version of the English grand suburban villa
shows Prospect House placed centrally,
dominating the neat garden and its newly
planted flower beds with staked shrubs or
vines along the edges. The exaggerated
perspective of the paths gives a sense of
the extent of the land which was 'an
estate of 52 acres, of which 32 are laid
out as flower, fruit and kitchen gardens
and paddocks, including a great variety of
trees of choice description' according to
the Land Agent's advertisement when the
property was bought by W.H. Clark, a
brewer, in 1853 for £4,300.

Gill has placed garden seats casually on
the sunny paths, where the umbrella-
shaded figure strolling about the property
adds to the feeling of summer. Gill's
faithful dog guards the portfolio leaning
against the garden seat which the artist
may have just vacated.

All the paintings in this series have a
decorative label fixed centrally below the
image with the title designed by Gill. This
painting also has a decorative border
simulating a frame.

Art Gallery of South Australia, Adelaide;
Gift of Mrs F.M. Graham and family 1947

                                   (AGSA 0.1348)

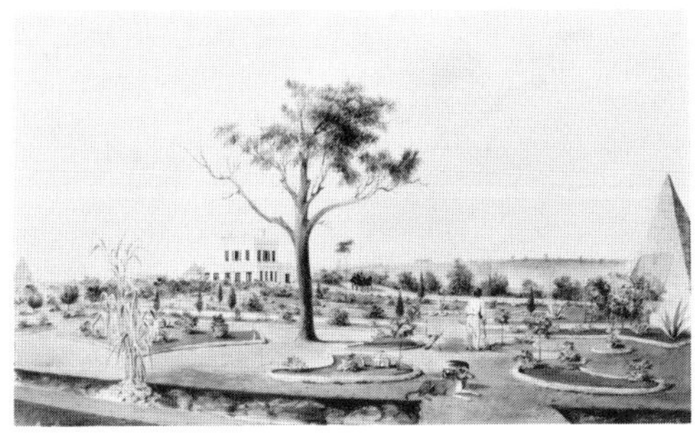

107 *Prospect House, The Seat of J.B. Graham, Esqr., near Adelaide, South Australia* 1850

watercolour on paper, mounted on linen
40.5 x 68.6 cm (image), 50.5 x 75.5 cm
Signed and dated, l.l. corner, brush and brown watercolour *S.T.G/ 1850.* Inscribed decorative label affixed to sheet centrally below image, pen and brown ink, brush and brown watercolour *PROSPECT HOUSE/ The Seat of J.B. Graham, Esqr, NEAR ADELAIDE S. AUSTRALIA.*

A more detailed view of the garden with another aspect of the house in the background. The large tree may be one of the few original trees left growing when the land was cleared to make way for the formal flower beds edged with blue copper waste, and 'exotic trees replaced indigenous ones' as Max Lamshed records in his *Prospect 1872-1972, a Portrait of a City.* The gardener, one of a large entourage of servants kept at the house, leans on his spade in a patch of welcome shade, an Australian touch noted by Gill's observant eye. The pyramid-like structure at the right is a hessian shade house.

Art Gallery of South Australia, Adelaide;
Gift of Mrs F.M. Graham and family 1947
(AGSA 0.1345)

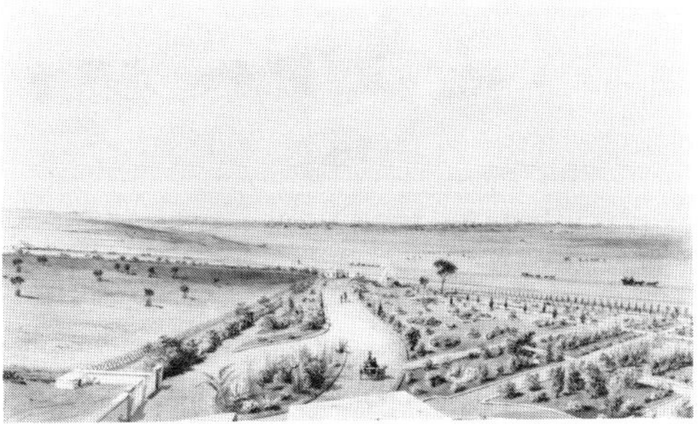

108 *View from the Leads of Prospect House, Looking towards Hindmarsh* 1850

watercolour, body colour on paper, mounted on linen 40.5 x 68.8 cm (image), 49.5 x 74.9 cm
Signed and dated bot. c., pen and brown ink *S.T.G. 1850.* Inscribed decorative label affixed to sheet centrally below image, pen and brown ink, brush and brown watercolour *VIEW/ FROM THE LEADS OF PROSPECT HOUSE/ Looking towards Hindmarsh and showing main Approach S.S.W./ portion of Garden Grounds &c/ ADELAIDE S°. AUSTRALIA 1850.*

From a vantage point on the leads (a term used to describe a roof made of lead sheets), Gill looks over the parapet to the formal garden below, along the winding driveway with its carriage and small gatehouse beyond. In the distance the brown, sun-dried land stretches away to Hindmarsh, an industrial suburb on the plain below Prospect. Gill has managed to suggest a sense almost of folly in trying to recreate such an English lifestyle in what is still a relatively desolate landscape.

Art Gallery of South Australia, Adelaide;
Gift of Mrs F.M. Graham and family 1947
(AGSA 0.1346)

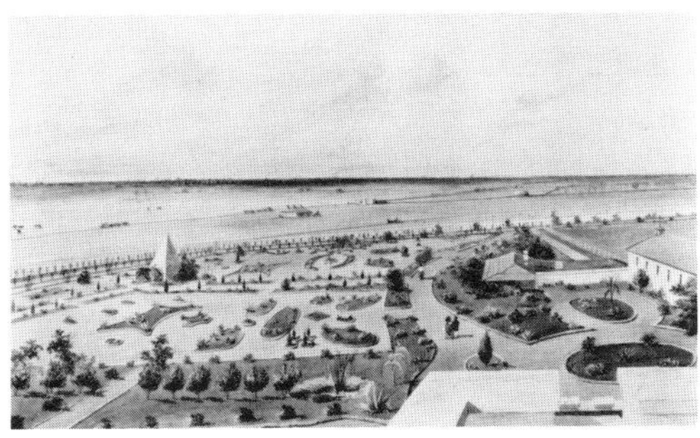

109 *View from the Leads of Prospect House, Showing west-north-west portion of Garden Grounds* 1850

watercolour on paper, mounted on linen
40.6 x 68.6 cm (image), 49.7 x 75.2 cm
Not signed. Dated in title . . . *1850.* Inscribed decorative label affixed to sheet centrally below image, pen and brown ink, brush and brown watercolour *VIEW/ FROM THE LEADS OF PROSPECT HOUSE/ Showing W.N.W. portion of Garden grounds &c/ ADELAIDE S°. A USTRALIA/ 1850.*

Another aspect of the grounds viewed from the leads. At the right the stables and coachhouse with coachman's cottage and, to the left, part of the new orchard. Distant smoke on the horizon gives a hint of civilisation and bullock teams carting produce on the dusty road hint at the prosperity of the colony. Gill still evokes a sense of incongruity between the two worlds of untamed, dry landscape and over-organised, formal landscape garden.

Art Gallery of South Australia, Adelaide;
Gift of Mrs F.M. Graham and family 1947
(AGSA 0.1349)

Portraits of the Colonists

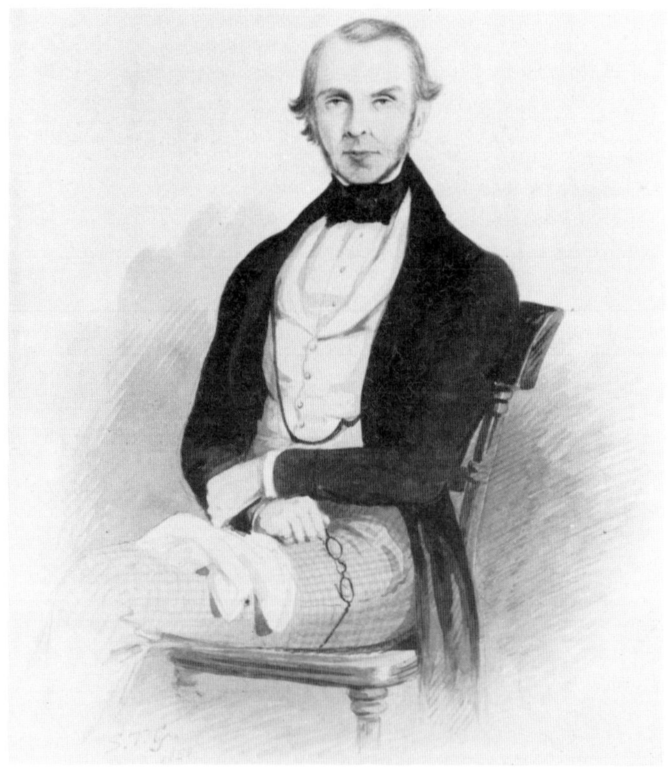

Gill launched his artistic career in Adelaide in March 1840 with a press announcement that he was 'late Draftsman and Water Color Painter to the Hubard Profile Gallery of London' and solicited 'the attendance of such individuals as are desirous of obtaining correct likenesses of themselves, families or friends' (see p.9). Apparently none of the colonists responded because the small painting *R.F. Macgeorge* (cat. 112) dated 1850, ten years later, is one of the earliest known portraits in watercolour.[1]

Gill was a competent and rapid watercolourist, but his style and the medium were probably considered unsuitable by the colonists, who may have preferred more formal portraiture in oils, a medium Gill rarely used. However, his first known work, a *Self portrait* (see p.viii) was painted in oils at Plymouth in February 1835 when he was sixteen years old.

There is no record of Gill's employment with the Hubard Profile Gallery,[2] but his experience as a silhouette artist, cutting out paper profiles, head, bust or full-length usually in black, with the details of the features and costume picked out in white, silver or gold, is evident in the pose and treatment of his first Adelaide portraits, the unique series of *Heads of the People*.[3] Published in 1849 this was his first venture into lithography. Drawn directly on the stone, in profile, rather flat and reminiscent of the silhouette, the twenty-two bust-sized portraits 'ventured on a touch of satire, with a spice of caricature'[4] and, judging by the press reaction, appear to have been a fairly shrewd observation of the character and physical features of some of Adelaide's leading colonists.

Gill really seemed to have a preference for sketching groups of people and for capturing the atmosphere of an event. A contemporary in discussing his success with groups of figures remarked that Gill was 'rapid—perhaps too much so—in the execution of his works: but this quickness produces that character of life and spirit which always distinguishes his performances and which is the chief charm about them'.[5] An atmosphere of restraint pervades his lithograph *Fete at Prospect House on the occasion of the consecration of Christ Church, North Adelaide, 20th December 1849*, (cat. 111) which would have been a fairly sedate affair, attended by His Excellency the Governor, the Lord Bishop of Adelaide and clergy and some three hundred of the most important colonists. In contrast, the six hundred colonists portrayed in *The Old Colonists' Festival Dinner* (cat. 113) of 1851 appear in a much more boisterous mood.

Gill certainly had an ability to observe and characterise people and an occasion such as the Festival Dinner would have provided ample material for the two later incisive satires of 1852 *The Chair* (cat. 114) and *The Vice* (cat. 115).

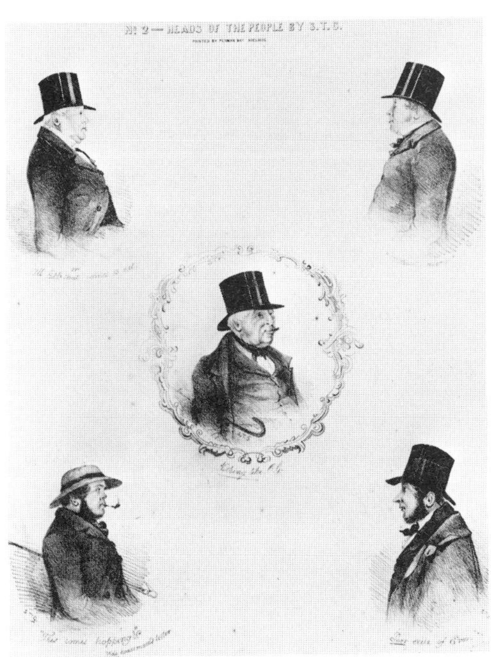

110 No. 2 — Heads of the People by S.T.G. 1849

lithograph 34.7 x 27.1 cm
inscribed on stone top c. as title, below title *PRINTED BY PENMAN & CO ADELAIDE.*

Signed on stone, l.l. or l.r. of each of the five images, *S.T.G.* and inscribed on stone below each image with a motto which is set out in the following text.

The second set of *Heads of the People* was described as 'cleverly got up, and, upon the whole, fair likenesses'[6] when published in July 1849. Comprising five portraits on one sheet, the group included from left to right:

or
All fish that comes to net
James Hurtle Fisher (1790-1875) the colony's leading barrister. Resident Commissioner 1836-38. First Mayor of Adelaide in 1840.

'Without reserve'
Nathaniel Hailes (1802-1879) auctioneer, journalist and author of the mottos for *Heads of the People.*

Nothing like O.G.
Osmond Gilles (1788-1866) merchant, land owner and mine owner.

'This comes hopping &c' vide housemaid's letter
John Ewart (1815-1872) who was lame and kept a livery stable.

'Poor exile of Erin'. Campbell
George Strickland Kingston (1807-1880) surveyor, engineer, architect and a director of the South Australian Mining Association.[7]

Art Gallery of South Australia, Adelaide;
South Australian Government Grant 1961

(AGSA 6112G94)

111 Fete at Prospect House on the occasion of the consecration of Christ Church, North Adelaide, 20th December 1849 1849

lithograph, two stones 28.6 x 44 cm
Signed l.l. corner, on stone *S.T.G.*; inscribed below image, l.r. corner *Printed by Penman & Co. Adelaide*, bot. c., *Fete at Prospect House/ on occasion of the Consecration of Christ Church N. Adelaide Dec[r] 20th 1849/ This print is respectfully dedicated to the very Rev[d]. the Lord Bishop and Clergy of So. Australia by their/ Obedient and humble servant/ Sam[l]. Tho[s]. Gill.*

The fete was given by Mr and Mrs John Adams on Thursday 20 December 1849 to celebrate the consecretation of Christ Church by Bishop Short in the presence of His Excellency the Governor and a large group of influential colonists. After the ceremony some 300 guests 'partook of a handsome *dejeuner*' at Prospect House, whilst some 350 children, who had walked in procession carrying banners from the

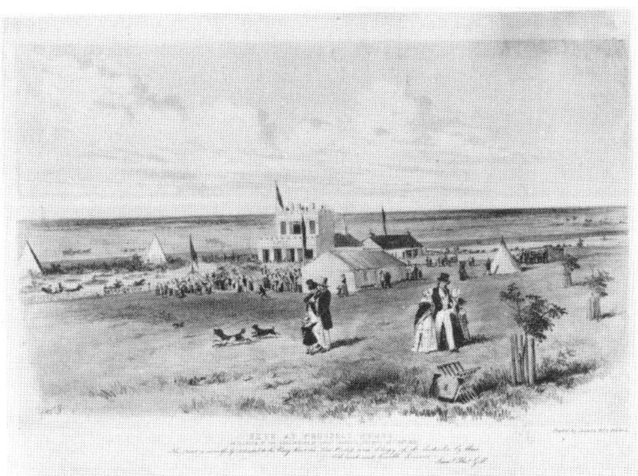

Church to Prospect House, were 'regaled with a profuse dinner, suited to their juvenile tastes'.[8]

Gill published the lithograph within five days of the event which suggests he may already have made and used one of the preliminary sketches for the large watercolours of Prospect House, dated 1850, presumably commissioned by Mrs Adams on behalf of her son J.B. Graham (see Houses p.89 and cat. 106-109). Note the artist's portfolio leaning against the stool, a device repeated in *Prospect House, The Seat of J.B. Graham, Esqr.* (cat. 106).

National Library of Australia, Canberra

(NLA 605/S919)

112 R. F. Macgeorge 1850

watercolour on paper 17.6 x 13.8 cm
Signed and dated, l.l. corner, brush and pale brown watercolour *S.T.G./ 1850.*

Robert Forsyth Macgeorge (1795?-1859) timber merchant and member of the first or Common Council of Adelaide 1841-42 and 1842-43. In May 1853 S.T. Gill mortgaged his properties at Coromandel Valley to Macgeorge for £500.[9] Macgeorge

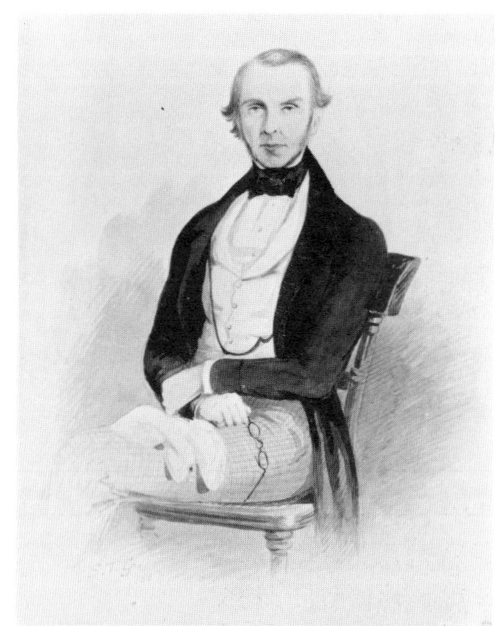

was drowned in the wreck of the *Royal Charter* 26 October 1859.[10]

Art Gallery of South Australia, Adelaide;
South Australian Government Grant 1962

(AGSA 0.1949)

113 *Old Colonists' Festival Dinner*

1851

lithograph, two stones, 40.2 x 52.9 cm
inscribed, l.l., *ON STONE BY S.T. GILL*,
l.r., *PRINTED & PUBLISHED BY PENMAN
& GALBRAITH ADELAIDE*, bot. c., *OLD
COLONISTS FESTIVAL DINNER/ HELD AT
THE REAR OF THE CITY-BRIDGE HOTEL
MORPHETT STREET ADELAIDE SOUTH
AUSTRALIA ON THURSDAY THE 27TH
MARCH 1851/ IN COMMEMORATION OF
THE FIRST SALE OF TOWN LAND 27TH
MARCH 1837.*

Credit is due to Gill for his original
presentation of what must have been a
difficult and tedious subject. Some 600
colonists attended the Old Colonists'

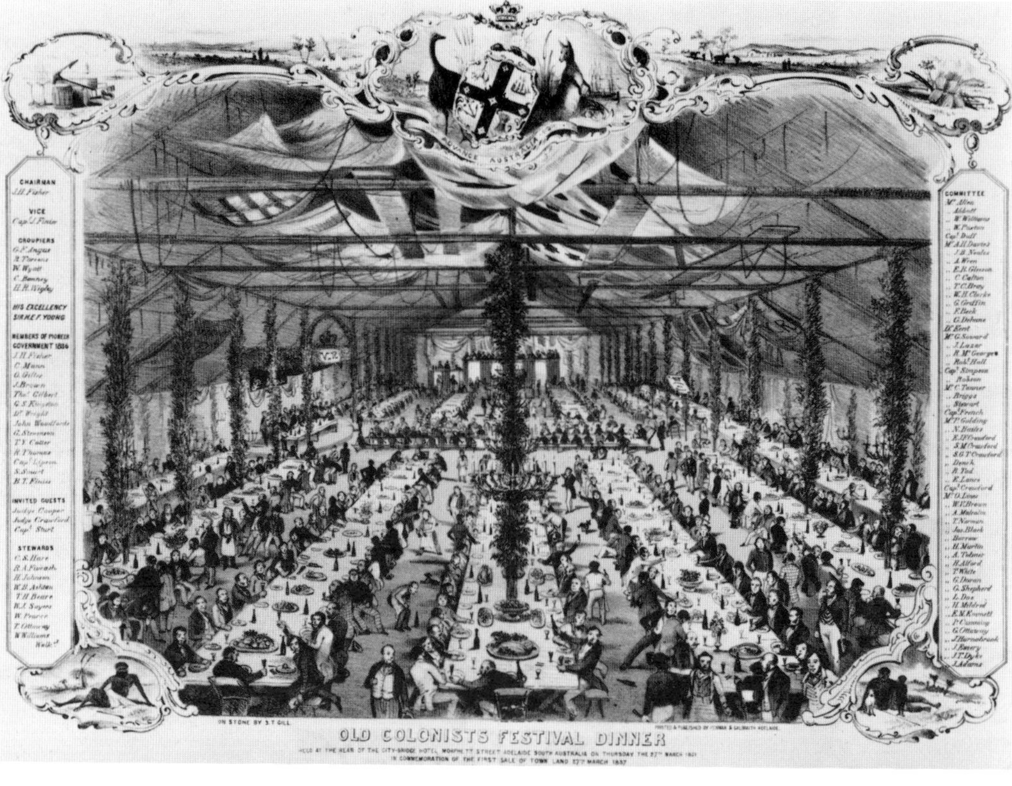

Festival Dinner and any attempt at
individual portraiture would have been
impossible. However he has surrounded
and embellished the scene with small
landscapes, port scenes and vignettes
alluding to the source of the colonists'
wealth and to the dispossessed noble
savages, the whole surmounted by a coat
of arms and ADVANCE AUSTRALIA.

The dinner was held in a canvas-
covered pavilion, 120 feet by 80 feet,
erected at the rear of and between City-
Bridge Hotel and Holy Trinity Church.
Some 22 toasts were proposed during the
evening and the colonists must have been
in a self-congratulatory mood considering
the success and prosperity achieved in the
fourteen years since the first sale of land.
We overlook them towards the eastern
end where the Adelaide Amateur Band
provided music whilst on the left, under
the royal insignia 'V.R.' is the Chairman's
table. Supporting posts were decorated
with greenery and the whole interior was
brilliantly lit by 'fanciful and rich
candelabra'. Amusement, additional to the
band music and songs was provided by
two large emus, a kangaroo and a wallaby
which were allowed to hop or walk about
at will.[11]

Art Gallery of South Australia, Adelaide;
Bequest of V.K. Burmeister 1957   (AGSA 575G464)

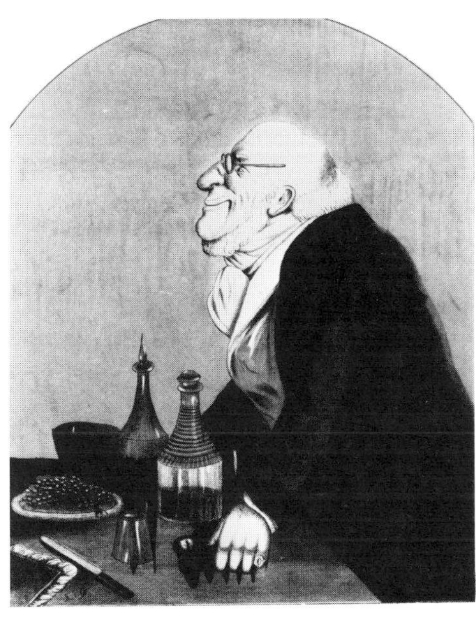

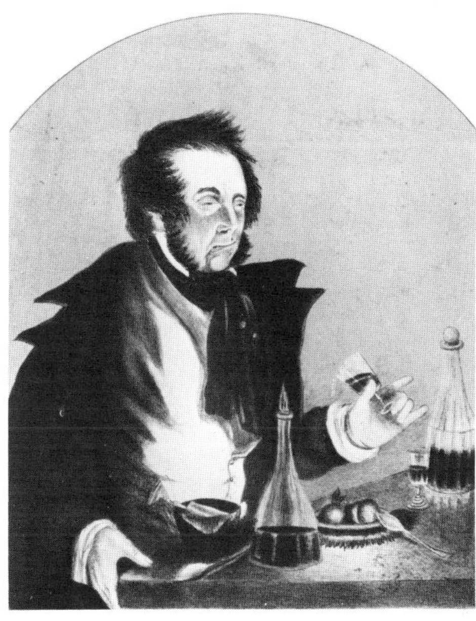

114   *The Chair*   1852

lithograph two stones
Signed l.l. corner on stone *S.T.G*;
inscribed below image l.r. *Drawn by S.T.
Gill 1852* centre, *THE CHAIR./ Gentlemen
— This is the very happiest moment of my
life.*

Gill possessed an innate ability to observe
human foibles. With a touch of satire he
portrays the smug self satisfaction of a
recently appointed chairman. This
lithograph pairs with *The Vice* (cat. 115).
Both subjects are probably fanciful and
since there is no publication line it is not
known where they were produced. Dated
1852 they may have been drawn in South
Australia or Victoria.

Mitchell Library,
State Library of New South Wales, Sydney

115   *The Vice.*   1852

lithograph two stones.
25.2 x 20.4 cm (image) 33.6 x 24.4 cm
Signed l.r. on stone *S.T.G.,*
below image l.r. *Drawn by S.T. Gill 1852,*
centre, *THE VICE./ Gentlemen — Feeling
as I do on the present occasion.*

A pair to *The Chair* (cat. 114). With a
subtle play on words Gill satirises the
vice-chairman who appears to be decidedly
queasy after too many toasts. Both subjects
could have been suggested by a function
such as The Old Colonists' Festival
Dinner, but whether they were drawn in
South Australia or Victoria is not known.

Art Gallery of South Australia, Adelaide;
South Australian Government Grant 1979
(AGSA 796HP52)

Conventions and abbreviations

Titles of works and dates of execution which are the result of Curator's research as distinct from those provided by the artist are enclosed in parentheses.

All measurements are expressed in centimetres, height before width, and signify sheet size unless otherwise stated.

All inscriptions by the artist are recorded and are on the front of the work, unless otherwise stated.

Pictures in the exhibition which are referred to in the catalogue and the accompanying notes are identified by the Catalogue Number e.g. (cat. 14) otherwise the Collection and the Accession Number are given e.g. (AGSA 0.1352).

p.	page
c.	*circa*
AGNSW	Art Gallery of New South Wales, Sydney
AGSA	Art Gallery of South Australia, Adelaide
ANG	Australian National Gallery, Canberra
NGV	National Gallery of Victoria, Melbourne
NLA	National Library of Australia, Canberra
NK	Rex Nan Kivell Collection, National Library of Australia, Canberra
ML	Mitchell Library, State Library of New South Wales, Sydney
SLV LT	La Trobe Library, State Library of Victoria, Melbourne
SLSA	State Library of South Australia, Adelaide
SAA	South Australian Archives, State Library of South Australia, Adelaide (SAA re-organised in November 1985 into two sections — the Public Record Office and the Mortlock Library of South Australiana)
UA	University of Adelaide
DG	Dixson Gallery, State Library of New South Wales
BDM	Registrar of Births, Deaths and Marriages, Adelaide

Appendix A

James Allen's commission to S.T. Gill for illustrations for a series of 'Lectures on South Australia' given in England 1846-47.

In 1845, James Allen[1] who had been Proprietor and Editor of *The South Australian Register* from 1842, sold the paper and visited England 'partly on a family errand, but chiefly to further the interests of the colony by popular lectures, accompanied by drawings and transparencies of colonial scenery, in the collection of which his own pencil has been assisted by that of an artist of first-rate ability'.[2]

Allen first made the proposal to devote some of his time 'to the diffusion of information about the colony by lectures or otherwise' in a letter dated 16 September 1845 to William Giles, the Adelaide Manager of the South Australian Company.[3] Although there is no record of a reply, Giles must have favoured the proposal and Allen must have immediately commissioned Gill to paint a group of watercolours and assist in the preparation of transparencies because he sailed for England late in December. During the voyage Allen gave a lecture on South Australia in Cape Town, 25 February 1846, where the sketches 'highly creditable to the artist' were displayed and where 'a live kanagaroo' was introduced 'to speak for itself'.[4]

On arrival in England the proposal was taken up by the South Australian Company. Its Committee for the Diffusion of Information respecting South Australia sought donations towards the cost of promoting a series of three *Lectures on South Australia* in an advertisement which stated 'Mr. Allen has brought with him a large number of Drawings, executed by a Colonial Artist . . . and is encouraged to exhibit them as a Series of Dissolving Views [lantern slides]'.[5] An editorial in the same paper gave the qualifications of the lecturer and stated that most of the paintings had been 'taken under his own directions, and from spots visited by himself and by Mr. Gill, the clever South Australian artist' and 'will all be made available to the illustration of this series of Lectures'.[6]

The first of the series of three lectures was delivered to 'a highly respectable audience at Crosby Hall', Bishopsgate Street, London on Tuesday 30 August 1846[7] and the next two were received on 7 and 14 July 'with marked approbation; and the beautiful dissolving views . . . were admirable for their fidelity'.[8] On 3 August Mr Allen gave 'a lecture devoted especially to the Mines of South Australia' when 'specimens of ore and drawings of the Mines were exhibited . . . and excited great interest'.[9] Between July 1846 and January 1847, in addition to Crosby Hall, the series of lectures was given at four other places in London and in eight cities in England.[10]

In October 1846, *The South Australian News*, London published a syllabus of the three lectures and the titles of the 'Dissolving Views . . . prepared from drawings executed in the Colony' (see List 1) and 'illuminated by the Oxyhydrogen Lime Light'.[11] Reference is often made in the newspaper reports to the dissolving views but it is not clear whether Gill's watercolours were exhibited during the tour. The only mention is of the 'drawings of the Mines' exhibited at the special lecture on mining in London.

When Allen returned to South Australia in mid 1847 the majority of the watercolours must have remained in England to become the property of the South Australian Company and many of them were eventually presented by the Company to the Art Gallery of South Australia (see List 2).

A list of the commissioned works, or of those acquired by the South Australian Company, has not been found, but comparison of the titles of the watercolours in the Art Gallery's gift from the South Australian Company (List 2) with those of the Dissolving Views (List 1) allows the reasonable assumption that sixteen of the watercolours in the gift were those originally commissioned from Gill by James Allen and used to illustrate his lectures. It also seems reasonable to assume that Gill developed his watercolours and the transparencies (dissolving views) in his studio from sketches made on the spot such as the twelve now owned by the National Library of Australia (see List 3). Of these twelve, eleven titles correspond to those of the Dissolving Views (see comparison List 1) and of these, six are dated in the signature 1845 and five are inscribed on the reverse in pencil by Gill *Mr. Allen*.

(Note: This appendix has been condensed from an extensive working paper now deposited in the Mortlock Library of South Australiana, State Library of South Australia).

LIST 1 *Titles of the Dissolving Views*

The title of each Dissolving View, or group of Dissolving Views is given as it was published 'to follow Mr. Allen's Illustrated Lectures on South Australia' (*The South Australian News*, London, 1 October 1846, p.77). Inset below the title, or group title, is listed a work, or group of works of similar title or subject from:

1 the watercolours by S.T. Gill owned by the Art Gallery of South Australia which were gifts from the South Australian Company in 1890 and 1931,

2 the wash drawings by S.T. Gill owned by the National Library of Australia, Canberra, or

3 watercolours by S.T. Gill in other collections.

Lecture I

1. Emigrants landing at Holdfast Bay.
2. The Surveyor General's boat going round to the Port.
3-4. Two views of Port Adelaide in 1846.
  NLA R.115 *Port Adelaide*
5. Government House as it was in 1837-9
  NLA R.112 *Old Gov[ernmen]t House*
6. Government House as it now is.
  AGSA 0.34 *Government House, North Terrace, Adelaide 1845*
  NLA R.114 *New Govt. House, [Adelaide] from So. East*
7. Adelaide, the capital of South Australia as it was in 1837-8.
8-12. Street Views of Adelaide as it now is.
  AGSA 0.642 *Hindley Street, Adelaide, looking West from King William Street 1845*
  AGSA 0.944 *Hindley Street, Adelaide, looking East 1845*
  AGSA 0.939 *North Terrace, Adelaide, looking South East from Government House Guardhouse 1845*
  AGSA 0.940 *Rundle Street, looking West from across Frome Street, Adelaide 1845*
  AGSA 0.648 *Trinity Church, North Terrace, Adelaide 1845.*

Lecture II

1. St John's Church with the Mount Lofty Ranges in the distance.
  NLA R.110 *St. John's Church, So. Adelaide, So. A.*
2. Frome Bridge, crossing the Torrens, in the neighbourhood of Adelaide.
  NLA R.111 *F[rome] Bridge from W[est] Side*
3. General view of a cattle station in the interior.
4. The Stringy Bark Forest.
5. Sketch of Ridley's Simultaneous Reaping and Thrashing Machine in full work.
6. Albert Town, a village on the road from the Port.
7. A view of North Adelaide.
  AGSA 0.645 *Kermode Street, North Adelaide, looking East, 1845*
8. The German Village of Klemzig, on the banks of the Torrens.
9. Moorundie, a village on the banks of the river Murray.
  AGSA 0.35 *Old Police Station and Edward John Eyre's House at Moorundie River Murray 1842*
10-12. Views of lead and copper mines of South Australia.
  AGSA 0.941 *Burra Burra Mine 1845*
  AGSA 0.942 *Kapunda Mine 1845*
  AGSA 0.943 *Glen Osmond Mine 1845*

Lecture III

1. View of North Terrace, with the Bank and Legislative Council Room, Adelaide.
  AGSA 0.938 *Bank of South Australia and Legislative Council Room, North Terrace, Adelaide 1845.*
2-3. Two Views in Rundle and King William street, Adelaide.
  AGSA 0.643 *King William Street, looking North 1845*
  AGSA 0.647 *Rundle Street, Adelaide 1845.*
4. Captain Sturt setting out on his exploratory Expedition
  AGSA 0.644 *Sturt's Overland Expedition leaving Adelaide, August 10th 1844.*
  NLA R.113 *Sturts Expedition [leaving Adelaide]*

5. The Adelaide Race Course
    UA   *A Race Meeting at Adelaide 1845*
    NLA R.118   *Adelaide Race Course /45.*

6. Meeting of the Hounds, at the Dry Creek, near Adelaide
    UA   *A Hunt Meet at Dry Creek, near Adelaide 1845.*
    NLA R.109   *Meeting of Adelaide hounds at Dry Creek, Northern Road.*

7. Crouching for and shooting the Emu, or Australian Ostrich.

8. Hunting the Kangaroo.
    NLA R.117   *Hunting the Kangaroo*

9. Whirlwind

10. Interior of a Settlers Hut.
    NLA R.116   *Interior of Settlers Hut*

11. Moonlight scene from the base of the Mount Lofty Ranges.

12. Agricultural and Horticultural Show, on the Park Lands, in the neighbourhood of Adelaide.
    AGSA 0.641   *Agricultural and Horticultural Show, Adelaide, 1845.*
    NLA R.108   *A[gricultural] & H[orticultural] Exhibition, Park Lands.*

LIST 2 Art Gallery of South Australia

The right hand column refers to the corresponding title in List 1, e.g. 3/12 = Lecture III, View 12.

Watercolours, gift from the South Australian Company 1890

0.641	*Agricultural and Horticultural Show, Adelaide 1845*	3/12
0.642	*Hindley Street, Adelaide, looking West from King William Street 1845*	1/8
0.643	*King William Street, looking North 1845*	3/2
0.647	*Rundle Street, Adelaide 1845*	3/3
0.644	*Sturt's Overland Expedition leaving Adelaide, August 10th 1844.*	3/4
0.645	*Kermode Street, North Adelaide, looking East 1845*	2/7
0.646	*Port Adelaide looking across Gawler Reach 1848*	
0.648	*Trinity Church, North Terrace, Adelaide 1845*	1/12

Watercolours, gift from the South Australian Company 1931

0.944	*Hindley Street, Adelaide, looking East 1845*	1/9
0.938	*Bank of South Australia and Legislative Council Room, North Terrace, Adelaide 1845*	3/1
0.939	*North Terrace, Adelaide, looking South East from Government House Guardhouse 1845*	1/10
0.940	*Rundle Street looking West across Frome Street., Adelaide 1845*	1/11
0.941	*Burra Burra Mine 1845*	2/10
0.942	*Kapunda Mine 1845*	2/11
0.943	*Glen Osmond Mine 1845*	2/12
0.34	*Government House, North Terrace, Adelaide 1845*	1/6
0.35	*Old Police Station and Edward John Eyre's House at Moorundie, River Murray 1842*	2/9

LIST 3 National Library of Australia

Twelve brown or grey wash drawings by S.T. Gill acquired in 1932. The right-hand column refers to the corresponding title in List 1, e.g. 3/12 = Lecture III, View 12.

R. 107	*H.M.S. Goal [sic] Adelaide, So. A.* no corresponding title in List 1.	S.T.G./45	
R. 108	*A[gricultural] & H[orticultural] Exhibition, Park Lands.*	S.T.G.	3/12
R. 109	*Meeting of Adelaide hounds at Dry Creek, Northern Road.*	Unsgd	3/6
R. 110	*St. John's Church, So. Adelaide, So. A.*	S.T.G.	2/1
R. 111	*F[rome] Bridge from W[est] Side.*	S.T.G./45	2/2
R. 112	*Old Gov[ernmen]t House.*	S.T.G.	1/5
R. 113	*Sturts Expedition [leaving Adelaide 1844].*	S.T.G.	3/4
R. 114	*New Govt. House, [Adelaide,] from So. East.*	S.T.G./45	1/6
R. 115	*Port Adelaide*	S.T.G./ 45	1/3
R. 116	*Interior of Settlers hut.*	S.T.G./ 45	3/10
R. 117	*Hunting the Kangaroo*	S.T.G./ 45	3/8
R. 118	*Adelaide Race Course/ 45.*	S.T.G./ 45	3/5

Six of the above sketches are inscribed on the reverse in pencil by the artist *Mr. Allen*, they are nos. R. 107, 108, 115, 116, 117, 118.

Notes
1. James Allen, a journalist and radical Baptist emigrated to South Australia from England in 1839. Editor *Southern Australian*, 1841 and Proprietor and Editor of the *S.A. Register*. 1842-1845. Visited England 1846-47.
2. *South Australian Register*, 5 November 1845.
3. South Australian Archives. B.R.G.42, South Australian Company Correspondence.
4. *South African Commercial Advertiser*, 25 and 28 February 1846, pp. 89, 93-4.
5. *South Australian News*, London, 1 June 1846, p.44a.
6. *Ibid.* 1 June 1846, p.41a.
7. *The Times*, London, 2 July 1846, p.5b.
8. *South Australian News*, London, 1 August 1846, p.60b.
9. *Ibid*, 1 September 1846, p. 68b, 69a.
10. *Ibid*, 1 October 1846, p.76a, 1 January 1847, p.99ab.
11. A magic lantern using the light produced by burning limestone under a current of oxyhydrogen gas.

Appendix B

Signatures and dating

S.T. Gill did not commence the practice of adding the date to his signature in Australia until 1844. Therefore the assignment of dates of execution to the many of his watercolours and wash drawings which are unsigned or not dated in the signature or inscription has been undertaken by studying the changing style of Gill's signatures and the changing style of his watercolour technique which became coarser as he grew older. It is also necessary to take both these factors into account when assessing works which are signed and dated, because there are some exceptions in which the date with the signature does not correspond to the date of execution of the work. In particular there are a number of late versions of the Burra Burra Mine series, painted *c.* 1865-70, which have been signed and dated *S.T.G./47*.

To assist in this assessment, a table of signatures with dates was assembled and a few examples grouped in periods have been illustrated below. Gill usually signs his work in the l.l. corner, rarely elsewhere, and usually with the initials *S.T.G.*, with or without stops. Early in his career he sometimes used his initials and surname *S. T. Gill* and on rare occasions abbreviated christian names and surname *Sam Thos. Gill* (cat. 62).

Plymouth, England — 1835-38 (Sketch-book)
Gill signed with initials in a variety of styles of script and Roman block letters with serif and in some cases used the style *S. T. Gill*. More than half of the works were dated with the signature.

Adelaide, South Australia — 1839-52
There are no examples of signature with date in the period 1839-43. These early works are signed in styles similar to those used in England in the Sketch-book. The group of *The Seasons and the Months* in the exhibition (cat. 2 to 16) are typical examples and are considered to date *c.*1840-42.

From 1844 Gill begins to add the date to his signature, but not regularly. The earliest example in the exhibition is no. *The Gawler River*, 1844 (cat. 22). The signature tends towards the Roman block style with or without serifs, and two types of *G* are employed, Roman, or script with a small hook or tail under the *G* itself.

Melbourne, Victoria — 1852-56
Similar to the final South Australian period with a greater tendency towards the Roman block sans serif, with the two styles of *G*. The tail under the *G* more emphasised see *Death of the Boomer, 1853* (cat. 79).

Sydney, New South Wales — 1856-64
The signature is generally Roman block, sans serif, except the *G* which generally has a small decorative hook to the tail extending back under the *T* and sometimes under the *S*.

Melbourne, Victoria — 1864-80
The characteristic signature with the decorative tail to the G sweeping back under the three initials is now fully developed on his watercolours and lithographs. One of the few exceptions is one of his last drawings *Bank Place, Melbourne, 1880* (DG). For a period from about 1867 Gill also impressed an embossed circular stamp *S.T. GILL MELBOURNE* onto some of his lithographs and watercolours, but the exact period of its use requires further investigation.

During this second Melbourne period, Gill began to repeat many of his earlier compositions possibly 'on spec' but often as commissions, the two series of the Victorian Gold Fields for the Melbourne Public Library in 1869 and 1872 being a case in point. Many South Australian subjects were also repeated at this time and several examples have been included in the group relating to *The Horrocks Expedition* (cat. 93, 95, 103). A further example is the Burra Burra Mine series which was mentioned earlier.

Pencil Drawings
The pencil drawings have presented a particular problem which needs further research. Most of the South Australian subjects seen appear to be either field sketches with artists' notes, or preliminary drawings and also appear to have come from sketch books. All are signed with the signature style of the second Melbourne period, 1864-80 and in some there are anomalies in the inscribed title or date. The best explanation seems to be that Gill retained his drawings for reference and after repeating some of the subjects in Melbourne from 1864 onwards would then sign the drawing, perhaps date it and add to the title from memory and sell it when in need of extra funds.

There are four pencil drawings in this exhibition which are signed with second Melbourne period signatures (1864-80) and some have apparent anomalies in the date or inscription. They are:

Rankine's Station, Mount Crawford, Barossa Range, South Australia. *c.*1842-43 (cat. 19)
The title is inscribed in pencil, part of which is faint and rubbed and appears to be contemporary with the drawing *c.*1842-43. The signature is in darker pencil and *c.*1864-80.

On the Onkaparinga River, above Horseshoe Township, South Australia, 1848 (cat. 29).
The title is inscribed in pencil on the reverse. The date 1848 appears to have been added later in a lighter pencil, similar to the signature, suggesting that it was added from memory when the work was signed in Melbourne *c.*1864-1880.

*On the River Broughton, Northward, South Australia. c.*1846 (cat. 85).
The title is inscribed in pencil, the first part *On the River Broughton/* is probably contemporary with the drawing, *c.*1846. The second part *Northward/ So Australia 18* is in a lighter pencil and could have been added later to more accurately identify the location. The *18* is rubbed and the last two digits have been omitted, suggesting that Gill could not recall the exact date. The signature is in darker pencil and was added *c.*1864-80.

*Depot Creek South Australia, looking West c.*1846 (cat. 94).
The title is inscribed in pencil and is probably contemporary with the drawing, *c.*1846. The signature is in a lighter, broader pencil and was added *c.*1864-80.

Plymouth, England — 1835-38. (*Sketch-book*)
Dogs meat
pen and ink. (AGSA D.759-57)

The Plowman
pen and ink. (AGSA D.759-33)

Country Courtship
pen and ink. (AGSA D.759-73)

Finis
pen and ink. (AGSA D.759-82)

Adelaide, South Australia — 1839-52.
(*Commenced dating from 1844*)
(*The Gawler River*) 1844
watercolour. (AGSA 795HP30)

Sturt's Overland Expedition leaving
Adelaide, 1844.
watercolour. (AGSA 0.1522)

(*Port Adelaide looking east along
North Parade*) 1846
watercolour. (AGSA 0.1181)

Penny's Stopes, Burra Burra Mine,
April 12th 1847.
watercolour (AGSA 0.649)

(*Port Adelaide looking north along
Commercial Road*) 1847
watercolour (AGSA 0.656)

Monument to Colonel Light.
watercolour (AGSA 0.654)

R. F. Macgeorge
watercolour (AGSA 0.1949)

Prospect House, the Seat of J. B.
Graham, Esqr. near Adelaide, South
Australia (AGSA 0.1348)

Views in Adelaide No. 1: Hindley Street
from King William Street.
lithograph (AGSA 684G11)

Melbourne, Victoria — 1852-56. (*First
period*)
Convivial Diggers in Melbourne,
lithograph

Forest Creek, Mount Alexander.
watercolour (LT, SLV)

Death of the Boomer, 1853.
watercolour (LT, SLV H.956)

McLarens (Main Road) Ballarat, June '55.
watercolour (AGSA 787HP16)

Sydney, New South Wales — 1856-64
Offices of the Sydney Morning Herald
pencil and wash drawing (NLA)

H. Noufflard's House in Bligh Street,
Sydney View from the Street.
watercolour (Private collection)

General View of Sydney from the North
Shore.
watercolour (DG, SLNSW)

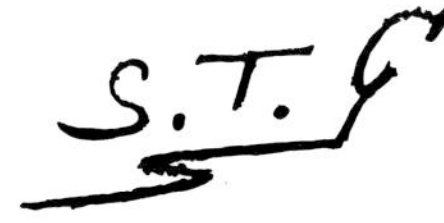

Embossed stamp

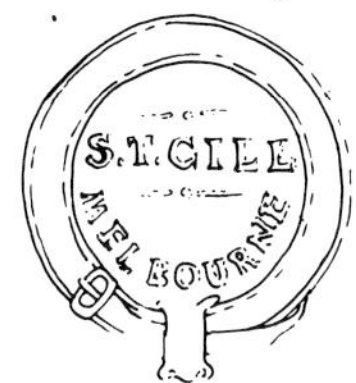

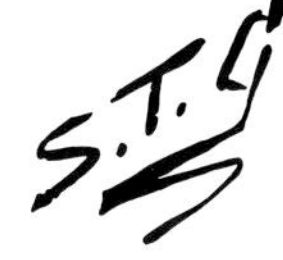

Melbourne, Victoria — 1864-1880 (*Second period*).
Cattle Branding
colour lithograph from *The Australian Sketchbook*
Hamel & Ferguson, Melbourne 1865.

Ease without Opulence
lithograph, lettered below image 'Melbourne, Printed for the Proprietor, DeGruchy, Leigh, 43 Elizabeth St.,' (This firm only traded under this name at this address in 1867)

Horrocks first interview with hostile blacks NW of Spencer Gulf.
watercolour   (NLA R.7619)

Wayfaring Diggers from *The Victorian Gold Fields during 1852-3.* A set of 40 watercolours commissioned by the Melbourne Public Library, 1869   (LT. SLV)

A Hilarious Dinner Party, or Convivial Diggers in Melbourne.
watercolour   (DG. SLNSW)

Major King's Head Sheep Station on Kapunda Creek, So. Australia.
watercolour   (NLA)

Melbourne, 1880, A Street Scene Bank Place.
drawing   (DG. SLNSW)

Grand Locomotive Race, 1880
watercolour   (AGSA O.   )

Pencil Drawings.
(Early South Australian drawings to which a late signature *c.*1864-80 has been added.)
*Rankine's Station, Mount Crawford, Barossa Range, South Australia. c.*1842-43.
pencil drawing   (AGSA 697HP9)

Depot Creek, South Australia, looking west. 1846
pencil drawing   (AGSA 697HP7)

Notes

Appreciation

1. Pastoral subjects were part of Australian imagery by the 1820s but the first known pictorial record of sheep-shearing is a tiny drawing by John Glover in the sketchbook he commenced on 19 December 1834 (National Library of Australia, Canberra). Cuthbert Clark, an amateur Tasmanian artist, produced small watercolours of shearing, harvesting and other rural subjects in the early 1840s which show Glover's influence; some are actually inscribed by the artist as being 'after Glover'.
2. This could be the first suggestion of a bushfire in Australian art, although there exists a watercolour by Frederick Garling in the collection of the Ballarat Fine Art Gallery of a bushfire subject which has been given the date of c.1840. Eugene von Guérard, William Strutt, J.W. Curtis, J.A. Turner and John Longstaff were all later in turn to paint their major works on this theme, which also became a popular subject in magazine illustrations.
3. This large oil (which was probably preceded by a small preparatory watercolour) is on long-term loan to the Art Gallery of South Australia from the South Australian Museum, Adelaide.
4. By the 1840s, however, Glover's vision was affected as he was approaching eighty and his few known works after 1842, including some watercolours, are clumsy compared with the fresh work by Gill of the same period.
5. The various visits to South Australia by the intrepid George French Angas are complicated and difficult to follow. Angas first arrived in Australia when he came to Adelaide in January 1844, but he left for New Zealand in July the same year. In November he returned to Australia this time staying in Sydney. He spent the first half of 1845 back in South Australia, but then left for Britain and later South Africa. Angas was again in South Australia in 1850 staying to mid 1851, when he moved to Sydney. He did not return to South Australia until 1860 and three years later he left Australia for Britain never to return. It seems likely that Angas's practice of consistently dating his works accurately set an example for Gill for whom no dated works in South Australia exist before Angas's arrival. Gill dates the majority of his South Australian works after this.

    There seems to be no evidence of Angas having any contact with Gill when the latter moved to Sydney from Melbourne in 1856.

Biographical Outline

1. Reverend Samuel Gill was born at Tiverton, Devon, 9 August 1793, the son of Robert and Mary Gill. A member of the Baptist Church, he studied at the Bristol Baptist College from December 1813 to November 1815 when he preached his first sermon. In April 1817 he married Winifred Oke daughter of William Oke, Collector of Customs, Falmouth, Cornwall, and his wife Nancy. In the same month (April 1817) a new Meeting House was opened at Perriton, near Minehead, Somerset, with Reverend Samuel Gill as its first Minister.
    References:
    Bristol Baptist College, Bristol, England.
    Mr A. Stubbings, Secretary, Minehead Baptist Church, Somerset, England.
    Mrs Jessie Thompson, *Samuel Thomas Gill*, unpublished ms. (Mrs Thompson was a daughter of John Ryland Gill and a niece of Samuel Thomas Gill.) Courtesy of Mr C.M. Thompson, Bridgewater, South Australia.
2. Public Record Office, London, chronological register of births, Dr Williams's Library, 1820-24 (Ref., RG 4/4664, entry 4692.) Dr Williams's Library, originally in Red Cross Street, is now at 14 Gordon Square, London. The Register of Births held there was established by the Protestant Dissenting Deputies in 1742-3 to record the births of Dissenters who would not be baptised in parish churches. After civil registration was established in 1837 the Register was closed and the records transferred to the Registrar General, London. (*National index of parish registers*, vol.2, pp. 558-64)
3. Mrs Jessie Thompson, *op. cit.*
4. John Ryland Gill, *Autobiography of John Ryland Gill 1821-1891*, unpublished ms., written 1891, two volumes (only one volume covering the period 1821 to about 1838 remains; the second volume was destroyed by bushfire 1948). Courtesy of Mr C.M. Thompson, Bridgewater, South Australia.
    Public Record Office, London, births, Dr Williams, *op.cit.*, entry 4693.
5. *Ibid.*, entry 4694.
6. John Ryland Gill, *op. cit.*
    Millbrook, three miles west of Plymouth, now in Cornwall, was in Devon until 1844. (Devon Record Office).
7. Public Record Office, London, births, Dr Williams, *op. cit.*, entry 4695.
8. John Ryland Gill, *op. cit.*
    In the 1820s and 1830s, Devonport, Stonehouse and Plymouth were three separate, but adjacent, towns united by docks, naval and military establishments and with a large population of service personnel of all ranks. Morice Town and Stoke were

smaller towns and closer to Devonport. In 1914, the towns amalgamated and became suburbs of Plymouth. Morice Town lost its identity. (Plymouth Central Library)

9. Mrs Jessie Thompson, *op. cit.*

10. John Ryland Gill, *op. cit.*

11. *Ibid.*
    See note 8.
    An 1830 Directory of Plymouth, Devonport and Stonehouse (Brindley) mentions in a list of schools, a ladies' school conducted by Mrs Gill in Navy Row, whilst in the list of residents the Reverend Samuel Gill appears as running an 'Establishment for Young Gentlemen'. (Plymouth Central Library).
    John Ryland Gill does not mention his father as having any connection with a school at this time.

12. John Ryland Gill, *op. cit.*

13. *Ibid.*

14. *Ibid.*
    John Ryland Gill mentions travelling with his father 'very often' and seeing London when he was 10 years of age. He does not mention his brother Samuel Thomas Gill as accompanying them, but it is assumed that the elder son would have been given the same opportunity.

15. Dr William Seabrook, a schoolmaster and dissenting Minister conducted his Academy at Park Street (1830) and later at Ebrington Street, Plymouth, approximately two miles from Navy Row, Morice Town. (Plymouth Central Library).
    Bowden, 1971; p.2, says Samuel Thomas Gill was a boarder at Dr Seabrook's Academy as 'the distance from Navy Row to Park Street was too far for daily travel'. Assuming this to be correct, Samuel Thomas Gill's formal education must have been completed before the closure of Mrs Gill's school when the family moved to Caroline Place, Stonehouse, which is about a mile from Dr Seabrook's Academy.

16. Mrs Jessie Thompson, *op. cit.* Mrs Thompson says that at an early age Gill was good at drawing and that his parents were advised to have him trained in art. She gives no details of his training. However, the Gills employed Masters of Painting and of Drawing in their school at Navy Row, and no doubt similar tutors were available at Dr Seabrook's and at the Naval and Military School of which the Reverend Gill was Principal from 1833. In his application for free passage to South Australia Gill gave his trade as 'Carver and Gilder'. (see Note 26.)

17. John Ryland Gill, *op. cit.*, Mrs Jessie Thompson, *op. cit.*
    It has not been possible to confirm the exact dates or sequence of events that are said to have taken place in or about 1833 as a result of the children contracting small-pox. The dates of death of the two brothers were recorded in the family bible which was destroyed in the 1948 bushfire and so far no official confirmation can be obtained in England. Some doubts are raised by the statement from the Devon Record Office that 'in 1831, following the outbreak of smallpox, there was a more devastating outbreak of cholera. This continued into 1832 and may have been responsible for the deaths of the two younger boys'.

18. John Ryland Gill, *op. cit.*

19. *Ibid.*
    The Plymouth Central Library has been unable to identify this school, saying it may be the Royal Naval and Military Free School, which was established in 1831, but no school accommodated 400 boys. Queen Victoria became the patron.

20. John Ryland Gill, *op. cit.*
    John Ryland Gill, who was also educated at Dr Seabrook's Academy, then at Ebrington Street, Plymouth (see note 15), assisted at his mother's school and was then articled for five years to Mr Rodd, Solicitor, Clerk of the Bench of Magistrates, East Stonehouse. He terminated his articles in the third year (*c.*1838) and his description of events reveal that at that time he shared a bedroom with his brother Samuel Thomas Gill and that his mother had two pupil boarders who had gone home for mid-summer holidays, confirming that the date was about August 1838.

21. *Self portrait* aged. 16 years 9 months, an early and rare work in oils, was painted at Plymouth about 21 February 1835 and was in the possession of the Thompson family at Bridgewater until destroyed with other original records in a bushfire in 1948.

22. The sketchbook was acquired by the Gallery in 1965 from Messrs C.M. and A.D. Thompson, grandsons of John Ryland Gill.
    Mrs Jessie Thompson, *op. cit.*, says that the Reverend Gill was 'a gifted artist', who gave his son lessons and took him sketching in Devon. Apart from the sketches by Reverend Gill in the sketch-book, several other examples of his work exist.

23. Mrs Jessie Thompson, *op. cit.*, makes the statement that Samuel Thomas Gill 'studied under leading masters in London, but [she] has no record of those masters'. Perhaps Gill was in fact working for the Hubard Profile Gallery, an aspect of his career she never mentions. (See note 24).

24. Quoted from Samuel Thomas Gill's advertisement in the *South Australian Register*, 7 March 1840 (see p. 00), which is the only factual record that he worked for the Hubard Gallery. The wording 'of London' is ambiguous, as the Hubard Gallery apparently went on tour. In Sue McKechnie's *British Silhouette Artists and their Work, 1760-1860*. London: Sotheby Parke Bernet, 1978, she states that the Hubard Gallery was founded in 1822 by Mr Smith to exploit the precocious talent as a silhouette cutter of W.J. Hubard (1809-62). It travelled in the United Kingdom, then went to the United States where in 1826 Hubard left to pursue a separate career as a portrait painter. Returning to England late in

1829, the Hubard Gallery was based at 109 The Strand 'some time in the 1830s', but was lost sight of by *c*.1845. The charge for a 'Likeness with Frame and Glass' was one shilling. McKechnie makes the following assumption:

As a young man, Gill, with his good training, was probably responsible for some of the better work produced by the Hubard Gallery, perhaps during the period 1836-39. It is impossible, however, to attribute to him with certainty any of the illustrated examples of the gallery's work. The fact that he began his career in London suggests that the Hubard Gallery may have been based there in the late 1830s.

25. Mr C.M. Thompson, Bridgewater, South Australia, family papers.

26. South Australian Archives, *Register of Emigrant Labourers applying for a Free Passage to South Australia*, applications 5291-6. The Reverend Gill, as purchaser of a Land Order for an 80 acre Section was entitled to free passage for dependants, providing they went out as bona fide labourers, and for servants and labourers at the rate of one per £16 expended in land. In this way in addition to Samuel Thomas Gill, he brought out his second son John Ryland Gill as an 'Accountant and Gardener', his daughter Winifred Mary Gill as a 'Sempstress', Emma Witheridge as a 'House Servant', and John Palmer and John Gidley as 'House carpenters'.

27. South Australian Archives, *Passenger Manifest*, Source 25, vol. 2, p.84.

28. *South Australian Register*, 21 December 1839.

29. Mrs Jessie Thompson, *op. cit.*

30. *Ibid.*
Date not confirmed as the records of the West Terrace Cemetery prior to 30 June 1840 were destroyed by fire.

31. General Registry Office, Lands Department, Adelaide, Memorial 459/88.

32. Details of the erection and completion of the building are not known. John Ryland Gill is said to have helped with its construction and later as an assistant in the school before becoming a clerk in a solicitor's office in Adelaide. Reverend Samuel Gill advertised a Classical and Mathematical Preparatory School at Coromandel House, Sturt Vale for young gentlemen under twelve in the *South Australian Register*, 13 May 1843, and again in the *Adelaide Times*, 25 December 1848. Reverend Gill also conducted Baptist services there (See note 35).

33. E.A.D. Opie, *South Australian Records prior to 1841*, Adelaide: Gillingham, 1917, p.104.

34. Bowden 1971, p.5 and Dutton 1981, p.14 both say that Gill visited Eyre at Moorundie in February 1842 but there seems to be no contemporary record of this. The two drawings said to have been made by Gill at this time and used by Eyre to illustrate his *Journals of an Expedition of Discovery into Central Australia* in 1845 are *Opossum Hunting near Gawler Plains* and *Mode of disposing of the dead at the Lower Murray*, but as Dutton points out they do not relate to the Moorundie area.
Two early watercolours in the exhibition, (*Natural avenue of trees, near Eyre's station at Moorundie, River Murray, c.1842-44*) (cat. 34) and (*Australian Aborigines river fishing from a canoe and from the river bank, River Murray, c1842-44*) (cat. 35) seem to provide the evidence that Gill was at Moorundie but the works are not inscribed nor dated. The Art Gallery of South Australia owns a pencil drawing by Gill (AGSA 697HP10) which is inscribed with the title 'Old Police Station/ Murunda [*sic*] S.A. 1843'. The style of signature and inscription, however, suggest that they may have been written later in his career and the date is therefore unreliable (see Appendix B). In fact the representation of the police hut is different from that in (*Old Police Station and Edward John Eyre's House at Moorundie, River Murray, 1842*) (cat. 26) signed and dated *S T G/44*, a watercolour which Gill copied from a sketch made by Captain Frome when the latter visited Eyre in March 1842.

This does raise the question of why would Gill copy Frome if he had visited the area himself, although it now seems reasonable to assume that Eyre commissioned watercolours by Gill (several after Frome and Hamilton) which he took to England in 1844. As yet it is impossible to establish an exact date for Gill's visit(s) to Eyre at Moorundie.

35. Elizabeth Murray was the sister of Alexander Murray (see note 47) who established a biscuit factory at Coromandel Valley. The Reverend Gill was by now Pastor of the United Churches of Christian Brethren of Clarendon and Coromandel Valley, an offshoot of the Baptist faith. The Murrays were also Baptists. There is no official record of the marriage which may have been held at Coromandel House, where services were usually held. Until the passing of the Marriage Act in 1842, marriages performed by dissenting clergy were illegal, although marriages performed hitherto were validated by the Act. (cf. Douglas Pike, *Paradise of Dissent*, M.U.P., 1957, pp. 276-9)

36. Births, Deaths and Marriages, Adelaide (Births vol. 1, p.31) The *South Australian Register*, 30 August 1843, p.2c announced under Births 'Mrs Gill of Sturt Vale on Wednesday 23rd ultimo — a daughter'.
Eliza Jane Gill married (Colonel) J.L.R. Fiveash, brother of Rosa C. Fiveash, a South Australian botanical artist, on 27 December 1865. (B.D.M., Adelaide, ref. 3574/65).

37. National Library of Australia, Canberra, owns a preliminary sketch (NLA R.113) titled *Sturt's Expedition*, and the Art Gallery of South Australia owns three watercolours, cat. 80 and 81 and *Sturt's Overland Expedition leaving Adelaide 10th August 1844* (AGSA 0.1522).

38. From research documents relating to John Howard Angas now in the possession of the National Trust, Collingrove. This

commission is also confirmed in a document in the possession of Mr C.M. Thompson, Bridgewater, South Australia.

39. The two works are the same subject from different viewpoints. Section 471 was part of the Angas holding in the Barossa cf. 'Agricola', *Description of the Barossa Range* etc, London: Smith Elder, 1849, plan facing p.8.

40. Allen, *The Royal South Australian Almanack,* 1845.

41. The exhibition was held in the Legislative Council Chamber from 18 to 20 June 1845, cf. an advertisement, and a paragraph *South Australian Register,* 18 June 1845, pp. 2c and 3b, and a review, *South Australian Register,* 21 June 1845.

42. George French Angas, *South Australia Illustrated,* London: Tho.⁵ MacLean, 1846-7. Sixty hand-coloured lithographic plates with text. Angas painted the original watercolours for 57 of the plates and used three watercolours by Samuel Thomas Gill for Plate 7, *Port Adelaide,* Plate 41, *Adelaide, Hindley Street from the corner of King William Street* (cat. 44) and Plate 54, *The Departure of Captn. Sturt, August 1844.* (cat. 81).

43. Frederick Robert Nixon, a Surveyor in the Surveyor General's Department, etched and printed a set of *Twelve Views of Adelaide and its Vicinity, South Australia,* which for many years was wrongly attributed to Francis Russell Nixon, the first Bishop of Tasmania. See R.G. Appleyard, 'Frederick Robert Nixon', *Bulletin of the Art Gallery of South Australia,* vol. 28, October 1966, p.6.

44. *The South Australian,* 17 June 1845, 'Correspondence' — letter signed 'N.R.F' *South Australian Register,* 18 June 1845, p.3c.

45. Many of the watercolours became the property of the South Australian Company and are now in the collection of the Art Gallery of South Australia (see Appendix A) and (cat. 26, 42-47, 56-58, 69 and 81).

46. *South Australian Register,* 8 November 1845, p.2b. Gill is said to have been the first to acquire daguerreotype equipment in Adelaide and that he very soon sold it to professional photographer Robert Hall (*c.*1821-1866) (*South Australian Register,* 22 April 1846).

47. Alexander Murray, M.P., J.P., (1803-80) emigrated to South Australia in 1840 with his wife, two children and a sister, Elizabeth, who in 1842 married Reverend Gill (see notes 35 & 36). In 1844 Reverend Gill sold 10 acres at Coromandel Valley to Alexander Murray on which he established his biscuit factory.

48. *The Glasgow Herald,* 10 November 1845, p.3, advertises the exhibition *South Australia as it is,* opening Tuesday 11 November 1845. As well as drawings by Alexander Murray and Gill there were working models of reaping and thrashing machines from South Australia. Sixpence admission was charged and a catalogue was available at twopence. The exhibition was visited by Edward Jerningham Wakefield, who makes comments in his Journal, *The London Journal of Edward Jerningham Wakefield 1845-46,*

Ed. Joan Stevens, Wellington, New Zealand: Alexander Turnbull Library, 1972, pp. 71-73, 147.

49. *The Glasgow Argus,* 17 November 1845, p.3, confirms that the exhibition was 'brought to this country by Mr Alex. Murray'. The Art Gallery of South Australia has three watercolours by him which show him as a capable amateur.

50. *The Glasgow Herald,* 10 November 1845, p.3.

51. *The South Australian News,* London, 1 May 1846, p.40b. '*South Australia as it is* will be on view early in May, 75 original paintings . . . to be sold along with two working models of reaping and thrashing machines . . . Price 400 guineas. If not disposed of in one lot — they will be sold separately. For particulars apply to Mr. Hailes, 27 Leadenhall Street.'

52. Stephens, *The Royal South Australian Almanack.* 1846.

53. *South Australian Register,* 4 July 1846, p. 2d, 15 July 1846, p.3e; *Adelaide Observer,* 18 July 1846.

54. *The South Australian Gazette and Colonial Register,* 10 October 1846.

55. Stephens, *The Royal South Australian Almanack,* 1847.

56. *The South Australian,* 5 January 1847.

57. *The Adelaide Observer,* 9 January 1847, p.2a.

58. *The South Australian Gazette and Mining Journal,* 23 January 1847, p.2d and 20 February 1847, p.1c.

59. See the introduction to the Horrocks Expedition p. 00.

60. *A Catalogue of the Exhibition of Pictures, the Works of Colonial Artists,* Adelaide: Dehane, 1847. (Mortlock Library, State Library of South Australia).

61. *The South Australian Gazette and Mining Journal,* 30 January 1847, p. 1d, 6 February 1847, p. 1e., 20 February 1847, p. 1c.

62. *The South Australian,* 12 February 1847, 5d; *South Australian Register,* 13 February 1847, p. 2e; *The Adelaide Observer,* 13 February 1847, p.5a.

63. Gill's hand-lettered titles below the images are dated April 12th 1847 (cat. 59-65).

64. *South Australian Register,* 14 August 1847, p.3c (see cat. 59-65).

65. *The South Australian Almanack,* 1848. *The Royal South Australian Almanack,* 1848.

66. *The South Australian,* 21 January 1848, p. 1a.
The Mortlock Library, State Library of South Australia, holds one sheet of a catalogue similar to that produced in 1847 listing 55 items, whilst the press (*The South Australian,* 15 February 1848, p.2f) reviews the exhibition stating that works of Messrs Gill and Hamilton 'are to be seen on every side'. The mention of catalogue number 97 reveals that the exhibition was larger than the surviving fragment of the catalogue suggests.

67. *The South Australian,* 15 February 1848, p. 2f; *South Australian Gazette and Mining Journal,* 19 February 1848.

68. *The Adelaide Times,* 12 May 1849, p. 4a; *The South Australian,* 15 May 1849, p.2e.

69. *The South Australian*, 25 May 1849, p.2d.
   Other newspaper references: *South Australian Register*, 26 May 1849, pp. 2c, 2d; *The Adelaide Times*, 28 May 1849, pp. 2d, 3f. See also John Tregenza, 'S.T. Gill's "Heads of the People"', *Bulletin of the Art Gallery of South Australia*, vol. 35, 1977, pp. 26-35.

70. *South Australian Register*, 18 July 1849, pp. 3a, 2d.

71. *South Australian Register*, 1 September 1849, p. 3c; *The South Australian*, 4 September 1849.

72. *The Adelaide Times*, 13 August 1849, p.3f.

73. *The South Australian*, 25 December 1849, p.3c. (see also cat 113).

74. J.B. Graham, a Director of the South Australian Mining Association, returned to England in 1848. His mother, Mrs John Adams, and her husband, took up residence at Prospect House. These eight pictures are part of a gift to the Art Gallery of South Australia in 1947 from Mrs F.M. Graham and family, descendants of J.B. Graham. (see cat. 67 and 106-109).

75. *The Adelaide Times*, 11 March 1850, p. 3d.

76. *The Mercury and South Australian Sporting Chronicle*, 25 May 1850, p.485b.

77. *The Adelaide Times*, 7 January 1851, p.3d.

78. General Registry Office, Lands Department, Adelaide, Memorial 140/28. 53 acres, Section 1089, Hundred of Adelaide. Cost £150.17.0.

79. Gill's advertisements appeared in the *South Australian Register* and *The Mercury and South Australian Sporting Chronicle*.

80. *The Mercury and South Australian Sporting Chronicle*, 22 February 1851, p.801c. *The Adelaide Times*, 4 March 1851, p.3a.

81. *The Mercury and South Australian Sporting Chronicle*, 21 June 1851, p.939a, 28 June 1851, p.947c, 19 April 1851, p.865b and p.867c; *The Adelaide Times*, 19 April 1851, p.5d; *The South Australian*, 18 April 1851, p.3d.

82. *The Mercury and South Australian Sporting Chronicle*, 21 June 1851, p.939d.

83. *The Adelaide Times*, 10 July 1851, p.3b; *The South Australian*, 15 July 1851, p.3c.

84. *The Mercury and South Australian Sporting Chronicle*, 2 August 1851, p.986b.

85. *South Australian Government Gazette*, 11 September 1851, p.634b.

86. *South Australian Register*, 3 October 1851, p.2c.

87. *The Adelaide Times*, 20 December 1851, p.5c.

88. The Index of Passengers for Interstate Ports (Mortlock Library, State Library of South Australia), lists the following to Melbourne during this period, T. Gill, *Seabird*, 29 Dec. 1851; Thomas Gill, *Cantaro*, 15 Jan. 1852; Thomas Gill, *Anna Dixon*, 5 Feb. 1852; Thomas Gill, *Margaret Brock*, 30 March 1852. It is possible that S.T. Gill could be one of these passengers to Melbourne, since he was listed as Tho.⁵ Gill in the Passenger Manifest from England in 1839.

89. Gill may have travelled overland with the gold escort heading for the goldfields, or he could have travelled via Mount Gambier if the pencil inscription on the reverse of the oil painting "Mount Gambia [*sic*] 1852", (cat. 30) can be considered accurate.

90. See note 92.

91. Two plates in Part I, titled *A Bendigo Mill, June 20 1852*, and *Approach to Eagle Hawk Gully from road to Bendigo, June 27 1852*, and one plate in Part II, titled *Zealous Gold Diggers, July 1 '52*.

92. Mrs Jessie Thompson, *op. cit.*, states that Samuel Thomas Gill, John Ryland Gill and James Thompson, the brother of John Ryland's fiancee sailed to Melbourne together in the *Hero*. The evidence in the Index of Passengers for Interstate Ports (Mortlock Library, State Library of South Australia) does not support this statement. The newspapers list Messrs. Gill and Thompson as sailing to Melbourne in the *Hero*, 16 September 1852. The names appear together in the Shipping List and it should be noted that only *one* Gill, with no initials is listed. Samuel Thomas Gill was already in Melbourne working on his lithographs (see note 91) and it seems more likely that he met his brother and James Thompson in Melbourne and then accompanied them to the goldfields, where, according to Mrs Thompson, *op. cit.*, the latter two 'were quite successful'.

93. *The Adelaide Times*, 18 December 1852, p.4f.

94. Registrar of Probates, Supreme Court, Adelaide. Mrs Elizabeth Gill, in her application for Letters of Administration declared that 'she is the widow and next of kin' of the late Samuel Gill who died 'without leaving a will or other testamentary writing' that 'there are now living two children' by a former wife, Samuel Thomas Gill, the eldest son and John Ryland Gill both resident in 'the Province of Victoria' and that 'there is now living one child of the said Samuel Gill by his marriage with this appearer, namely, Eliza Jane Gill'. (see also notes 35 and 36).

95. *The Argus*, Melbourne, 4 February 1853, p.5e. and Bowden 1971 p.45.

96. The Index of Passengers to and from Interstate Ports (Mortlock Library, State Library of South Australia) lists arrivals from Melbourne, Gill, *Phoenix*, 17 April 1853; Gill, *Freedom*, 28 April 1853; and departures for Melbourne: Gill, *Dreadnought*, 25 June 1853. No initials are given in the press lists. In view of his commitments in Melbourne, Gill could only have travelled to Adelaide by sea, arriving 17 or 28 April returning to Melbourne 25 June 1853.

97. Lands Department, Adelaide, General Registry Office. Memorials 360/51, 429/51, 457/89, 193/92, 9/105 and Packet 15942.
   Jessie Thompson, *op. cit.*, states that the Reverend Gill made a Will leaving the Coromandel Valley property to John Ryland

Gill and making a provision for his second wife and child. The widow, Mrs Elizabeth Gill is said to have destroyed the Will, therefore under the then laws of intestacy Samuel Thomas Gill, as eldest son, inherited all of the land and improvements. Probably as a result of this and S.T. Gill's disposal of the land the two brothers eventually became estranged and are said not to have communicated with each other thereafter.

98. *The Argus*, Melbourne, 21 June 1853, p.7g.

99. Bowden, 1971, p.82.
   This may have been a *de facto* relationship, as no record of the marriage can be traced in Melbourne, Adelaide or Sydney. (see note 100)

100. The Sydney Directory for 1863 lists Samuel Thomas Gill, artist, 67 Riley Street in the alphabetical section and also under 'Artists'. In 1864 Mrs Gill is listed at 73 Stanley Street in the alphabetical section. She continues to be listed variously as 'Mrs Gill', 'Mrs Gill, artist' 'Mrs S.T. Gill' or 'Mrs Elizabeth Gill', latterly at 87 Stanley Street until 1875, after which she disappears.

101. Bowden, 1971, pp. 105-11.

Landscapes and Rural Scenes

1. Mrs Jessie Thompson, *op. cit.*
2. See Biographical Outline, note 38.
3. Francis Dutton, 1846, p.144.
4. R.G. Appleyard, 'Captain E.C. Frome, R.E. and his sketches of South Australia 1839-49', *Bulletin of the Art Gallery of South Australia*, vol. 34, nos 1 and 2, 1972, p.5.
5. See Biographical Outline, note 38.
6. 'Agricola', *Description of the Barossa Range in South Australia*, London: Smith Elder & Co., 1849. Plan of Special Surveys facing p.8.
7. Rodney Cockburn, *Pastoral Pioneers of South Australia*, Adelaide: Lynton, 1974 (2 vols), vol. 2, p.84 mentions a Robert Heaton Rhodes, but there is no record that he worked for the Angas family.
8. See Biographical Outline, note 38.
   This watercolour was given to the owner's father by a member of the Angas family.
9. R.G. Appleyard, *op. cit.*, p.14.
10. E.J. Eyre, *Journals of Expeditions of Discovery into Central Australia and Overland 1840-41 including an Account of the Manners and Customs of the Aborigines*, London: Boone, 1845. The two illustrations after Gill are *Opossum hunting near Gawler Plains* (vol. 1 facing p.68) and *Mode of disposing of the dead at the Lower Murray* (vol. 2 facing p.344.)
    See also Biographical Outline, note 34

11. In addition to this picture and the illustrations for Eyre's Journal listed in Note 10 above, the Mitchell Library has four watercolours by Gill inscribed on the reverse in pencil by the artist '-Eyre Esqr-'. They are:
    PX*D73f5 *Crater of Extinct Volcano, From Hon¹ Capt Frome's northern Sketches,*
    PX*D73f6 *River Murray native women fishing for Crawfish — From sketch of Mr. G. Hamilton,*
    PX*D73f7 *Natives crouching Emu,* and
    PX*D73f8 *Native Fight.*
    This would seem to confirm that Eyre commissioned Gill to provide him with a number of watercolours to take to England for illustration and display.

12. See Biographical Outline, note 34.

13. Auhl and Marfleet, *Journey to Lake Frome 1843*, Adelaide: Lynton, 1977, pp. 70, 85, 100. James Henderson's pencil sketch is in the Mortlock Library, State Library of South Australia, and the watercolour by Frome in the Art Gallery of South Australia, AGSA 709HP14.

14. Mortlock Library, State Library of South Australia, photograph no. B43327.

15. Arthur H.S. Piggin, who emigrated from Braintree, Essex, arrived in Melbourne in February 1869 aged 22 and apparently formed a close friendship with Gill. Piggin was a commercial traveller who later became Manager of Robert Reid & Co., Little Flinders Street, Melbourne.

Mining

1. Auhl and Marfleet, 1975, describes the development of the mines and the effect on the colony.
2. Wheal derives from *huel* a Cornish word for a mine and owes its use in South Australia to the Cornish miners who came to work the newly discovered mines, some of which incorporated the word in their names, e.g. Wheal Gawler, Wheal Watkins, Wheal Fortune.
3. Auhl and Marfleet, 1975.
4. *South Australian News*, London, 1 October 1846, p.77a.
5. *ibid.*, 1 August 1846, p.60a, and 1 September 1846, p.68b.
6. 'Diary of Ann Jacob 1840-1848', unpublished ms., by permission Mrs Mary Horrocks, Adelaide.
   Ann Jacob, who married Arthur Horrocks, 1850, was a sister of John and William Jacob. The latter married Mary, the eldest daughter of Captain Bagot, one of the owners of the Kapunda Mine.
7. *ibid.*
8. Auhl and Marfleet, *op. cit.*, p.33.
9. *ibid.*, p.82.
10. *South Australian Register*, 14 August 1847, p.3c.

11. *ibid.*
    The Art Gallery of South Australia owns four of the original set (cat. 62 and 63 and AGSA 0.651, and 0.652) acquired in 1914 as gifts from the South Australian Mining Association and three of the 'copies' (cat. 59–61) acquired in 1947 as gifts from the family of J.B. Graham. Gill varies the composition of figure groups, animals, trees, carts, etc.
    J.B. Graham, the largest shareholder, owned 400 £5 shares at one time worth £200 each. He bought Prospect House on the northern outskirts of Adelaide (cat. 106–109).
12. *South Australian News*, London, 1 July 1848, p.248a.
13. The Art Gallery of South Australia acquired one of the original watercolours (cat. 67) as a gift from the South Australian Mining Association in 1914 and in 1947 as gifts from Mrs F.M. Graham and family three versions, no doubt commissioned for J.B. Graham:
    0.1350 *Burra Burra Mine, So. Australia, from the rear of P.C.C. Smelting works, near Kooringa, Feby 26th 1850.*
    0.1352 *Burra Burra Mine So. Australia, Showing chief portion of Surface Operations, Adelaide, Feby 26th 1850*
    0.1354 *Kooringa the Burra Burra Township from the Quarry at the rear of P.C. Comp's Smelting Works Feby 26th 1850*
14. Auhl and Marfleet, 1975, *op.cit.*, p.82.
15. *South Australian News*, London, 1 July 1848, p.284a.

Sport and Recreation

1. *History and Growth of the South Australian Jockey Club,* Adelaide: Griffin Press, 1955, p.3.
2. D.H. Pike, 'The Diary of James Coutts Crawford, 1839 and 1841', in *South Australiana,* vol. 4, no. 1, 1965.
3. Anthony Trollope, *British Sports and Pastimes* London: Virtue, 1868, p.5.
    The three references above appear in John A. Dayly, *Elysian Fields: Sport, Class and Community in Colonial South Australia 1836-1890,* Adelaide: published by the author, 1982.
4. *South Australian Register*, 15 February 1845.
5. *South Australian Register*, 21 February 1846.

Sturt's Expedition into Central Australia

1. *South Australian Register*, 14 August 1844, p.2e.
2. *ibid.*, 10 August 1844, p.30.
3. See Gill's watercolours of Eyre's house and of the natural avenue of trees (cat. 26 and 34).
4. Sturt illustrated his field journals with sketches. However, he also makes reference in his *Narrative* to sending his draughtsman, J. McDouall Stuart, to 'sketch in the hills'.

5. Two other watercolours in the gift from Her Majesty Queen Elizabeth II *Ana-branch of the Darling* (NLA R.344) and *The Depot Glen* (NLA R.355) correspond to two of the illustrations facing pp. 103 and 266 respectively in vol. 1 of the *Narrative*. Both are inscribed 'Captn Sturt, del'. The former, NLA R.344, is the original for the illustration and in 1983 the National Library reattributed the work from Sturt to Gill. The latter, NLA R.355, is attributed by the National Library to Sturt. However, its style indicates that it could have been painted by Gill and some subject differences between it and the illustration suggest that Sturt's original may have been the one copied by the engraver. At least two other illustrations *King William Street, Adelaide* and *Port Adelaide* facing pp. 147 and 167 respectively in vol. 2 are engraved from works by S.T. Gill, the original of the former being AGSA 0.643.
6. Langley 1969, p.255 quotes a letter to Captain Sturt from E. Portman (Emma, Baroness Portman, Lady of the Bedchamber to Queen Victoria), dated 29 January 1849, Windsor Castle, concerning his 'presents to the Queen' and expressing the gratification and interest 'which both Her Majesty and His Royal Highness Prince Albert have felt in looking at the drawings'.
7. The gift comprises five works relating to Sturt's Expedition, (cat. 82, 83, 84 and the two listed in note 5 above), and eight works relating to the Horrocks Expedition (see Horrocks Expedition note 16).
8. *South Australian Register*, 14 August 1844, p.2e.
9. See Appendix A, James Allen's 'Dissolving View', Lecture III, no. 4 which is titled *Captain Sturt setting out on his exploratory 'Expedition.*
10. Sturt, 1849, vol. 1, p.166.
11. Sturt, 1849, vol. 1, pp.253-5.
12. Sturt, 1849, vol. 1, pp.337-45.

The Horrocks Expedition 1846

1. *South Australian Register*, 4 July 1846, p.2d.
2. *South Australian Register*, 15 July 1846, p.3e.
3. S.T. Gill 'Progress of Discovery — Expedition to the North-West', *South Australian Gazette*, 10 October 1846.
4. 'John Ainsworth Horrocks' Journal' *Proceedings of the Royal Geographical Society of Australasia (S.A. Branch),* vol. 8, pp. 36-47.
5. Both Dr John Tregenza of the History Trust of South Australia and also Ralph Grandison have spent many days in the field tracing the route of the expedition and locating the scenes painted by Gill, the titles of many having been lost. Grandison has published his findings to date in an article 'The relocation of fifteen sites painted by S.T. Gill whilst accompanying the Horrocks' Expedition of 1846' *Proceedings of the Royal Geographical*

Society (S.A. Branch), vol. 83, 1985, pp. 12-21.

6. 'John Ainsworth Horrocks' Journal' *op.cit.*, pp. 36 and 37. Several mistakes and omissions appear to have been made when Horrocks's journal was copied. It states that the expedition departed on '29 July, 1846, Monday'. A calendar will reveal that Monday fell on 27 July in 1846, which was in fact the date of departure.

7. John Henry Theakston (*c.*1810-1878), stone mason, said to have worked for Sir Francis Chantrey in London before emigrating to South Australia. Worked for Horrocks, carved family crest, coat of arms and motto in stone at Hope Farm.

8. *South Australian Register*, 15 July 1846, p.3e.

9. Edward John Eyre established a base at Depot Creek twice during his exploration in the area in 1839, and was there again in 1840 and 1842.

10. S.T. Gill 'Progress of Discovery', *op.cit.* 12 and 13 August.

11. *The South Australian*, 5 January 1847, p.6a.

12. *The Adelaide Observer*, 9 January 1847, p.2a.

13. *South Australian Gazette and Colonial Register*, 23 January 1847, p.2d.

14. *Ibid*, 30 January 1847, p.1d.

15. *A Catalogue of the Exhibition of Pictures, the Works of Colonial Artists*, Adelaide; Dehane, 1847. Mortlock Library, State Library of South Australia.

16. The gift from Her Majesty Queen Elizabeth II comprised thirteen watercolours, eight by Gill relating to the Horrocks expedition (NLA.R.347-354) and five watercolours developed from sketches by Captain Sturt to illustrate the latter's *Narrative of an Expedition into Central Australia* (NLA R343-46 and 355). (see Sturt notes 5 and 7).

    The assumption that Sturt won the Horrocks pictures in a raffle is based on the fact that as Chairman of the Committee organising the *Exhibition of Pictures*, Adelaide 1847, he was closely associated with Gill in this capacity, as well as in having his sketches developed. Also the raffle took place in the Government Offices and Sturt was Colonial Treasurer. For details of Sturt's presents to Queen Victoria, see Sturt note 6.

17. Ralph Grandison questions whether during the course of the expedition Gill had time to visit all of the sites he has located, particularly in the lower Flinders. He could have made another visit to the area between the time he painted a group of watercolours at Bundaleer Station in March 1847 and the seven watercolours at Burra Burra Mine dated 12 April 1847. The date, 2 April 1847 inscribed on the photograph of the watercolour *Stoney Creek Mt. Remarkable Survey, Sketch taken from above the fall* (see note 27), if authentic, supports this theory. (See also notes 5, 46, 47 and 48.)

18. See cat. 95 and 103 and particularly the comments on cat. 93.

19. 'John Ainsworth Horrocks' Journal', *op.cit.*, 31 July (actually 29 July).

20. Ralph Grandison, 'The relocation of fifteen sites painted by S.T. Gill whilst accompanying the Horrocks Expedition of 1846, *Proceedings of the Royal Geographical Society (S.A. Branch)*, vol. 83, 1985, pp. 12, 13. (see note 5)

21. Ralph Grandison, *op.cit.* Grandison has located the sites depicted in seven watercolours (sites 1-7) which Gill probably sketched between 3 and 6 August (see note 17).

22. 'John Ainsworth Horrocks's Journal', *op.cit.*, 4 August.

23. See Horrocks note 27 for derivation of the 'Great Fall'.

24. Ralph Grandison, *op.cit.*, p.13, site 2.

25. Ralph Grandison, *ibid.*, p.13, site 4.

26. Ralph Grandison, *ibid.*, p.13, site 3.

27. A set of albumen-paper photographic prints (pre 1875) of watercolours by Gill once in the possession of the Horrocks family in England, and now lost, includes another sketch of this same scene which is inscribed by the artist l.r. corner *Stoney Creek, Mt. Remarkable Survey/ sketch taken from above the fall*. An inscription, probably by Celia Horrocks, on the reverse of this photograph which is in the possession of Mrs M. Horrocks, Adelaide reads *Sketch taken from the 'Great Fall' distant from White's C. Station 10 miles and from Adelaide 178 miles. S.T. Gill artist. 2 April 1847.* The date may be a mistake, or Gill may have made another visit to the area (see note 17).

28. 'John Ainsworth Horrocks' Journal', *op.cit.*, 9 and 10 August.

29. S.T. Gill, 'Progress of Discovery', *op.cit.*, 10 August.

30. Ralph Grandison, *op.cit.*, p. 17, site 10. See also his acknowledgement to Dr John Tregenza who first located this site.

31. 'John Ainsworth Horrocks' Journal', *op.cit.*, 19 August.

32. Ralph Grandison, *op.cit.*, p.17, site 12.

33. S.T. Gill, 'Progress of Discovery', *op.cit.*, 22 August.

34. 'John Ainsworth Horrocks' Journal', *op.cit.*, 22 August.

35. *The South Australian*, 5 January 1847, p.6a.

36. S.T. Gill, 'Progress of Discovery', *op.cit.*, 24, 25 August and 9 September.

    Ralph Grandison located the site of this view at Depot Creek in January 1986.

37. S.T. Gill, 'Progress of Discovery', *op cit.,* 24 August.

38. 'John Ainsworth Horrocks' Journal', *op.cit.*, p.44.

39. S.T. Gill, 'Progress of Discovery', *op.cit.*, 30 August.

40. *Ibid.*, 30 and 31 August.

41. *Ibid.*, 1 to 4 September.

42. *The South Australian*, 5 January 1847, p.6a., describes the picture as 'one representing the extreme point attained by the party. In the foreground appears the invalid's tent, with Mr. Gill

watching outside — the country in the background presenting a most inhospitable and desolate appearance.'

Ralph Grandison has located the approximate site of the camp by studying the land forms, in particular the relationship between the closer South Point and the more distant Oakden Hills.

43. S.T. Gill, 'Progress of Discovery', *op.cit.*, 5 September.
44. *The South Australian*, 5 January 1847, p.6a., describes the picture as representing 'Mr. Horrocks returning, after having sustained that distressing accident which hurried him to a premature grave'.
45. S.T. Gill, 'Progress of Discovery', *op.cit.*, 9 September.
46. Ralph Grandison, having located many of the sites in this area, considers that it was physically impossible for Gill to have reached all of the sites in the time available during the expedition and suggests that the artist may have made a subsequent visit. See notes 17 and 47.
47. The expedition was near Mount Brown on 19-20 August and again on 10-11 September. Grandison doubts whether Gill had the time to reach this vantage point and others at Woolundunga which would point to the possibility of a subsequent visit. See notes 17 and 46.
48. See notes 46 and 47.

Portraits and People

1. The only other known example of a watercolour portrait is in the Art Gallery of South Australia (AGSA 0.494) *Portrait of a man*, signed and dated 'S.T.G. 1868'.
2. See Biographical Outline, note 24.
3. John Tregenza, 'S.T. Gill's Heads of the People', *Bulletin of the Art Gallery of South Australia*, vol. 35, Adelaide, 1977, pp.26-35. Tregenza illustrates the whole series, gives a full account of its publication and details of the subjects, with references.
4. *The South Australian*, 25 May 1849, p.2d.
5. *The South Australian*, 17 June 1845.
6. *The South Australian Register*, 18 July 1849, p.3a.
7. John Tregenza, 'S.T. Gill's Heads of the People', *op.cit.*, p.32, for biographical notes.
8. *The Adelaide Times*, 24 December 1849, p.3f.
9. See Biographical Outline for 13 May 1853.
10. *The South Australian Register*, 9 January 1860, p.2c.
11. *The Adelaide Times*, 28 March 1851, p.3, describes the pavilion and gives a full account of the evening. Other references are listed at Biographical Outline, note 81.

References

Auhl & Marfleet, 1975
Ian Auhl and Denis Marfleet, *Australia's Earliest Mining Era, South Australia 1841-1851, Paintings by S.T. Gill*, Adelaide: Rigby, 1975

Francis Dutton, 1846
Francis Dutton, South Australia and its Mines, London: Boone, 1846

Geoffrey Dutton, 1962
Geoffrey Dutton, *Paintings of S.T. Gill,* Adelaide: Rigby, 1962

Geoffrey Dutton, 1981
Geoffrey Dutton, *S.T. Gill's Australia*, Melbourne: Macmillan, 1981

Bowen, 1971
K.M. Bowden, *Samuel Thomas Gill, Artist*, Melbourne: Privately published, 1971

Sturt, 1849
Charles Sturt, *Narrative of an Expedition into Central Australia*, London: Boone, 1849 (2 vols. + maps)

Langley, 1969
Michael Langley, *Sturt of the Murray*, London: Hale, 1969

Exhibition of Pictures, Adelaide 1847
A Catalogue of the Exhibition of Pictures, the Works of Colonial Artists, Adelaide: Dehane, 1847 (Mortlock Library, SLSA). (Gill exhibited 62 of the 178 works listed. The exhibition was held in the Council Room, North Terrace, Adelaide, from 10 to 17 February, 1847.)

Exhibition of Pictures, Adelaide 1848
Another Exhibition of Pictures was held in the Council Room, North Terrace, Adelaide from 10 to 19 February, 1848. A fragment, one page of the catalogue listing 55 works, of which Gill exhibited eleven is held in the Mortlock Library, SLSA. (A contemporary newspaper report reveals that there were at least 97 items in the exhibition.)